GODFATHERS OF CRIME

FACE-TO-FACE WITH INDIA'S MOST WANTED

Sheela Raval is an investigative journalist with nearly three decades of experience in print and television media. As a special correspondent with the India Today Group (1993–2004), she specialized in reporting on the underworld. She is currently an investigative editor at ABP News. She is also a political commentator and business analyst, and has appeared on several international news networks such as CNN, ABC News, Sky News, Star Asia and BBC Radio. She has a Master's degree in Economics and Sociology from Mumbai University. *Godfathers of Crime: Face-to-face with India's Most Wanted* is her first book.

GODFATHERS OF CRIME

FACE-TO-FACE WITH **INDIA'S MOST WANTED**

SHEELA RAVAL

First published in 2015 by Hachette India
(Registered name: Hachette Book Publishing India Pvt. Ltd)
An Hachette UK company
www. hachetteindia. com

SRD

All photographs courtesy Mahendra Parikh and ABP News

ISBN 978-93-5009-976-6

Hachette Book Publishing India Pvt. Ltd
4th & 5th Floors, Corporate Centre,
Plot No. 94, Sector 44, Gurgaon - 122003, India

Typeset in Linux Libertine 10.5/13.9
by Saanvi Graphics, Noida

Printed and bound in India
by Manipal Technologies Limited, Manipal

To my parents, Harshadrai and Pragya, for bestowing a free mind, spirit and a blazing fire inside me that has always helped me find my way through the battles of life.

And to my dear stepmother, Indira, for her encouragement and unwavering support.

Contents

Prologue

MARIO PUZO WOULD HAVE BEEN proud of the scene.

In a ballroom chock-full with guests an opulent wedding reception was being held in all its finery. The large hall had been divided into smaller sections to create an intimate ambience for some of its special guests. In one such cordoned-off section, at the extreme right of the ballroom, a burly man in his fifties with a thick trademark moustache sat in a huge Chesterfield armchair, exuding authority. The armchair had been placed facing the podium where the bride and the groom were seated. From his vantage point he could see the guests were milling about and celebrating, but the guests could not see him. The dark suit fitted him perfectly, and he looked impeccable in it. The stark contrast between the colourful celebrations in the ballroom and the dark, subdued tone of the antechamber could not be more compelling.

Across the distance, our eyes met, and I mouthed 'hello'. He nodded in response. For a brief second, my mind went numb. I could hardly believe that the man had returned my greeting.

I was living the wedding scene that opens the 1972 classic film *The Godfather*, based on Mario Puzo's novel. I remembered a line from the movie that had introduced me to the mafia, the underworld, in my college days: 'No Sicilian can refuse a request on his daughter's wedding day.' I really wished at that moment, in Dubai, that the don would follow the Italian-American mafia tradition and accept my request to interview him. But this was not *The Godfather*, nor was he the fictional Don Corleone. The man sitting in the plush armchair was none other than India's most-wanted man, Dawood Ibrahim Kaskar, overseeing the reception of his daughter Mahrukh's wedding in the summer of 2005 – and while the rest of the world's media feverishly reported the don's absence from the event, I was the only journalist to see him there in flesh and blood.

Writing from the Bylanes of the Underworld

IT SEEMS STRANGE NOW FOR me to think that I stumbled into covering the underworld by default.

I had joined the Mumbai edition of *Gujarat Samachar*, the largest-selling Gujarati daily, as a subeditor-cum-reporter in 1988, while simultaneously pursuing a postgraduate degree in Economics and Sociology from Mumbai (then Bombay) University. I had initially gone to the *Gujarat Samachar* office to learn how a newspaper office functions, in order to complete the final submission for the part-time diploma course in journalism I was taking at the time. There I happened to meet Mr Vraj Matari, the resident editor. Mr Matari asked me why I was inclined towards journalism instead of an academic career after completing my Master's degree. My response was that my parents were already in the teaching profession, and I had an urge to look beyond my daily surroundings and open myself up to some adventures in life. The idea of becoming a journalist had arisen from that. My answer probably nailed it for me, and I got a job offer on the spot, starting immediately. I requested Mr Matari to give me some time to get back to him, as I had to first take my father's permission. When I told my father, he was a bit apprehensive as my profile would require me to pull night shifts, and my extended family had cautioned him that the media was a risky proposition for girls. Nevertheless, I began my journey in journalism the next day on the two conditions that I would not be required to work a night shift and that my timings would be fixed between 1 p.m. and 8 p.m.

My first major story was about the spectacularly lavish wedding between the children of two of Mumbai's leading diamantaire families: those of Bharat Shah and Kishore Mehta. I had received the most-coveted wedding invite and was given access to the *sangeet* ceremony. Bharat Shah was an icon in Gujarat, known for his meteoric rise in the diamond and film industries. Originally from Palanpur, Bharat and his brother, Vijay, both college dropouts, went on to become diamond czars within the short span of a decade. They founded India's largest diamond empire, a ₹35 billion conglomerate (then known as B. Vijaykumar in India and Vijaydimon in Belgium) with interests in diamonds, construction and films. They had established diamond-cutting and polishing factories in Bangkok, Antwerp, Tel Aviv, Mumbai, Surat and Palanpur.

Bharat Shah's 18-year-old daughter, Reshma, was getting married on 21 December 1989, but the preparations had begun a month earlier. Shah had a designer of film sets set up a Rajasthani palace at Wankhede Stadium. Reshma's wedding *mandap* was the replica of a fairytale palace with heavily encrusted pillars, entwined with tulips from Holland and orchids from Thailand. Traditionally, among Gujaratis, the bride's father makes all the wedding arrangements, and Shah wanted to make sure it would be a wedding to remember. The event lasted seven days with pre- and post-wedding theme parties, a black-tie James Bond and an Indiana Jones party being among the highlights. Nearly 20,000 guests were invited, including the entire diamond and film fraternity. Fireworks and laser shows, *mehendi* for the ladies, music and *dandiyaraas*, complimentary Indian wedding attire for international guests – the entire staff of B. Vijaykumar had gone into overdrive to ensure everything went off smoothly.

The ostentatious wedding was met with massive protests. Demonstrations were held outside the stadium while elite guests in designer wear and exquisite jewellery stepped out of limousines, BMWs and Mercedes. Khadi-clad activists from groups such as the Mumbai Sarvodaya Mandal, the Janmukti Sangharsha Vahini, the Chhatra Yuva Sangharsha Vahini and the Stree Mukti Sangathan chanted, '*Yeh shaadi nahin, tamasha hai. Tamashe ko bandh karo, bandh karo*! (This is not a wedding but a spectacle; stop the spectacle now!)' at the gates. The stark social contrast was played out for a week, which I reported in a series of articles that rewarded me with instant recognition in Mumbai and Gujarat.

Shah had once been called Bollywood's 'one-man industry' and he had reportedly spent ₹30 crore on the wedding. If somebody had told me then that I would be writing about the darker side of his business or his alleged links with the D Company a decade later, I would have laughed it off. Yet, 11 years later, in January 2001, when details about the involvement of the underworld in the making of the film *Chori Chori Chupke Chupke* were made public, I was the one reporting on the arrest of Bharat Shah (who had produced and financed the film) and his relationship with the Mumbai mafia.

For a Gujarati girl like me, 'mafia' and 'underworld' were dreadful words. This was a strict no-go zone. By and large, women in media at the time were expected to write on softer issues such as social welfare, women-related topics or lifestyle, rather than indulging in hard, mainstream reportage. When I began my career, I could not have imagined that I would be writing extensively on Mumbai's gang wars and chasing global terrorists across continents in search of scoops and stories a decade later. I began my career reporting on, as I regularly do even now, several areas such as politics, business, environment, cricket, cinema, sexuality, spirituality, women's emancipation, lifestyle and adventure sports. Crime reporting was just one of the many areas I covered, and I like to think I began reporting on crime more extensively because of my strong sense of adventure. My first meeting with a real-life gangster, Arun Gawli, in the early 1990s came about as a result of this, when I simply accepted the offer to interview him to test the waters. It was later, when I joined *India Today*, that I began covering the underworld in earnest, specializing in investigative reporting. When in 1994 I got access to Chhota Shakeel, dreaded don Dawood Ibrahim's lieutenant, it became my regular beat.

Through the 1960s and 1970s, gangsters like Karim Lala, Varadarajan Mudaliar and Haji Mastan held a vice-like grip on most illegal businesses in Mumbai. It was a different era of organized crime that thrived on the License Raj. Prohibition was in force in Maharashtra, and these outlaws concentrated on illicit liquor businesses, gambling, prostitution and *vasooli* for industrialists and traders. When prohibition was lifted, the gangs took to smuggling electronic goods, clothes, yarn and gold, and theft of valuable cargo from the docks. They operated within areas they had earmarked for themselves. Businessmen took the help of these gangsters to settle real estate and financial disputes, and recover debts. This fuelled the growth of gangsterism in the city.

Iqbal Mirchi, the notorious gangster who had been mentored by Karim Lala, once told me, 'All the smugglers at the Mumbai Port Trust (uneducated youth who could go to any extent to make money) were actually used by the well-heeled *sethjis* of Mumbai. They were the main beneficiaries and brains behind subverting laws and manipulating the port system and customs officials to evade taxes.' Mirchi was a classic example of the old generation of criminals. He learnt the tricks of the trade at every stage and went on to become a notified narcotics kingpin. He gave me his first-ever television interview in November 2011 to announce his desire to surrender before an Indian court to seek justice and 'clear' his name of all criminal taint, which he had been tagged with since his escape to Dubai in the 1990s. When I met him for the first time at his sprawling villa in Essex, London, in November 2011, Mirchi introduced me to his children and grandchildren and talked about his life and happier times in Mumbai of old. His death in August 2013 marked the end of the smugglers' era of old Mumbai.

Between 1981 and 1982, a prolonged textile workers' strike left nearly 1.5 lakh mill workers jobless, causing untold hardship among their families. The strike forced mill hands and their children to join gangs to make ends meet. Many children of mill workers, such as Arun Gawli and Ashwin Naik, are involved in gang activities even today. Getting involved in trade union activities was a natural transition for these gangs. The Gawli gang infiltrated labour unions to influence the management, and then became a part of the management for a price. It was also in 1981 that Mumbai's gang wars began with the killing of Shabbir Ibrahim, Dawood's older brother, by members of the Pathan gang. The incident set off a spate of killings as each gang vowed endless vengeance for the death of its members.

When I began my career as a journalist, the Mumbai underworld was undergoing a transition. The old school of gangsters was fading away, and a newer order was shaping up. Old hands like Haji Mastan had turned to politics and financing films; Tamil gangster Varadarajan Mudaliar, who died in 1988, had shifted to Chennai (then Madras); and Karim Lala had reconciled with Dawood and withdrawn from the active crime scene.

The first sensational gang murder discussed in office at the time was that of Arvind Dholakia, killed by the Rama Naik gang at Hotel Caesar Palace in Khar in November 1988, reportedly at the behest of Dawood Ibrahim. Dholakia was suspected to be the brain behind gangster Babu Reshim's murder. Around the time, I was told by a senior crime reporter in office that most gangs operating in Mumbai, such as the Rama Naik gang, the Babu Reshim gang, the Arun Gawli gang (operating from Dagdi Chawl), the Sharad Shetty gang (Jogeshwari), the Chhota Rajan gang (Chembur) and the Ashok Joshi gang (Kanjurmarg), were active under the overall tutelage of Dawood Ibrahim. They thrived on providing safe passage to illicit liquor, smuggling contraband, land grabbing and extorting protection money. Dawood had already emerged as the tallest criminal among all these gangs. He had jumped bail in 1984 and made Dubai his home, and in the late 1980s was known as the 'Dubai Don' who controlled operations in India through his hirelings.

Through the 80s and the early 90s, people were more scared of receiving a phone call from him than being shot. The words 'Bhai *ka phone*' were enough to scare the Mumbai business community. A call from Dubai could be made to extort money, settle a land dispute, or to issue a threat to stay away from a certain deal. But there were friendly calls as well; people proudly announced they had been invited by 'Bhai' from Dubai to attend his lavish parties. The don's *mehmaan-nawazi* was much talked about, albeit in hushed tones, in socialite circles of the time. All those who attended the don's parties at his palatial residence, which he had named 'White House', were given generous gifts. Some went willingly and enjoyed the power trip, while others went out of fear as they could not refuse his invitation. Knowing 'Bhai' was a symbol of power in the film industry, and in the real estate and trading communities, and it was openly flaunted.

In December 1992, communal riots broke out in Mumbai following the demolition of the Babri Masjid in Ayodhya. It was a painful experience to see a cosmopolitan city like Mumbai burning up in communal hatred. The Shiv Sena was at its most aggressive, while Muslims seemed scared and shaken. I had by this time moved to the *Times of India* group at their offices in Bori Bunder in south Mumbai. A second round of communal riots began on 6 January 1993. The D Company gangster Feroz Kokani killed three *mathadi* (labourer) workers near Pydhonie in a retaliatory act. This was perhaps the don's way of showing the south Mumbai Muslim ghetto, where he had grown up, that he still had the power to avenge the riots. Kokani was arrested in Bangalore in October 1994 and brought to Mumbai. He escaped from custody in 1998 and joined the gang in Karachi, where he is believed to have been killed.

The second round of riots was followed by the worst act of terror in India's history. On 12 March 1993, 13 blasts rocked Mumbai, killing more than 250 people and injuring more than 1000. As I went around reporting from the various sites and hospitals, I was shocked by the sheer blood and gore I saw. Since the police had restricted the movement of people and the media after the blasts, I tagged along with the late Congress leader Murli Deora in his car. The city I loved had been torn to shreds. It felt like I was living through a terrible nightmare.

The blasts saw the leading dons of the Mumbai underworld being given the tag of 'terrorists' when the Crime Branch named Dawood and Anees Ibrahim as the masterminds, and their henchmen Tiger Memon and his brothers as the main conspirators and executors of the blasts. The underworld was now perceived to be a threat to the nation, and the investigation into the blasts brought many skeletons tumbling out of the closets of otherwise respected dignitaries and government officials, and filmstars like Sanjay Dutt.

The blasts also led to a shift in alliances within the underworld. Chhota Rajan split from the D Company quite dramatically, forming his own gang. His efforts to project himself as an enemy of the Pakistani Inter-Services Intelligence (ISI) and the D Company, and as a patriot who was determined to avenge the blasts, was strategically aimed at winning the support of politicians and authorities, who seemed to believe Rajan's 'Hindu' spin could be an answer to Dawood's Muslim identity. The gang feuds intensified after that, with both sides using every opportunity to attempt to eliminate key members of the other over the years. Some of these have been successful and have become common knowledge; some have been dramatic and made headlines (like the D Company's attack on Chhota Rajan in Bangkok); and some have fallen below the radar (like the little-known but multiple attempts on Dawood's life by Rajan's men) as they have remained unsuccessful due to various circumstances. I have reported on most of these incidents, and those stories and their backgrounds are in this book.

In May 1993, I joined *India Today*'s Gujarati edition, where I reported on Dawood's links with a high-profile stockbroker and a big industrial house via the Delhi-based power broker Romesh Sharma after police raids recovered incriminating evidence suggesting that Sharma and the corporate sector used the Dubai route to secure the movement of funds. The story brought to light Dawood's reach in Delhi and his links with the corporate world. At the same time I contributed articles to the English edition of *India Today*, where one of the major stories exposed a certain Raj Rajaratnam, who bore an uncanny resemblance to the hedge-fund manager convicted of insider trading, and his fraudulent and hostile ways of taking over companies.

Investigative stories began to attract me as I found them challenging and interesting. As the links of film stars attending parties in Dubai were closely scrutinized in the backdrop of the serial blasts, I explored Dawood's Bollywood links in detail and reported extensively on Bollywood's clandestine affair with the underworld's money and how it had returned to haunt the film industry. It was at this time that I began interacting with Chhota Shakeel. At the end of 1995, I switched fully to the English-language edition of *India Today* and continued reporting on, among other things, the ever-increasing menace of extortion that was plaguing Bollywood at the time. Creating fear is, after all, essential for the crime business to thrive.

The underworld–Bollywood nexus reached a crossroads with Gulshan Kumar's gruesome murder in August 1997. Kumar's killing made the film industry realize for the first time that the extortion threats they regularly received were for real. It created an atmosphere of fear and panic. The industry, which never tired of pomp and show, now swore by sobriety. BMWs and Mercedes sat in garages, while old Maruti 800s, Esteems or 118 NEs began to be used by producers in fear of calls from Dubai. In January 2000, filmmaker Rakesh Roshan was shot as he left his suburban office. Fortunately, he survived, but for Bollywood, this was a distressing phase – one whose lowest point came when Bharat Shah was arrested.

Shah's liaison with Dawood allegedly went back to the 1980s. The common platform between them was *hawala* dealings, but their relationship had deepened over a property dispute involving the late smuggler Yusuf Patel, Dawood and a third party. Before his arrest, Shah had vehemently denied any underworld involvement in *Chori Chori Chupke Chupke*. The night he was taken into custody, I went to his residence, Swapnalok, in Breach Candy, to meet his family. Vijay Shah, his brother, claimed that Bharat-bhai was being framed and people in power from 'top to bottom' were asking for money. He also claimed that they had already paid for *chhoti-moti* (small-time) demands so that his brother would be safe in custody, but now the dons were asking for over ₹100 crore! He gave me some names but Bharat's son Rashesh Shah asked me not to publish anything that his *kaka* (Vijay) had mentioned, as it would risk his father's life. Shah's real life was racier than any of the films he had produced! Chhota Shakeel had interesting things to say about the Company's connections with Bollywood and the Rakesh Roshan shooting in an interview I did with him, published in *India Today* on 1 January 2001, elaborated on in a later chapter.

By this time one big change had occurred. As most gangsters operated from foreign lands through phone calls and other electronic networks, Maharashtra had enacted the Maharashtra Control of Organized Crime Act (MCOCA) in 1999 to counter organized crime and terrorism. Unlike normal laws, under this Act, a confession before senior police officers is admissible not only against the accused providing the confession but also against others accused in the same case. Under this Act, there is no provision for granting anticipatory bail to the accused for six months and 'voice on the tape' is considered as evidence.

While the dons began to feel the heat once the Act came into force, I too felt its effect when my January 2001 interview with Shakeel landed me in an MCOCA Court as a state witness. The case and the trial turned out to be the experience of a lifetime. For a week, as I stood before some of the most high-profile and veteran criminal defence lawyers in the country, being cross-examined for around four hours daily, I learnt a few important lessons about crime reporting. From then on, I began thinking of every story I did on the underworld in legal terms. I realized that there is nothing in the digital world that can be deemed private. There is always someone listening in, snooping on your digital footprints, and sometimes also physically following you. To me it felt like a test by fire – an *agnipariksha* – and it taught me to stick to my professional boundaries in a more disciplined manner and conduct myself as a journalist within legal parameters.

I also understood that one of the major factors that provides a fertile ground for organized gangs to thrive is the lengthy and time-consuming legal process in our country, due to which people are averse to approaching courts of law for recovery of their dues or for getting justice. Instead, they turn to the mafia. Harassed creditors, landlords and tenants often approach goons for help; even banks and leasing companies take the help of gangsters for the recovery of loans. In the process, gangsters become relevant to the social system and they begin to run a parallel system of dispute resolution with considerable monetary gains for themselves. The cumbersome tenancy law and the Urban Ceiling Act have also, in some ways, been responsible for the growth of gangsterism in Mumbai. With big industrial houses plunging into real estate with huge investments, the prices of property have skyrocketed. A persisting nexus between builders, real estate agents and underworld gangs continues to be a social menace, and sometimes even the judiciary is not spared. The revelation of a nexus between a Sessions Court judge in Mumbai and an underworld don sent shockwaves through Indian legal circles in 1999. The irony of the situation was that a distressed judge had called the don for help!

In 2004, I joined broadcast journalism full-time. My first story was the sensational arrest of Kanchi's Shankaracharya, Jayendra Saraswati, who was charged with the murder of a priest. Television was not unfamiliar to me as I used to appear as an expert reporter on the underworld on Aaj Tak for many years. However, working for a Hindi channel and understanding the technicalities of television reporting took me a while. Television is an essentially visual medium, but for my kind of investigative stories my editor Uday Shankar broke all norms. He believed that a powerful story could be presented in many creative ways without an actual visual of the event. We did not have enough visuals of Dawood's daughter's *walima* (reception) or Samira Jumani's interview, for instance, and yet the two stories managed to create television history by topping all-time TRP (television rating points) charts at the time.

Over the last four decades, alliances in the underworld have been through various permutations and combinations. Partners within the same gang have fallen out to form their own splinter gangs. The political affiliations of the gangs have also shifted. Through the 2000s, in particular, there has been a paradigm shift, and the Mumbai underworld has now become a global story. I would never have known the extent and reach of the operations run by the Mumbai underworld had I not travelled to Bangkok in September 2000 to cover the attack on Chhota Rajan at his partner Rohit Verma's house, carried out by D Company gangsters under instructions from Chhota Shakeel. I landed in the Thai capital without knowing the language and with access to just a single contact for logistical support, but it turned out to be a landmark assignment for my career. Coming face-to-face with a badly wounded Rajan at the hospital and interacting with his good-looking lieutenant Santosh Shetty and other gangsters from his gang who had arrived from Mumbai was an eye-opener (detailed in later chapters in the book). I witnessed a completely different side to the two multinational crime empires that was hardly visible or known to India before this. The Bangkok episode compelled me to modify my perspective on the Mumbai underworld. The once small-time local gangsters, I realized, had become global players, and now ran trans-national operations involved in arms trafficking, drug-running and counterfeit currency.

Chasing the mafia across continents and countries – from Mumbai to Bangkok, Dubai, Lisbon, London, New York, Atlanta, Morocco and Nepal – has been an adventurous and intriguing journey. In my long pursuit of understanding the phenomenal path towards global infamy taken by some of India's most wanted criminals, I have discovered the finer nuances of global strategic manoeuvres and attempts to change the political geography of different countries through overt and covert means, as well as the supremacy of regional colonialism to economic and military dominion. In the wider global context, I have discovered the intricate connections between the Pakistani ISI, the British MI6, the US Central Intelligence Agency (CIA), the Saudi Intelligence and al-Qaeda in promoting terrorism in the name of *jihad* in the subcontinent. The darker side of spy games are played with pawns such as the underworld.

In my interactions with nine of India's most wanted criminals I gained insight into different aspects of their work, their connections and their lives. Each of my interactions – from my first interview with Arun Gawli in 1990 to the interviews I have conducted of Iqbal Mirchi, Abu Salem (and his first wife, Samira Jumani, and paramour Monica Bedi), Santosh Shetty, Ashwin Naik, Chhota Shakeel, Chhota Rajan – has been unique. Of these, my meeting with Mirchi was perhaps the most vivid and insightful. We interacted for about nine days during which not only did I get to know him better but he too grilled me on my knowledge of the underworld and its workings. Only after he was satisfied with what he heard did he share some valuable insights into the politics that govern the underworld. In fact, I was in half a mind to begin the book with an account of this interview. Yet, when I thought about it, although my brush with Dawood Ibrahim was short, the circumstances under which it happened were crucial. Like Osama bin Laden was to America, Dawood has been branded the biggest threat to India, and it was getting to know his business and reach closely, whether in person or through my interactions with his lieutenant Chhota Shakeel, that I got a truly wide perspective of the nexus that holds the underworld together and perpetuates it. It was imperative then that the book begin with him.

During my first big story on the underworld – my interview with Gawli in early 1990 – I did not know how to deal with a gangster, nor was I aware of the protocols to follow, but by the time I encountered Dawood Ibrahim I had become a seasoned underworld reporter. During my interviews I have also witnessed the emotional side of these hardcore criminals, particularly when they reminisced about their initial days in Mumbai and their families. Their voices softened when they spoke about the safety and future of their children and grandchildren. Some proudly shared how their children have become doctors, engineers, MBAs, fashion designers and legitimate businesspersons. When I was allowed to see their romantic sides, they blushed and looked elated. Even after having everything that money can buy and enjoying power through their ability to create dread, I saw in them an acute craving for social dignity and acceptability – none of them wanted their grandchildren to know them as a 'terrorist' or a 'gangster'.

When stories are told several times over, they become myths and legends and the truth often gets hidden within layers. In many ways this has happened with the dons of Mumbai's underworld. In this book I have attempted to not only make sense of the evolution of the godfathers of Mumbai's underworld by communicating their stories by piecing together facts from various sources, but to also present to the reader through accounts of my personal interactions with them over three decades an insight into the minds and personalities of these men, the ways in which they operate, and the deeper nexus of cooperation from the most unlikely sources that perpetuates their stature as formidable forces and keeps their business going.

In my long innings, I have not faced any major issues with the underworld despite my testimony against them in court. After my appearance in court, I did not hear from Chhota Shakeel for four years. I am sure he conducted all possible checks on me and my testimony in court and resumed talking to me only after his doubts were cleared. But it would be wrong to say that there were no problems at all. Intimidations, veiled threats and subtle harrying tactics are common professional hazards in this field, and I have had my share of them too. Knowing you have been under the surveillance of the mafia or government agencies is not a very good feeling. The political class and the bureaucracy are equally, if not more, adept at flexing their muscles. In fact, officialdom is more brazen and arrogant – phone-tapping and dropping clues that one is being watched are common ways to create pressure or fear. And if you do not heed such warnings, you might just find a dead cat outside your house, as I have!

A senior colleague at Star News once joked about reporting on the underworld, suggesting that stories on gangsters sounded more fictional than real and no one would know the difference as no gangster would come forward to deny or confirm the veracity of a story. Soon, he got proof of how seriously the underworld took their projection in the media, as a don called me to point out a serious issue over the language used in his profile that had recently been aired and threatened the person responsible with consequences if the profile was not corrected during the repeat telecast.

For me, working strictly within my professional limits while adhering to all legal parameters has been a tightrope walk. I am aware at all times that any tilt towards a particular side, whether the criminals or the official forces, could cost me dearly. Camaraderie on either side, the agencies or the gang world, would add to the risks involved. Sharing my experiences and stories is my way of communicating to the next generation of journalists what it takes to be an investigative reporter and how underworld reporting, as adventurous and thrilling as it may seem, is no cakewalk. It is essential to build up a relationship of trust with your sources within agencies and in the gang world, and you have to be ready for any kind of scrutiny at any given point in time.

The murder of Jyotirmoy Dey by the Chhota Rajan gang and the subsequent arrest of reporter Jigna Vora under MCOCA have irrevocably altered the way reporting on the underworld is done in India. Power equations have become irreparably skewed and journalists are now treading on a slippery slope. I think in the future there will broadly be two kinds of underworld or crime reportage – puff pieces orchestrated by the system (basically stories that depict what the government wants people to see or the media to showcase in the name of the greater good), and no-holds-barred Internet journalism that consists of stories largely from anonymous sources.

Reports, both for print and television media, cover basic facts. How those stories were unearthed and investigated – the stories behind the stories, that is – are rarely discussed or told. This book contains those stories.

It is not just about mobsters, their alleged crimes and the clashes between gangs. It tells the story of how Mumbai's petty outlaws and smugglers went on to become global mobsters, narco-arms kingpins and even global terrorists with the help of their respective mysterious benefactors. Equally, it is about major intelligence outfits across the world using these fugitive mobsters as potent tools for subversive activities to achieve territorial dominance and financial supremacy. India has a tough task ahead in balancing its position amid all these overt and covert activities.

My journey would not have been possible without the support of editors who believed in me: Aroon Purie, Shekhar Gupta and Prabhu Chawla at *India Today*; and Uday Shankar and Shazi Zaman at Star News, which was renamed as ABP News in 2012, converted a print journalist into a television presenter and anchor. I thank them all for their help and encouragement. In this endeavour, there have also been many known and unknown people who have helped me generously, and though some of them have to remain unnamed, my gratitude extends to them all.

Sheela Raval
13 November 2015

PART 1
Encounters with the D Company

Enemy Number One

THE GRAND HYATT ON SHEIKH Rashid Road, Dubai, is a magnificent property that stands out even among the glittering skyscrapers of this oil-rich city. Its Baniyas Grand Ballroom is fittingly opulent – an ideal place to hold a spectacular ceremony. On the evening of 22 July 2005, the huge hall had been decorated in an elegant and classic style, in white, gold and dashes of pink here and there. The tables across the ballroom were each set for eight guests and had large candelabras at their centres with four candles each. The stage was set for a grand candlelit dinner. The bases of the candle-stands were covered in pink and white roses. Each table had eight packets of *chhuwaras* (dry dates) and other dry fruits traditionally served at weddings. The stunning chandeliers created dramatic light effects. Huge screens were placed in all corners so that guests could follow every detail of the ceremony. The stage for the couple had been draped in white, with its approach decorated with orchids and pink roses. A pair of green Chesterfield armchairs were placed at the centre of the stage for the newly-weds to sit on and greet the guests. The event was being captured live by over 1000 cameras positioned strategically, not just around the ballroom but also in the corridors leading to the hall.

I was at this venue to cover the high-profile and closely monitored wedding reception of Dawood's eldest daughter

Mahrukh to Junaid, the son of former Pakistani cricketer Javed Miandad. That evening I had come to the *walima* on behalf of Star News (now ABP News), responding to an invitation issued by Miandad to the channel during an interview aired a week earlier. Though there were plenty of other reporters from other channels who wanted to cover the wedding, they had all been turned down. I had not expected Miandad's invitation to be honoured or that I would be allowed inside. But here I was, although getting in had hardly been a cakewalk – but more on that later.

While I waited to be taken on-stage to greet the couple, I scrutinized the hall, watching out for familiar faces and levels of security. It was at this time that I noticed Dawood Ibrahim, the don himself, sitting in an enclosed area, as narrated in the beginning.

Till the time I got a glimpse of the don, the only image of him that Indian television channels repeatedly aired was that of Dawood sitting in the gallery of Sharjah's stadium, watching a cricket match, surrounded by his cronies and Bollywood celebrities. He looked a bit different in real life, I thought.

Instinctively, I turned to walk towards him, but the two men beside me – Fayaz and Jaber, my escorts at the wedding – immediately sprung into action. They stopped me, saying that he was sitting in an all-male section and I could not go there.

I said I just wanted to say hello to Dawood Bhai.

They turned towards the don, and after some sort of communication between the two men and Dawood, Jaber told me he would talk to me later, once the function had ended. It was 1.30 a.m. already, and the event would go on for at least another hour. I would have told him if I could that all I wanted were some visuals that would prove my presence at the *walima* of Dawood Ibrahim's daughter's wedding. I tried again, asking him if I could have my pictures taken or perhaps shoot some footage while I wished the couple. I promised I would not make the images public until I had their permission. But Jaber was unrelenting. He told me, as he had before, that he would ask and let me know.

While we waited, I asked him how they would like me to report about the event. Jaber reminded me that I was the only journalist who had been allowed inside, and then looked at the wall-mounted CCTV camera. I suppose someone from security must have given him further instructions through the Bluetooth device plugged into his left ear, because when he turned back to me he simply said, '*Aap jo theek samjho.* (Do what you think is right.)'

It was a simple yet loaded answer. The million-dollar question for me was: should I go on air and say that Dawood Ibrahim himself was present at the reception, or not? Since the morning, all of Indian media, including my channel, had been reporting his absence at the wedding. The venue for the event was closely guarded, but those who had made their way through other nearby ports to Dubai had started beaming peripheral information quite early on. Dawood had been placed on the US Treasury watch-list of global terrorists in 2003 for his links with the al-Qaeda and it was indeed surprising to see him at the venue. The don had evidently hoodwinked intelligence agencies across the world and stepped out of the crosshairs of rivals' guns to be present at the *walima.* My sources had informed me earlier that the *nikah* had been solemnized at Mecca on 20 July. I had no doubt whatsoever that he had been present there as well.

I had heard that Dawood had been moving around freely as a Pakistani businessman in the UAE and Saudi Arabia at the time. The D Company had many legitimate businesses there, some allegedly in partnership with the upper echelons of power, including the royalty. His presence at the *walima* clearly indicated that he was not hiding. In fact, he was simply not flaunting his presence so as to avoid creating any sort of diplomatic trouble for the Dubai authorities.

I continued to be in two minds about whether I should stick my neck out and report his physical presence at the venue right then, or wait for him to meet me later. It was a matter of chance, and I wanted to take it. If I had managed to enter the don's well-guarded venue and spotted him there, the possibility of a meeting and interview still existed. His lieutenant, Chhota Shakeel, had been promising to set up an interview for me with Dawood since 1994; every time I received his call, I would remind him of his promise. And every time, in his filmy style, Shakeel would say, '*Ek baar aap ko commit kiya hai to phir aap hi ko* first interview *denge jab woh tay karenge.* (Whenever he chooses to speak, the first interview will be with you.)'

Dawood had spoken to *India Today* soon after the blasts in Mumbai in 1993, but had gone into silent mode after that; he had given very few interviews to the press since. Not only did he stay away from the media, but he was also said to have ordered his brothers to refrain from communicating with any media outlet as conversations on the telephone give away location details as well as voice samples that could be admissible as evidence against them in the court under laws dealing with organized crime, such as the MCOCA which had been brought into effect in 1999. His spokesperson Chhota Shakeel and younger brother Iqbal Kaskar had both been located several times by Indian authorities while conducting business on the phone. This was followed by long legal battles that Dawood liked to avoid as they simply meant adding more cases to the already long list of criminal charges against him.

In any case, I decided to wait and see if my luck would play out and I would get to interview the don later that night.

Once the news of Dawood's daughter's wedding reception broke, everyone wanted to cover the event. There was a rush for visa applications, and many were disappointed as an equal number of rejections came through. At Star News, we applied for six visas eight days before the event, but could not secure any. Our passports were returned without any explanation. Some media persons took flights to Sharjah and others flew from Abu Dhabi to reach Dubai.

Meanwhile, Star News had roped in Sathish V.M., a freelance journalist in Dubai, to cover the event. On 22 July (the day of the *walima*), at the afternoon editorial meeting, the decision was taken to fly me to Dubai as a stopover option. I had valid visas to travel to the Schengen countries and the US at the time and was booked on the 8 p.m. Lufthansa flight to London via Dubai. My editor, Uday Shankar, insisted this was a last chance and it had to be taken, but I still did not know how to get out of the Dubai airport without a visa for the UAE. At around 3 p.m., I received a call from RS, a social activist and politician. I must have been sounding low, because he asked me what the matter was and when I told him I had to reach Dubai in the evening for an important coverage but did not have travel permits, he promptly offered to help.

RS was an angel! He gave me a number in Dubai and asked me to fax a copy of my passport to that number. He said his relatives owned a hotel in Dubai and they could help get a visa processed the same day as they were quite influential. He guaranteed my visa letter would arrive in an hour's time, and assured me I would be able to enter Dubai.

On his assurance, I went home, packed my bags and desperately waited for his call. He called me again to ask if I had travelled to Dubai earlier and whether I had any issues with the authorities there. I told him this would be my first trip to Dubai. He informed me that the process was taking a while as my name was on the blocked travellers' list (it seemed Dawood had sufficient reach with the Dubai authorities to get them to deny visas to journalists), but his relatives had personally vouched for me and the visa would be released in an hour. He asked me to proceed to the airport and wait for the letter.

The clock was ticking and the pressure was now building up. I left for the airport and on my way there I got a call from the Dubai hotel that was working on my travel permit. A lady on the line said she wanted to fax it to me. I found a shop that had fax services and received my letter there, and felt heartened. This was indeed a positive sign.

When I landed in Dubai at 10.30 p.m., RS called me again to ask if I had reached safely. There was a car waiting for me outside, he said. I was extremely relieved when the immigration officer stamped my passport without asking me any questions. It had been a tense day but now I had reached my destination. Outside, the temperature was 48 degrees and I felt like I was walking straight into an oven. A black Mercedes was waiting for me and the driver asked me if I wanted to go to my hotel first. I chose instead to head to the venue of the *walima*. The event had begun an hour ago, and now my mind was focused on just one thing: how would I gain entry into the banquet hall at the hotel?

A luxurious hotel in the Burj Dubai district, the Grand Hyatt towered over Dubai's historic creek. That evening, as my car entered the foyer, it wore a festive look. The separate entrance to the banquet hall was already crowded with dozens of television crews waiting to catch a glimpse of the invitees. The red carpet had been rolled out; the main entrance to the ballroom was decorated with fresh flowers, and candles flickered all around. As expected, elaborate security arrangements had been made both inside and outside the hotel, with uniformed and plain-clothes guards keeping an eye on the proceedings.

As I walked up to the reception, I could sense undercover agents from several intelligence agencies lurking around. Sathish came to receive me. He had been reporting on the event for the last two days and informed me that he had managed to book a room for me in the same hotel. This was very good news, as I had been told by intelligence sources that the entire hotel had been sanitized and booked only for the Kaskar–Miandad guests.

Sathish updated me on the happenings so far. He said that Miandad and his wife had arrived at 9.30 p.m. sharp, followed by the bride and groom, who had arrived in separate Hummers. Guests had started trickling in much before Miandad's arrival. The cameraperson – a young Palestinian lad in his twenties, who had amazingly been standing, recording the proceedings in the heat since 4 p.m. – said that he had noticed several guests, mostly single males dressed in Pathani suits, arrive at the venue in batches, but he had not spotted anyone important coming in before my arrival. Many Arabs wearing *kanduras* and women wearing fancy and expensive *abayas* milled around. The hotel staff later informed me that even Anees Ibrahim was wearing a *kandura* as a disguise. Sathish told me that the media had been asked to stay away from the guests and the hosts, and photographers had been strictly warned against clicking pictures. Sathish's sources at the hotel had refrained from revealing the guest list or sharing information on where the invitees were staying.

I checked into my room on the first floor and changed into a more suitable dress for the occasion. Sathish and I then proceeded to the main lobby and from there to the lower-level Baniyas ballroom, which was not crowded but cordoned off by security. As we approached the doors, the men on duty asked us to show our invitation cards for security reasons. I told them that we had come from Mumbai and did not have an invite, but I was Miandad's guest. I wrote a note for Miandad that I was here to honour his invitation and would report on the event only if he wished. One of the men wearing a black suit went inside with my note and returned with two more men – both with Bluetooth headsets plugged into their ears. They looked like suave agents straight out of some James Bond movie.

One of them, a beefy man in a cream-coloured crisp linen suit, introduced himself as Jaber (the police would tell me later that Jaber Ali Motiwale was from Karachi and a close confidant of Dawood). He began to berate me for our channel's reportage, which he said had hurt both families as the names of their children had been dragged into the dealings of the D Company's criminal empire. Sathish and I exchanged worried looks at the thought that it would now probably be impossible to convince these men to allow us inside.

I requested Jaber to ask his bosses about me and my decade-long history of reportage. If his bosses thought I was not credible enough to grace the occasion, I would leave, I told him. I suspected we were being watched on closed-circuit cameras. All Hyatt ballrooms included a state-of-the-art media room, and I had a hunch that Chhota Shakeel was handling this one himself, monitoring every movement via the footage. My thoughts were confirmed when, almost immediately after I had spoken, Jaber responded to one of his two cell phones. In response to whatever was told to him, his body language suddenly changed and he seemed to ease up. My gut told me I was in luck. Jaber scanned me from head to toe with a scanner and said into one of his phones that I was 'clean'. When he spoke to me now, his tone had changed and said politely, '*Aap chaliye aur bachhon ko dua dijiye.* (You may come in and bless the couple.)' Sathish was asked to wait outside.

I walked into the hall with Jaber on my right and the other security personnel, Fayaz, a slim, athletic-looking man in his early fifties, on my left. Fayaz looked like he could be a former military officer, and later the same evening I would find out that he had spent 20 years in the Pakistan Army. In the ballroom, Junaid and Mahrukh were already on the stage, and there was a long queue of invitees and guests waiting to wish them. Javed Miandad, who had once enthralled the crowds in this city with his magical willow, was welcoming guests from the groom's side along with his wife who was dressed in a silver sari. From a distance, I could see the bride's mother, Mehjabeen, sitting next to her. Dressed in a glittery white georgette suit Mehjabeen graciously received guests on the podium.

Since the stage was crowded, Fayaz and I sat at one of the tables while Jaber went to the stage to inform Miandad that they had brought me in. I looked around to see if I could find any familiar Indian or Pakistani faces. Sathish had told me that high-profile guests, among them the elite of Pakistan and the UAE, including the members of the royal family, were in attendance. None of the big names from Bollywood or the cricketing world was there except for former Pakistan captain Asif Iqbal. The only thing that linked the *walima* to Bollywood was the popular Hindi film songs that continued to play in the background. Dawood himself was there, though invisible to the guests, and we exchanged a brief, silent greeting.

Once the stage was relatively empty, Jaber came down to fetch me. Miandad welcomed me on the stage and introduced me to Junaid and Mahrukh and the other relatives, including Mehjabeen and her other daughter Mahreen. He told them that I had been writing about the D Company for a decade in *India Today* magazine and was now working for Star News in India.

While Junaid wore a dark blue tuxedo, Mahrukh wore a red *sharara-lehenga* heavily embroidered in gold. Both spoke in Hindi and British-accented English. Those on the stage greeted me individually and Miandad told me, '*Dekho, bachhe kitne masoom hai. Bas media lagi padi hai* label *lagane ke liye. Inka kya kasoor? Inko baksh dena chahiye.* Professional *aur* personal life *alag rakhni chahiye.* (Look at the children – they are so innocent. What is their fault? It's just the media that always needs a label. They should be spared. Professional and personal lives should be kept separate.) You must respect my family affairs.' He said the two had met while studying in the UK, but Dawood's wife Mehjabeen and his wife were also related, so the families had known each other for a long time.

I was then asked to sit between the bride and the groom for a photo session. After 15 minutes, I was escorted down from the stage and Jaber insisted that I eat dinner. I told him I would, but in a while, and sat down at a table absorbing the moment. Fayaz sat with me while Jaber went to attend to other guests. We chatted for a bit and he mentioned that I must have won great respect and trust as a journalist as it would not have been possible for me to get in otherwise.

I looked around the hall. What I found striking was that the gaiety one associates with weddings was absent here. The non-stop chit-chat among friends and relatives meeting after a long time, the back-slapping and the loud guffaws, the general merriment that accompanies a happy occasion were all missing. Guests were engaged in conversations in hushed tones. I could see security personnel in civilian clothes all around us. I had heard that a private security agency from Dubai – Vanguard Security Service – had been hired for the event. There were female security guards, too.

Meanwhile, Fayaz was telling me that they kept tabs on all Indian channels and recorded everything that was said about the D Company. I was surprised to learn that he knew the names of our newsreaders across the channels and their characteristic styles. He told me that he admired a particular lady anchor and asked me to pass on his regards to her and tell her that she was beautiful. Cheekily, he added that I should tell her to wear a *bindi* as he thought she looked better with one. I learnt too that Fayaz came from a small Himalayan village near Pakistan-occupied Kashmir, and had three daughters. He claimed to be a lower-ranking officer in the Company, and was in charge of the security of Dawood's family. He gave me his number on the condition that I call him from a Dubai phone and never from India or an Indian number.

My biggest concern at this point was that while I had a story, I had no visuals to support it. Fayaz had confirmed what Satish had told me earlier – that guests were not being allowed to take pictures. He pointed towards the family-appointed cameramen at the stage and at the hall entrance, indicating that only these photographers could take pictures. I had my phone in my handbag but I knew many eyes were watching me closely. I also observed that any attempts to capture the bride and groom or other guests on mobile cameras were being politely but firmly dissuaded. At the table across from mine, a woman took out her mobile phone from her handbag and aimed the camera at the couple but she was immediately asked to desist.

It was now time for me to leave. I was not left alone even for a moment so I knew I would be escorted to the lobby as well. Jaber asked me if I wanted to have dinner, retire to my room and wait there. The ball had been thrown in my court as to how I would report the event, and in the hope of getting an interview of Dawood later I chose to play the long shot instead of giving into the urge of breaking the news of the don's presence at the event.

At around 2 a.m., I called the assignment desk in Mumbai, where Rajneesh Kumar was on night duty. I reported that I had managed to attend the event but since cameras were not allowed inside, the story would reach him in the form of walk-throughs (description-based visuals) and some piece-to-cameras (PTCs), which would come to him in the next hour. He informed me that the Dubai story would play on the first morning bulletin at 5 a.m. The pressure of the deadline was now on my mind. Since cameras were not allowed inside the venue, I would have to describe the scenes in detail and make the story as visually graphic as I could with limited resources.

I called the cameraperson to the garden, where I was waiting. Even at 3 a.m. the heat was unbearable. As he was positioning his tripod, some of the hotel staff came running to tell us we could not shoot in the premises without permission. It was late and no senior staff was available to grant us the permission either. We still managed to get some footage at the hotel and, for the rest of the story, drove around the city's landmarks and completed our work.

The uplink centre was about 45 minutes away, and I was racing against time. I had to file my story in time. At the same time, I wanted to get back to the hotel as soon as possible since I had been offered a chance to meet Dawood after the function was over. Unfortunately, by the time the uplink was done and I got back, it was already 6 a.m. and most of the guests had left. I tried Fayaz's number from the lobby, but nobody took the call. I was primarily there to cover the *walima*, and while I felt some satisfaction at having covered the event successfully I was upset that I missed a golden chance to meet the don separately for an interview.

I slept for a few hours before I got back to work. More PTCs and phone-ins went on throughout the day. My cameraperson that day was an Indian called Prashant, who said he was one of the video-recorders on duty the previous night in Baniyas. I thought I had struck gold and asked him to share some visuals, but my happiness was to last only for a few seconds. He informed me that the entire crew had been strip-searched before and after the event. They had not been allowed to take their own equipment; the cameras had been given to them, only to be taken back after the function was over. Such were the security arrangements, he said, that the kitchen had been sanitized a day before and no hotel staff had been allowed inside the ballroom or the kitchen areas before and through the event. Private cooks, security personnel and service staff had been brought in to maintain secrecy. The family members and close guests had been checked into the hotel the previous day. Dawood, his brothers and other close aides had entered from the back door that opened out into the parking area.

As luck would have it, I was stuck in Dubai for two more days due to the cloud burst of 26 July 2005 in Mumbai, when the city had come to a standstill and the airport had been shut down. I still held out some hope of meeting the don. Fayaz called me back to tell me that even though he was not in a position to talk to 'Bhai' directly, he had relayed the information to him every time I had called. There did not seem to be a way of getting to the don this time, though.

Meanwhile, I tried to be careful yet truthful in my reporting. I had informed Uday about my dilemma and he had agreed that I had made the right decision; yet both of us knew that I had to report the truth. Eventually, I found a way out – I reported that Dawood's 'presence had been felt at the venue'. In my report I commented on two things. One, that the don was a father who could not come out into the open even at his own daughter's wedding. The second was on the secrecy around the wedding and the guests. Times had changed, I felt. There was once a time when people proudly announced they had been invited by 'Bhai' from Dubai. 'Now, nobody was willing to acknowledge his invitation and people were avoiding his functions,' I noted.

After that evening, whenever I spoke to Chhota Shakeel, he would remind me that I was the only Indian journalist to be allowed to attend the *walima*. I had come close to interviewing 'Bhai', he told me, but it just had not worked out. And he reminded me that a 'commitment' had been made that when 'Bhai' was ready to reveal the truth behind the 1993 Mumbai blasts, he would speak to me.

In 2006, I tried once again to reach out to the don through his trusted lieutenant. This was soon after the first verdict on the 1993 blasts was pronounced by the Terrorist and Disruptive Activities (Prevention) Act (TADA) Court in Mumbai on 12 September that year. This time, Chhota Shakeel assured me that he would speak to 'Bhai' and get back to me as the latter was currently in a place where he could not be reached on the phone. As promised, Shakeel called me back, but said that things were not working out and it would not be possible for the don to meet me at the moment.

In the same conversation, Shakeel insisted that the D Company had not executed the 1993 blasts and that the truth behind it needed to be exposed. He claimed, as we had heard earlier through rumours, that 'Bhai' had been kept in the dark about the plan as he was averse to hurting the city that he loved and the plan had been executed without his knowledge. He maintained that the 'facts' would be exposed in time. I contested Shakeel's claim and said that all the evidence had pointed towards Dawood and his brother Anees being a part of the conspiracy hatched in Dubai. Even confessional statements from those arrested and other evidence in the special TADA Court had indicated the same.

In the worst-ever bombing in the history of India, 257 people were killed in a series of explosions in Mumbai on 12 March 1993. This was the first terror attack of its kind believed to have been carried out as revenge for the riots in Mumbai in January 1993 after the demolition of the Babri Masjid in December the previous year. Charge sheets drawn up by the Mumbai Police and the Central Bureau of Investigation (CBI) state that the conspiracy had been masterminded by the Inter-Services Intelligence (ISI) in Pakistan and Dawood Ibrahim, and the plan was executed by Tiger Memon. Assistant Commissioner of Police (ACP) Sunil Prataprao Babar investigated the case under the direct supervision of the then Joint Commissioner of Police (Crime) M.N. Singh and the then Deputy Commissioner of Police (DCP) Rakesh Maria. Investigations revealed the direct or indirect involvement of 204 people, including film star Sanjay Dutt. Out of the 204 accused, 165 were arrested and the remaining 39 – including Dawood, his brother Anees, and Ayub Abdul Razak Memon aka Tiger Memon – were declared as offenders. Of those arrested, the special TADA court, constituted to conduct the trial in this case, acquitted 28. The trial went on in the special court set up at the Arthur Road Jail compound in Mumbai for 13 long years, until Judge P.D. Kode began to deliver his verdict from 12 September 2006 onwards. He convicted 100 men, of whom 12 were awarded the death penalty, including four members of Tiger Memon's family. Twenty others were given life sentences, and the remaining got varying jail terms under the anti-terror law, the Indian Penal Code (IPC) and other relevant penal laws.

In March 2013, the Supreme Court confirmed the judgement of the special court. The apex court, which acquitted two people, upheld the conviction of 84 others. Of the 12 who were awarded the death penalty, the sentences of 10 were commuted to life imprisonment, and of the two who were awarded death sentences, one died a natural death during the course of the trial. The Supreme Court also directed those out on bail to serve their remaining jail terms, and clarified that the convicts undergoing life imprisonment were expected to remain in custody till death. On 30 July 2015, Yakub Memon, Tiger Memon's brother, was hanged for his role in the blasts after multiple petitions and clemency pleas on his behalf were rejected by the Supreme Court and the President of India.

The penalty stage of the longest-running trial in India's history is still on-going, as some of the conspirators who managed to flee the country after the bombings were arrested and extradited to India later on. They include Abu Salem, Mustafa Dossa, Firoz Khan, Taher Merchant, Riyaz Siddiqui and Abdul Qayoom, among others. Dawood Ibrahim, Anees Ibrahim and Tiger Memon are yet to be brought to book. Since 1993, successive governments at the centre have been trying to bring the three back to the country, but in vain. In an interview for ABP News around this time (4 July 2015) Chhota Shakeel told me, 'We wanted to come back, but your government didn't allow us to face the case. *Advani ka game hai.* (It is all Advani's game.) Your government did not want us back. Bhai had himself spoken to Ram Jethmalani (the noted lawyer) in London that time. *Ab daana daalne se koi fayda nahi hai.* (There's no use crying over spilt milk.) We know they will want to trap us and not give us a fair chance to prove our side (of the story in court).'[1]

Jethmalani later confirmed to ABP News that he had indeed spoken to Dawood in 1994 after the blasts.[2] Dawood had apparently told him that he had not been involved in the incidents as it was being made out and that if he was given an assurance of fair treatment he was ready to come to India and face trial. Jethmalani said that he had written to Sharad Pawar, then chief minister of Maharashtra, about Dawood's offer to return. 'The government of that time did not accept Dawood's offer to return as they feared exposure. Obviously, they had something to hide. Something that would have been exposed had Dawood come back... Refusing Dawood's proposal wasn't Pawar's decision alone; the Congress government led by P.V. Narasimha Rao was also a part of it,' Jethmalani told the channel.

In response to Jethmalani's statements, former Maharashtra Chief Minister Sharad Pawar said in a press conference,[3] 'Yes, Ram Jethmalani gave me a proposition but it was conditional. Dawood Ibrahim is facing charges in the Mumbai serial blasts in which hundreds of people lost their lives. With serious charges against him, was it appropriate to get Dawood to India and make five-star arrangements for his stay? The law is the same for all.'

In my interview of 4 July 2015, I asked Shakeel if Dawood, Anees and the Kaskar clan would consider returning to India and facing the law. Shakeel said that no Indian government, including the current one, has been serious about taking up the dons' offer of returning to the country. 'They make statements about Dawood Bhai such as they will smoke the gang out like

Osama and so on. We don't trust anyone any longer and are not buying any bait from Indian authorities.'[4] He went on to relate the troubles that Yakub Memon and his family faced after returning to India. He said that Yakub had surrendered in all earnestness as he had hardly known what his brothers Tiger and Ayub were up to, and yet he faced the gallows and was hanged. Shakeel claimed that the Indian government's promise made to Yakub was not honoured and, therefore, none of them would now think of returning to India.

Soon after this, on 15 July 2015, news broke that Yakub Memon would be hanged at 7 a.m. on 30 July in Nagpur Central Jail, where he had been lodged.[5] The dismissal of his review petition had paved the way for his execution, which had been stayed by the Supreme Court when the petition was filed. His pleas for mercy had already been rejected by President Pranab Mukherjee in April 2015 and again in July. The next morning, Shakeel messaged me: '*Dekh liya? Bharosa kaise karein aur kis pe*? (Now do you see? Tell me, whom should we trust, and how?)'

Indian authorities have, however, maintained their stand that no promises had been made to Yakub or his family – verbal or otherwise – about showing leniency. CBI Joint Director Shantanu Sen, who was responsible for arresting Memon, told ABP News, 'We don't negotiate with criminals and no promise was made to Yakub before or after his arrest. He chose to face the law and went through the trial along with his family as he had faith that he would get justice. I think justice has been done. His parents were spared by the court. One of his brothers was also acquitted as he has mental issues. (Memon) was given capital punishment by both the courts for his role in organizing finances and getting arms for the other accomplices because they felt that it was the rarest of rare situations. He stayed in the same house as Tiger and Ayub, the main conspirators and accused, and he was in the know of the conspiracy.'[6]

Except for Tiger and Ayub, the rest of the Memon family had returned to India from Dubai in 1994 and were promptly arrested by the CBI upon landing. The same year, Yakub was also arrested at Kathmandu airport while boarding a Lufthansa flight to Karachi. During security check, his briefcase revealed a huge bundle of passports, and he was taken to Ramesh Chandra Thakuri, then Kathmandu airport's security chief. When I met Thakuri at his residence in Kathmandu on 29 July 2015, a day before Yakub was hanged, he told me the ten passports found in Yakub's luggage looked authentic. In fact, he had been surprised to see Yakub travelling on an Indian passport when he was arrested and that his other passports had recently been 'renewed'. Yakub's insistence that the other passports belonged to his family members made Thakuri call up the Nepal Inspector-General of Police Motilal Bohara, who in turn called up the Indian Embassy in Nepal to verify the passports and establish Yakub's identity. A certain Mr Ashok Kumar from the embassy identified Yakub and, on India's request, Nepal Police escorted Yakub to Bihar. From there he was brought to Delhi on a special flight. Thakuri told me there was another passenger travelling with Yakub, but he had already checked in and was therefore allowed to leave, perhaps to pass on the message to the Memon family that Yakub had been taken in and they, too, could return to India. Yakub had been in custody since then and was awarded the death sentence by the TADA Court after being held guilty for financing operations in the blasts conspiracy, even though he had consistently maintained that he had returned because he was innocent. Two of his brothers, Essa and Yusuf, and his sister-in-law, Rubina, were also sentenced to life imprisonment.

In response to Shakeel's message, I reminded him once again about his two-decade-old promise and asked if Dawood would speak to me or the media any time soon about what really happened in 1993. To which Shakeel reiterated his old promise and we left it at that.

In the early 1980s, the Mumbai Police dossier on Dawood Ibrahim described him as: 'Height: 5'6"; build: medium; face: round; complexion: shallow; eyebrows: thick; moustache: drooping; no beard. "I" mark mole on the left eyebrow. Type of criminal: cheat, gangster and smuggler. Father's name and occupation: Ibrahim Kaskar, Constable, Crime Branch, CID.'

A decade later, in October 1994, M.N. Singh, then joint commissioner of Mumbai Police, wrote a comprehensive report titled 'Growth of Gangsterism in Mumbai City', which stated similar details about Dawood Ibrahim but added another word in the description of crimes committed by him: 'Terrorism'. In his introductory note Singh wrote, 'Investigations into the 1993 serial bombings in the city brought to light the linkage between Dawood Ibrahim and Sikh militants. Gangsterism, therefore, has acquired an extended dimension of subversion, posing a threat not only to the law and order in the city but also to the security of the entire country, thus making the problem far more sinister and dangerous.'

I was working with the *Times of India* group at Bori Bunder, Mumbai, at the time and had reported on the 1993 blasts. The Crime Branch had already begun to suspect Dawood and his gang's involvement in the blasts, and after visiting their offices the day after the blasts I joined my colleagues for lunch at a nearby restaurant in Crawford Market. The city was still reeling from shock. We were greeted by the restaurant owner, who was seated behind the counter. Since he knew we were reporters, he asked us who we thought was responsible. A friend working for a Marathi daily dropped the Dawood bomb. On hearing his name, the restaurateur, who was also from the Bhendi Bazaar area, said, 'I am shocked he could be involved in such a dastardly act. Had he not gone rogue, he could have been like Tata, Birla or Ambani. I have seen him growing up in our area. He was recklessly daring and an ambitious Muslim boy and was in a hurry to become *raees* (rich). He was sucked into the whirlpool of this city's underworld.'

A TV grab showing Dawood with his family at a birthday party in Dubai in the early 1990s.

Even before the blasts, Dawood had become a classic Mumbai figure in the public imagination, someone who had used his artistry to exploit cracks in the system and within the gangland to become the underworld's boss. The Muslim restaurateur was shaken and scarred by the two ugly rounds of communal riots backed by Hindu fundamentalists that had taken place in the city after the demolition of the Babri Masjid; I had begun to notice armed guards outside his restaurant since December 1992.

Joint Commissioner M.N. Singh's report echoed this perception about Dawood when it was published a year later. It stated, 'Sitting in Dubai, Dawood controls the operations of his gang in Mumbai through his hirelings. With the help of money and muscle power, he has not only maintained his hold over the gang but has also expanded its activities and emerged as the most powerful among all the gangs operating in Mumbai city. He has also emerged as something of a hero-figure for Muslims who look up to him as a saviour of the community. This probably explains why, instead of being condemned for his role in the serial blasts of 12 March 1993, he has earned the admiration of his community for restoring its honour after the Babri Masjid demolition and the Mumbai riots. When Mr Khuddus Kashmiri, president of the Ulema Council, publicly called him his son, he was probably expressing his community's admiration for Dawood Ibrahim.'

Born on 31 December 1955 in a Konkani Muslim family from Mumke village in Khed taluka of Ratnagiri district, Dawood was the second of twelve children. His father, Ibrahim Kaskar, popularly known as Ibrahim *Chacha*, was a police officer who retired as head constable from the Crime Branch, CID, Mumbai. His mother, Aminabi, was a housewife. In Mumbai, they used to reside at 33 Pakmodia Street, which later became the headquarters of his gang.

As per official records, Dawood studied up to the eighth standard at the Urdu-medium Ahmed Sailor High School in Nagpada. He dropped out of school in 1969 and started hanging out with other Muslim boys at Musafir Khana in south Mumbai, where smuggled goods were sold. He closely watched how the black market operated and saw a way to make money without putting in too much effort.

From here Dawood began his criminal career as a conman. The modus operandi was to show a potential customer an imported wristwatch or sometimes even a gold biscuit. After the initial haggling over the price, he would take the money and, in return, hand over the 'object' wrapped in paper. The customer was told to walk away quickly as the police were coming. Upon opening the wrapper, the aghast customer would find either a stone or an inferior-quality wristwatch inside. When his father heard about his son's wayward behaviour, he took the help of Haji Mastan to set up a small shop of electronic items for his sons Shabbir and Dawood to make money in a more respectable way. Most of the items sold in the shop were smuggled, and Dawood's sharp attitude and shrewd salesmanship landed him a role in Mastan's electronic smuggling business. He then graduated to transporting, protecting and delivering smuggled goods from Musafir Khana to various destinations. He formed a small core group of mainly Konkani Muslim boys to facilitate the operations.

The Ibrahims were always in need of money and other resources. His father's respectable job did not earn him enough to sustain the large family. The erstwhile smuggling kingpins Mastan and Karim Lala, who had labelled themselves messiahs of the poor, occasionally supported Ibrahim Kaskar by way of some *baksheesh* for his community services, which kept the family going. After tasting success with their shop and odd jobs for Mastan, Shabbir and Dawood took to smuggling textiles and low-value goods on the sly without informing Mastan, while the younger brothers, Noora and Anees, worked in a garage nearby. Dawood built a small office near their residence, and an unauthorized extension of the residential building allowed him to virtually build a fort on Pakmodia Street. The entry into the building complex was controlled through a main gangway protected by a huge gate, which was always kept closed and guarded. Dawood posted his trusted men at this entrance, the only one to the building. He also arranged for an intercom facility so that whenever a stranger wanted to enter the building, the men posted at the gate would collect his details and communicate the same to Dawood in his office or residence by using the intercom. This was unique in those days, even for a gangster.

As his ventures became successful, Dawood tried out newer crimes. Dawood and his associates, it is said, looted a boat carrying contraband off the Haji Ali coastline, and nearly a dozen partners distributed among themselves goods valued at around ₹15 lakh. The family suddenly had money, and soon Dawood was driving a second-hand Chevrolet Malibu and wearing branded suits stitched by expensive tailors. Like a film star, he could be spotted at night clubs, wearing the oversized dark-glasses that have now become his trademark. His one-time friend and smuggler Iqbal Mirchi, who owned a night club in Mumbai, spoke to me about this flamboyant lifestyle and attitude resembling that of a Bollywood star. His penchant for the good life was his driving force to make more money. His extravagance and charm won him many associates, and he made enemies as well among those who were threatened by his rapidly growing influence.

According to records of the Mumbai Police, Dawood's first major quarrel was with the Syed Batla gang, who also worked for Mastan. Batla suspected that Dawood was getting negative stories published against him in a local Urdu newspaper through his friend and editor Iqbal Naatik, and he got Naatik killed. The incident led to enmity between the two gangs. Mastan tried to resolve the matter, but Dawood was not happy with an apology. He parted ways with Mastan to start an independent outfit. Batla, in turn, joined hands with the Pathan brothers – Alamzeb and Amirjada – whose father, Changrez Khan, a retired watchman, was an associate of Karim Lala, the overlord of the crime world in south Mumbai at the time.

A Pashtun Pathan, Karim Lala had come to Mumbai in search of a good life, but lack of education and any special skills forced him to serve wealthy traders and textile industrialists. His services were used for *vasooli* (debt collection) and as he gathered people to do what he did under his tutelage, it marked the beginning of the Pathan gang. Soon, Lala diversified into bootlegging, gambling, prostitution and drug trafficking, along with local Gujarati banias Madhubhai and Madhavji Thakkar in Israeli *mohalla* in Dongri. With a thriving illegal business, Lala became the lord of the poor, unemployed and unskilled Muslim youth of the south Mumbai port area.

The 1972 general elections saw the birth of the Young Party, which mostly had as its members fanatical Muslim youth. It was formed by the late Maulana Ziauddin Bukhari in order to counter and eliminate Bashu, a notorious gangster from Teli *mohalla* who had worked against Muslim League candidates in the elections, and Yunus Ansari, an important witness in a petition against Bukhari. Dawood, then 17 years old, and Shabbir were key members of this party, and were joined by Samad Khan, the nephew of Karim Lala, and a few other Pathan youths like Alam Zeb (later killed in an encounter with the Gujarat Police), Amirjada (later killed in a shoot-out at the Sessions Court in Mumbai) and Mehmood Kaliya (later killed in a police encounter).

Bukhari contested in the assembly elections and won from the Khara Talab area, today's Mumba Devi, defeating Shauket Chagla, the Congress candidate. But he lost the seat within six months due to an election petition made by a citizen, inter alia, alleging that Bukhari had appealed to the voters to refrain from voting for Chagla on the grounds of religion and that Bukhari promoted feelings of enmity or hatred between different classes of citizens of India on the grounds of religion. Bukhari's election was set aside by the Mumbai High Court and when the verdict was also upheld by the Supreme Court, Bukhari began to withdraw his patronage and support to the party.[7] Shabbir and Dawood sensed an opportunity and began to take control. As money was needed to run the organization, Dawood, with the help of other party associates, committed his first major crime: a ₹4 lakh dacoity at Carnac Bridge on 4 December 1974.

The armed robbery turned the fortunes of Dawood Ibrahim Kaskar, causing his crime graph to climb continuously from that time on, and the Young Party became a gang of hardcore anti-social elements. Dawood's services began to be utilized for the safe landing and delivery of gold and silver and, later, electronic goods smuggled into the country by Haji Mastan and Yusuf Patel, the other big player at the time. With a clear eye on the profit margins such activities yielded, Dawood began poaching clients from Mastan, Patel and Lala by offering them competitive rates on the safe landing and distribution of smuggled goods. Contraband was being smuggled in bulk with the cooperation of customs officials and the police. Dawood's smooth dealings with the elite and influential merchants of Mumbai as well as with corrupt officials gave him an edge over the competition. What made him stand out was his bold attitude in commanding higher 'service' prices for illegal jobs for which he guaranteed successful results. Further, he would contribute to the cost if the job was not fulfilled or the goods got damaged. He was also ingenious in finding new smuggling routes, even taking to air routes that were much faster than the tried-and-tested traditional sea routes. Essentially, Dawood cut off all middlemen in the business. He knew very early on where his bread and butter would come from, and gradually his client list came to include influential textile and yarn industrialists, bullion and diamond traders, and builders and politicians who were also served by an umbrella outfit of local, smaller criminals. No other gang in the entire west coast of India could match Dawood's acumen in running illegal and criminal operations.

The stringent 1968 Gold Control Act triggered illegal imports of metal from the Gulf countries in the 1970s and 1980s, particularly from Dubai. Dawood knew that Dubai gold dealers had monopolized the smuggling business and dictated the terms of engagement. He, therefore, went to Dubai to figure out a way to get a direct supply of bullion. Here, his craftiness came in handy and he got some of the top bullion dealers in Dubai on board as he promised them a one-stop smuggling operation (supplier-cum-smuggler-cum-distributor) to offload goods in the grey market. His frequent visits to Dubai drew the attention of the authorities, and in 1982 he was arrested by customs officials at the Santacruz Airport with gold worth ₹25 lakh and detained under the Conservation of Foreign Exchange and Prevention of Smuggling Activities Act (COFEPOSA). He was, however, acquitted of these charges in 1983. Once the Act was abolished in the early 1990s, the D Company continued to smuggle drugs and arms through the same routes and networks.

Although initially the Kaskar brothers and the Pathans worked together, they parted ways owing to differences of opinion over the functioning of the Young Party and distribution of the loot. The Young Party thus gave birth to two gangs: the Dawood Ibrahim gang and the Pathan gang, who remained in direct conflict with each other. The Pathans were known for their violent ways in business, while Dawood presented himself as a civil and courteous gangster. He gained the support of many *galli* (street) gangs who were directly involved in protection-money rackets, settling land and financial disputes, and *vasooli.* As the interests of the two gangs clashed, they began to move into more violent territory, acquiring sophisticated firearms and killing off rival members. What changed the politics of the underworld in Mumbai, and introduced bloody violence to the business, was the killing of Shabbir Kaskar. A retired senior police inspector from the Crime Branch who has dealt with most of the gangsters (from

Dawood in the 1980s to his brother Iqbal in 2003) and witnessed their evolution, told me that it was Shabbir's ghastly murder and the subsequent attack on Dawood's younger brother Noora that steered the don's career towards more violent crimes. The incident marked the beginning of a succession of long and bloody gang wars that, in many ways, continue today.

On 12 February 1981, Shabbir is known to have picked up a dancer from Kennedy Bridge, Opera House, and proceeded on a drive. The two brothers, Alamzeb and Amirjada of the Pathan gang, followed his car, and when Shabbir stopped at a petrol pump opposite the Siddhi Vinayak Mandir in Prabhadevi they shot him seven times, killing him instantly. The motive behind the killing was to clip Dawood's wings. Shabbir's killing triggered a series of murders of members of the Pathan gang. Amirjada was ultimately arrested, while, according to official records, Alamzeb escaped and took shelter in Ahmedabad with the notorious Pathan gang member Gulab Khan. A furious Dawood waited for an opportunity to take revenge. He began by entering into direct competition with Gulab Khan in the smuggling and bootlegging business in Gujarat, and audaciously got Amirjada killed on the premises of the Sessions Court in Mumbai through a hired assassin, David Pardeshi of the Bada Rajan gang. Both Pardeshi and Rajan were arrested while Dawood was granted anticipatory bail as his lawyers expressed apprehension about the danger to his life at the hands of members of the Pathan gang.[8]

Meanwhile, realizing the growing power of Dawood and his gang, Karim Lala, the head and founder of the Pathan gang, approached Dawood for a settlement, but the very next day, Samad Khan, Lala's nephew, attempted to kill Noora, Dawood's younger brother. Dawood and Anees got Samad Khan murdered in October 1984, which marked the beginning of a spate of killings in Mumbai in which Dawood emerged as the ultimate victor after he killed Karim Lala's brother Rahim and brought the other active gangs of Mumbai – those belonging to Rama Naik, Babu Reshim, Arun Gawli, Sharad Shetty, Chhota Rajan and Ashok Joshi – under his control. All these gangs thrived on providing safe passage to illicit liquor businesses, smuggled contraband, land grabbing and extorting protection money. The Mumbai underworld first made its entry into the real estate business due to the tenancy laws and the 1976 Mumbai Urban Ceiling Act. These legislations led to the landlords paying hefty sums of money to gangsters to forcefully evict their tenants and to avoid harassment by the law. Builders, developers and even industrialists hired gangsters to forcibly evict recalcitrant occupants or to grab land.

One of the few existing visuals that show Chhota Rajan, Dawood Ibrahim and Chhota Shakeel (in the back row) together.

The murders of Babubhai Shah of Sheetal Stores on 6 March 1994 and of the textile mill owner Sunit Khatau on 7 May of the same year, both over land disputes, clearly exposed the growing nexus between gangsters and the business community. A known sympathizer and financier of Arun Gawli's gang, Sunit Khatau was preparing to sell surplus land around his mill and eventually shift his mill to Borivali. Knowing that Arun Gawli would receive a sizeable amount after the sale of the land, Amar Naik, a member of Gawli's rival Ashwin Naik's gang, decided to eliminate Sunit Khatau. On 7 May, Sunit Khatau's Mercedes was intercepted near Mahalaxmi Railway Station. A group of Naik's men attacked the car with heavy hammers and after breaking the windshield and the windows, shot Sunit Khatau in the car. The case was tried under the TADA but the accused were eventually acquitted by the TADA Court as Khatau's wife did not support the prosecution.

Real estate had become an exciting investment opportunity for the gangsters, and Dawood, too, acquired a number of properties in his name and in the names of his relatives and others. According to the information provided by the Directorate of Revenue Intelligence and gathered by Mumbai Police, Dawood owned over 76 properties in Mumbai and Maharashtra, which were attached by the order of the trial TADA Court when he was declared a proclaimed offender in the Mumbai blasts case.

In 1984, after his release on bail following the murder of Samad Khan, Dawood managed to obtain a new passport (his own having been deposited with the authorities by order of the court) and fled to Dubai. He has not returned to India since. Official records indicate that Dawood had managed to get a few other Indian passports issued to him. He would later admit, in an interview with *India Today* in 1993, that he travelled 'unofficially' around the world but avoided countries that had an extradition treaty with India.[9] (While Dawood's brothers fled to Dubai once he left the country and settled there, two of his sisters have passed away; four currently live in Mumbai, while one has settled in Dubai.)

Dubai now became Dawood's home. For a man who had lived in a congested locality and a dingy apartment with a dozen family members, Dubai turned out to be a dream city. Here, he established a legitimate construction and trading company, popularly called the 'D Company', with its offices on the twelfth floor of the 17-storey Pearl building on Al Fahidi Street, also known to be a shoppers' paradise. He ran his operations – legitimate and illegitimate – from here. According to records maintained by the Mumbai Police, he finally fulfilled his childhood dream of staying in a palatial house when he purchased a huge mansion at Jumeirah, an upmarket area in Dubai, and called it 'White House'. The house went on to host many influential people who were regularly entertained with good food, the best of French wines and Cuban cigars. Surrounded by powerful and glamorous personalities, Dawood became a figure of glamour and power himself.

Dawood enjoyed flaunting his Bollywood and other connections, all of which served as a symbol of his power in a star-struck nation. Despite his criminal record, he seemed to have acquired a curious respectability. He regularly indulged in pomp and show by hosting extravagant events. His lavish birthday party on 31 December 1992 saw famous Bollywood stars like Sanjay Dutt, Feroze Khan, Mithun Chakraborty, Johnny Lever, Asrani, Govinda, Mazhar Khan, Anil Kapoor, Jitendra, Jaya Prada, Aditya Pancholi and popular singers and celebrities attending it. Some would continue to be regularly spotted at Dawood's parties in Dubai and Sharjah, to which he would also invite his business clients and negotiate deals that would earn him millions. It was at one such party that Dawood met Bollywood actress Mandakini, whose real name was Yasmeen Joseph, with whom he allegedly had a child whom he supports to this day.

Whether the film stars attended the events because they were pressurized to do so or to flaunt their connection with the don remains in the realm of speculation. After the Mumbai blasts, many of them would be questioned by the police for their alleged links with the underworld. Dawood also went on to finance films through his chosen producers and directors, such as Hanif

Kadawala and Samir Hingora, accused in Mumbai blasts case, who allegedly ploughed back his money into the film industry through their company, Magnum Video, which has also been suspected to be involved in piracy. Hingora and Kadawala were arrested in April 1993 for their involvement in the blasts; Kadawala was shot dead in his office in February 2001 by unknown assailants, while Hingora was sentenced to nine years' rigorous imprisonment. According to official records, the police suspected Chhota Rajan-aide Guru Satham of engineering Kadawala's murder.

Dawood is said to be addicted to Hindi movies. According to those who know him personally, his habit of watching 'first-day, first-show' screenings of newly released films has apparently not changed over the years. Thanks to his widespread piracy business across India, Asia, the UK and the US, new releases reach him every week. Once, during an interview with me, Shakeel highly recommended I watch *Black Friday*, based on the 1993 blasts and the subsequent investigations, which had not released at the time.

My sources, some of whom have observed Dawood from very close quarters, say Dawood is himself quite filmy in many ways. According to them, he can outdo even the legendary actor Rajinikanth in style. The few video clips of Dawood at various family functions and parties from the 1990s (that are available with ABP News) show him wearing a white *sherwani*, with a cigarette in one hand, moving around smoothly in a crowd. At some point, he looks up and blows smoke into the air like Rajinikanth. A series of smoke rings rise above the crowd and glide across the room. This act is an attention-grabber, even in a room filled with smokers from the D Company. The ability to blow thick smoke rings that float confidently in the air is his trademark. Then come his branded suits, the dark glasses, the thick gold chain and his expensive diamond watch. A courteous mafia boss, 'Dawood Bhai' appears well-mannered yet intimidating. He speaks softly but sounds menacing.

Besides Bollywood, the don is also passionate about cricket. Images from the Sharjah Cup held in November 1985 – of a smartly dressed Dawood, wearing his trademark oversized shades with a phone in one hand and his Rothmans cigarette in the other, relaxing with his close associates and a few top stars from Bollywood stars in a special box at the stadium – have repeatedly been used by the Indian media when reporting on the don. The image is a powerful testimony of Dawood's strong hold over the game and the film world in Mumbai, even from faraway Dubai. He is known to open the betting price bid before a game, and punters in India, Pakistan, Bangladesh, Sri Lanka and Africa follow suit, placing bets ball-by-ball for a match. The bookie syndicate that he established and ran from Dubai evolved into an organized betting racket that allegedly fixed matches. Dawood's name cropped up in the cricket scandals of the late 1990s when he threatened Mumbai bookie Shobhan Mehta, and his brother Anees Ibrahim is suspected to have been involved in the match-fixing scandal of 2000, when South African captain Hansie Cronje and Indian captain Mohammed Azharuddin were charged with their connection to match-fixing via the bookie Sanjay Chawla. At the time, the Delhi Police revealed they had a recording of a conversation between Cronje and Chawla, the alleged representative of an Indian betting syndicate linked with the D Company. Cronje confessed that Azharuddin had introduced him to bookies, and the latter was banned from the game for life by the International Cricket Council (ICC) and the Board of Control for Cricket in India (BCCI). At the time, Dawood was blamed for laundering money via Internet sites that helped transfer funds from Dubai or London-based banks. In the 2000s, he was charged with enticing cricketers in the Indian Premier League (IPL) and was also suspected of investing in the league's teams through front partners. (These and related events are elaborately discussed in the following chapters.)

While media obsession over his Bollywood and cricket connections still continues, film stars who once flanked Dawood's side have for a while kept their distance from the don in fear of the law. Those who continued to maintain contacts kept it a secret and met the mobster and other gang members only on shoots or stage shows abroad. Sanjay Dutt's conviction on charges of illegal possession of firearms by the TADA Court in 2007 turned out to be a glaring example for all of them. It is believed that in the 1990s Dawood had invested at least ₹500 crore in Bollywood films. If the actors he had chosen refused to act in his films, his cronies would coerce them into doing so. *Chori Chori Chupke Chupke* was a classic example where the movie producer Bharat Shah was convicted for having links with the D Company. I have elaborated on the latter episode in a later chapter.

A retired Research & Analysis Wing (R&AW) official who handled underworld issues had once told me that Dawood was a keen observer, a quick learner and had an elephantine memory. He imbibed all the things that impressed him in life – from mannerisms and trade tactics to the lifestyles of the elite he would come across while moving around the world. He was very much an 'alpha male', the official maintained. His games and gambles were always big, and he specifically considered this to be his trademark style.

An encounter specialist who is responsible for eliminating many gangsters told me that Dawood controls the largest network of underworld operatives due to his extraordinary man-management skills. For Dawood, loyalty matters the most. He generously rewards his loyal army of followers and never abandons them. He takes care of their families after their deaths or while they are in jail, and in turn his men are willing to lay down their lives for him. Gang members who have been caught by the police have spoken both about his large-heartedness and his ruthlessness. He is known to be intolerant of treachery, and for betrayers the punishment is nothing less than a bullet to the heart or the head.

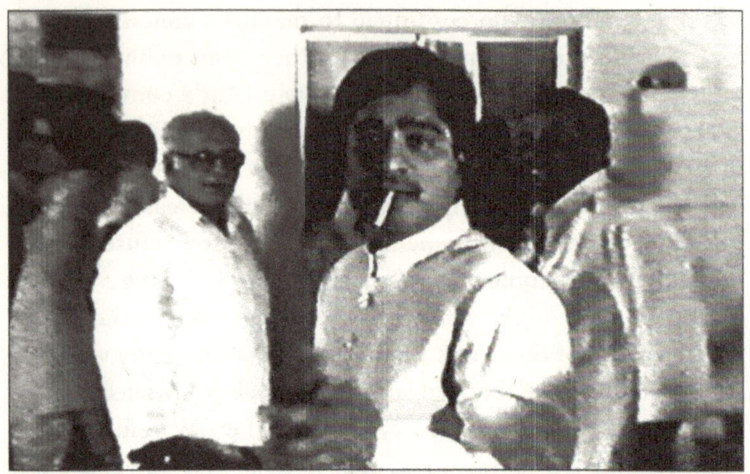

A TV grab showing Dawood Ibrahim at a wedding function in the late 1980s. Photo courtesy ABP News.

The last was confirmed to me by Riaz Jallianwala, the son of Dawood's Pakistani smuggling partner Taufiq Jallianwala, in a recent conversation. 'Dawood Bhai killed my father and uncle brutally and chopped off another uncle's legs,' Riaz said. 'His brother Mustaquin tried to kill my brother and me but we managed to escape. It was my father who gave Dawood his bungalow at Clifton in Karachi after his arrival from Dubai. In return, he killed him and his two brothers for suspected treachery.' Riaz is currently on the run, hiding from Dawood and his organization as he fears for his life. It has been argued that Taufiq, at the ISI's behest, had coordinated the Mumbai blasts from Pakistan with the help of Tiger Memon in India. Despite being friends and partners in the narcotics smuggling business, Taufiq is believed to have kept Dawood in the dark about the plans till the day of the blasts while using his name and network all the while. It was for this that Dawood had allegedly vowed to kill Taufiq's '*khandaan* (family)'.

It has also been heard from several quarters that both Dawood and Chhota Shakeel, his second-in-command, are known to be men of their word. A veteran police officer who knew Dawood's father Ibrahim Kaskar, told me that the older generation of Mumbai gangsters – mostly of Pashtun Pathan descent – culturally and traditionally believed in honouring their promises in the business. From the 1960s to the 1980s, he said, all *do numbri* (illegal) businesses were conducted solely on the basis of this business ethic, and dishonouring one's promise meant a bad name and losing business forever. Groomed under the Pathan boss Karim Lala, Dawood perhaps imbibed this underworld practice to the core. His close associate Chhota Shakeel echoed it in one of my interviews with him when he said, '*Zabaan di hai to di hai.* (My promise will be honoured, no matter what.)'

Initially, in Dubai, Dawood's gold-dealer friends helped him make an entry into the city's power corridors. The don's charming ways and craftiness found expression once again in his ability to impress the high and mighty of Dubai's power circuit, sheikhs and emirs from the Gulf and the elite of India, Pakistan, Africa and Russia. These connections opened up a new horizon in crime for him. After meeting known Pakistani smugglers like Yusuf Godhrawala and Taufiq Jallianwala, originally Memons from Mumbai who had settled in Karachi after the Partition of the country in 1947, Dawood found the narcotics business in the subcontinent to be more enticing than smuggling bullion and electronic goods. He was first introduced to Taufiq by a common friend at a party in Dubai when he visited the city in the early 1980s. After he escaped to Dubai, he met Taufiq again at a social gathering, where the latter invited Dawood to visit Pakistan and promised him great *mehmaan-nawazi.* Taufiq, with the help of his connections in the ISI, is said to have received Dawood right on the tarmac when he flew in, and escorted him into the country without any immigration procedures, which impressed the don. The story goes that Taufiq and Yusuf offered Dawood a supply of 'real gold' (heroin) if he was interested in using his networks to smuggle it into Mumbai through the sea route; he was told he could be a billionaire in no time. The offer sounded like a big business opportunity and, subsequently, Dawood stepped into the ISI's veiled world of deception. His new set of smuggler friends from Pakistan and Afghanistan are said to have advised him to go for a new identity and a passport from a Muslim country in order to have free movement within the region. Dawood's Saudi Arabian and Pakistani passports helped him conceal his travels and his identity from Interpol and India. Later, Dawood said in his 1994 interview to *India Today* that he was allegedly shocked to find out from Yakub Memon's interview that Taufiq Jallianwala had played an important role in the serial blasts. Dawood also admitted in the interview that he had known Jallianwala for over a decade and had travelled to Pakistan to attend his daughter's wedding because they were friends.

With the 'D Company' established in Dubai, Dawood was now competing with some of the world's most accomplished outlaws. The task before him was to consolidate his position and expand his base across the subcontinent. From Dubai, with the help of money and muscle he not only maintained his hold over his gang but also managed to expand its activities and have it emerge as the most powerful among all the groups operating in Mumbai. In addition to smuggling, illegal gambling, and an unlawful country liquor business, the D Company began to indulge in drug trafficking, *hawala*, land grabbing and forcible evictions, video piracy, prostitution, contract killings and extortion rackets. Dawood believed that creating more terror in his name in Mumbai would generate a greater brand value for his company in the international market, which would in turn fetch him more lucrative contracts related to India.

Over the years, investigations have revealed that the don has his fingers in virtually every pie connected to a range of crimes. Information connected to the Mumbai blasts has brought to light Dawood's network of *hawala* racketeers working for him throughout India to launder his funds to multiple countries, including Dubai. These *hawala* channels have also facilitated absconders in the Mumbai blasts case through various states such as Delhi, Rajasthan, Uttar Pradesh, Gujarat and Karnataka. The Mumbai Police has long suspected that Dawood had invested in travel agencies and recruitment companies operating in Dongri, Nagpada and Colaba areas to facilitate his gang's travel and migration processes. The D Company was reported to have considerable stake in East-West Airlines, the first private airline set up in India after the liberalization of its economy in 1991. The company's managing director Takiyuddin Wahid was shot dead in 1995, presumably by Dawood's rivals. In 2005, Jet Airways was to face problems in flying to the US due to reports of its alleged links with the D Company.

Then there are Dawood's forays into politics. He is said to have started funding Indian political parties from the early 1990s. In the *India Today* interview of 1993, Dawood admitted to funding all big political parties. It was rumoured then that around 70 members of Parliament owed their election to Dawood, although no one could confirm his clout because there was nothing on paper. Gangster-turned-politicians such as Bhai Thakur and Suresh alias Pappu Kalani were arrested at around the same time for having links with Dawood.

Once Dawood moved to Dubai to escape the law, other gangsters in Mumbai such as Chhota Rajan, Guru Satam, Chhota Shakeel, Sharad Shetty, Abu Salem and Sunil Sawant, all of whom owed their allegiance to the D Company, followed suit and fled

India. Like Dawood, though they left the country, their operations continued in India through their local henchmen. Arun Gawli and Ashwin Naik were the only two gangsters to give him a tough fight in Mumbai with the tacit support of local politicians, particularly in the Shiv Sena. Dawood also had differences with the Rama Naik gang, which separated from the D Company due to differences over a plot of land. Initially, the dispute was between Rama Naik and Sharad Shetty, a Dawood confidant. When the dispute was brought before Dawood for a settlement, he decided in favour of Shetty, and Naik fell out with his former associates. Naik was then killed in a police encounter in July 1988.

Dawood has also had a long-running feud with Arun Gawli over the control of the city. The feud cost Ismail Parkar, Dawood's younger sister Hasina's husband, his life. He was killed in his Nagpada hotel in 1991 as revenge for the killing of Gawli's brother, Papa Gawli, by the D Company. Dawood struck back by killing one of the killers, Shailesh Haldankar, in a raid on JJ Hospital in July 1992, where Haldankar was being treated for injuries. Dawood's associates stormed the hospital armed with automatic weapons, killing Haldankar and two policemen, and injuring five others.

When the gang wars escalated in Mumbai and the police began to kill known members of the gangs in encounters, the D Company found a new way to carry out assassinations. Dawood authorized a distinct group of hired killers who belonged to Uttar Pradesh and whose effectiveness stemmed from the fact that they were previously unknown in Mumbai and could thus easily enter the city, perform a 'hit' and leave the city without arousing any suspicion. This group included criminals like Subhash Singh Thakur, Brijesh Singh, Jai Prakash Bachhi of Varanasi, and Pradhan Singh and Mukhtar Ansari of Ghazipur. The other known operatives across the country included Latif Khan of Ahmedabad, Rusi Pathan of Bhopal, Subhash Singh Thakur of Varanasi, Babloo Srivastava who operated in Lucknow and Delhi, Sadhu Shetty of Mangalore and Hidayatullah of Calcutta. These smaller gangs were given contracts to eliminate rivals or provide protection as well as ensure smooth transportation of goods. They were allowed a certain degree of operational freedom and they helped the D Company expand its presence across the country, but Dawood saw to it that all of them remained totally dependent on him, especially for his networks. The don had always known how to enjoy the patronage of influential people and had tremendous clout in powerful quarters.

The first case of an organized gun-running racket in India came to light during the investigation into the 1993 Mumbai blasts, when it was found that shiploads of AK-56 rifles, 9mm pistols, Arges grenades, electric and chemical detonators, RDX, TNT and PETN explosives had been brought in consignments with the assistance of Abdul Razzak 'Tiger' Memon and Mohammed Mustafa Dossa along tried-and-tested sea-smuggling routes into Gujarat and Maharashtra and then transported down to Mumbai. The Mumbai blasts were the first instance of the underworld joining hands with the ISI to destabilize India. It further transpired during the investigations that Dawood and the ISI had allegedly hatched a conspiracy to train thousands of Muslim youths from different parts of the country to cause similar blasts elsewhere. Once India and the UAE began to discuss an extradition treaty, Dawood fled from Dubai with his entire family and was given shelter in Karachi by Pakistan. His henchmen Chhota Shakeel and Faheem Machmach followed suit and settled in Karachi. Dawood's associates and activities were spread across the subcontinent as well. Among other incidents, Nepali MP Mirza Dilshad Beg was shot dead in 1998 by Chhota Rajan's associates for having links with the D Company.

September 2014 was a time of joy and celebration in the D Company. The Mumbai-based Pir Saheb had approved a new alliance and given his blessings, and top-notch Bollywood designers had been consulted for a bridal trousseau without being told who the bride was. Expensive invites had been sent out with special accompaniments of baklava and gold coins. Despite his younger sister's untimely death in Mumbai due to a cardiac arrest in July the same year, Dawood Ibrahim's characteristic generosity towards his loyalists was on display when he came out of mourning for the special occasion, the first *nikah* in Chhota Shakeel's family. After all, the girl, Zoya Shakeel Babumiya Sheikh, called Dawood '*Bade Papa*'. Zoya, who had trained to be a doctor, was getting married to an American doctor of Indian origin, whose family had moved to Karachi after the Partition of the country in 1947. The *nikah* was to be a comparatively low-key function in Karachi, keeping in mind Dawood's personal loss.

While preparations for Zoya's wedding were on in Karachi and Dawood had been inviting guests, including the top brass of the Pakistan Army and the ISI, to a secure but plush venue for the reception post the *nikah*, in New Delhi Indian authorities were busy updating their dossier on the D Company. They were trying to persuade the US to clip its wings, curb its financial powers and pressurize its leader's host, Pakistan, to extradite Dawood to India.

The newly elected Narendra Modi-led BJP government had put this on top of the agenda from a security aspect, and Prime Minister Narendra Modi was meeting US President Barack Obama around the time Zoya was getting married.[10] The Indian government was aware of the don's plans, and in their talks on 30 September at the White House, Prime Minister Modi and President Obama committed themselves to joint and concentrated efforts to dismantle all safe havens for terror and disrupt all financial and tactical support to the al-Qaeda, Lashkar-e-Taiba,

Jaish-e-Mohammed, the Haqqani network and, most importantly, the D Company. National Security Advisor Ajit Doval, who had accompanied Prime Minister Modi to the US, extended his stay by two days to meet other leaders, including US Defense Secretary Chuck Hagel, to discuss common security interests between the US and India, their commitment to the strategic Indo-US partnership and future areas of bilateral security cooperation, including dealing with India's Enemy Number One and his possible capture in the future.

In Mumbai, meanwhile, the police kept a close watch on the airport, looking out for celebrities or well-wishers who would travel through to attend Zoya's *walima*. Dawood had managed to keep his presence at his elder daughter's *walima* a secret, but this time he not only graced the ceremony of Zoya's *nikah* on 19 September under the security cover of Pakistani authorities in Karachi, but also attended the *walima* on 28 September.

Despite such bonhomie, Pakistan has continued to officially deny Dawood's presence on its soil and has declared that it has no idea where he lives. For India, there might not be an easy solution as he has powerful patrons in the West and in the Gulf. In fact, there has been a clear pattern to Dawood's matchmaking strategy for his children. As mentioned earlier, Javed Miandad had told me his son Junaid and Dawood's daughter Mahrukh had met in the UK. The marriage fuelled reports of the don's black money investments and cricket match-fixing syndicate. Dawood's son, Moin, is married to Saniya, daughter of a London-based businessman. His youngest daughter, Mahreen, is the daughter-in-law of a rich businessman in the US. All three alliances indicate an attempt on Dawood's part to gain legitimacy in the West and strengthen his position in the hierarchy in Pakistan.

It is no mean feat for a lower middle-class school dropout to become one of the world's most infamous and powerful criminals. Dawood remains the only person with the dubious distinction of being designated both a 'global terrorist supporter' and a 'foreign narcotics kingpin'. In fact, he was ranked 57th on the list of the world's most powerful people by *Forbes* in 2011.[13] It takes a unique combination of business sense and ruthlessness to make it to the highest echelons of the crime world, and Dawood has both in plenty. As of May 2015, according to *Forbes* magazine, the D Company had an estimated net worth of $6.7 billion.[11] In June 2015, Dawood was seen in Sydney, Australia, scouting for a luxury apartment. According to the Australian magazine *Billionaire Newswire*, Dawood was spotted at Sydney's noted Golden Century restaurant in Chinatown along with other figures from the Sydney underworld and is said to have settled for a $5 million luxury property in the affluent locations around Sydney's Centennial Park, Kensington and Kingsford.[12]

The prelude to the *Forbes* listing was the first official announcement by the US Treasury on 16 October 2003 that it had labelled Dawood Ibrahim 'as a specially designated global terrorist under Executive Order 13224' and would request 'that the UN list him as well'. This finally vindicated India's stand at international platforms after a decade-long process of persuasion by successive Indian governments since the 1993 blasts.[14] With the announcement, not only did the American government finally acknowledge India's contention on Dawood and his syndicate but it also exposed Pakistan's clandestine support to the Dawood clan by providing details of Dawood's Pakistani passports, addresses of his residences in the country and his business interests. The label meant that all assets belonging to Dawood within the US are frozen and he is prohibited from conducting any transactions with US nationals.

The UN listing mentioned in the US treasury announcement

required that all UN member states take similar action. The fact sheet attached with the UN listing said: 'Dawood Ibrahim's syndicate is involved in large-scale shipments of narcotics in the UK and Western Europe. The syndicate's smuggling routes from South Asia, the Middle East and Africa are shared with Osama bin Laden and his terrorist network. Successful routes established over recent years by Dawood's syndicate have been subsequently utilized by Osama bin Laden. A financial arrangement was reportedly brokered to facilitate the latter's usage of these routes. In the late 1990s, Dawood travelled in Afghanistan under the protection of the Taliban. Dawood is currently wanted by India for the 12 March 1993 Mumbai Exchange bombings, which killed hundreds of Indians and injured over a thousand more. Information gathered by India's intelligence agencies indicates that Dawood has financially supported Islamic militant groups working against India, such as the Lashkar-e-Taiba (LeT), 'Army of the Righteous)', the armed wing of Markaz-ud-Dawa-wal-Irshad (MDI), a Sunni anti-US missionary organization formed in 1989. The United States added LeT to the list of designated terrorist organizations in October 2001. The group was banned by the Pakistani government, and its assets frozen, in January 2002.'

With the strong worldwide network he has established, Dawood's name has now become a byword in South and Southeast Asia's political, business, law enforcement and international spy agency circuits. Once a Mumbai street hoodlum, he now possesses international influence to the extent that he has earned the description of 'Osama bin Laden of South Asia' from Gilbert Anthony King, the American author of *The Most Dangerous Man in the World: Dawood Ibrahim.*[15] In his book, Gilbert has called Dawood an Islamic extremist, a nuclear black market entrepreneur and a protector of Osama bin Laden. The book shockingly reveals Dawood's alleged involvement in the kidnapping and death of the

US journalist Daniel Pearl, protecting Osama bin Laden after the fall of the Taliban in Afghanistan, and playing the establishment of the nuclear black market. Gilbert states that Dawood is closely linked with Bukhary Syed Abu Tahir, a Sri Lankan businessman of Tamil origin and a high-powered broker of nuclear technologies. Based in Malaysia, Tahir is referred to as the 'chief financial officer and money launderer' of Pakistan's nuclear scientist A.Q. Khan's black-market nuclear operations. Known as the father of Pakistan's nuclear bomb, Khan is said to have met Tahir at his Dubai-based company, SMB Computers, through an uncle. From then on Tahir is alleged to have helped the Pakistani scientist in his 'proliferation activities'. It is believed that by 1994, Tahir had started manufacturing centrifuges for uranium enrichment plants, and was asked by Pakistani officials to ship two containers of used centrifuge units from Pakistan to Iran. Dawood's shipping company had allegedly delivered the shipment, and he himself is known to have stayed in Malaysia as a guest of Tahir's son on at least one occasion in 2001, with the ISI secretly arranging for his safe passage.

The Indian media has very little access to knowledge on Dawood's life and activities in Pakistan but Western writers who have had access to their official agency sources have written extensively about his life in Pakistan, his connection with *jihadi* groups and the narcotics syndicates operating from Af–Pak via Dubai. Arguing that Dawood's drug trafficking syndicate was protected and used by the Pakistani intelligence establishment with tacit support given by US, UK and Saudi intelligence agencies to extract drug money from Afghanistan, American writer Peter Dale Scott wrote in his book *American War Machine: Deep Politics, the CIA Global Drug Connection and the Road to Afghanistan,*[16] 'In the 1980s, with CIA banking and the funnelling of massive amounts of US military aid...into parallel structures wielding enormous power over all aspects of (the Pakistani) government.

The ISI, in complicity with the United States, bestows protection on Dawood Ibrahim, lord of the Karachi and Mumbai waterfronts, who is simultaneously a drug trafficker, a terrorist, and a politically powerful financier.' The book claims that the benefits from the drug trafficking business were mutual and any damage incurred was considered to be collateral damage. It also argues that Dawood was a small cog in the giant narcotics empire that funnelled drug money into the big banks of several countries including the US and the UK. It reveals that it was only when Dawood started to realize the power he derived from keeping the secrets of the world's most powerful nations and began acting on his own that the US realized they had created a monster that needed to be tamed.

The information I personally had about Dawood and the D Company till September 2000 was mainly derived from details provided by official agencies, local associates, sympathizers, old-time neighbours and rival mobsters, and was essentially an Indian perspective on him. All reportage on Dawood in India was limited to his gang's criminal activities and the gang wars with his rivals. Not much was known about the D Company's international activities, and its size and scale. The official dossiers that I came across did contain some details, but they were very fuzzy. It was not until I went to Bangkok to cover the assassination attempt on Chhota Rajan and his subsequent hospitalization in 2000 (details about this appear in a later chapter) that I chanced upon information suggesting the mammoth scale of Dawood's illegal and criminal activities that had by then spread across Southeast Asia. This compelled me to update my views on Dawood and the D Company's reach and influence.

When I visited Bangkok in 2000 to cover the attack on Chhota Rajan (which he survived), officials in Bangkok shared information with me on Dawood and his associates' criminal activities, ranging from counterfeit currency rackets to the smuggling of illegal arms into the subcontinent, and I realized that the once small-time Mumbai mobsters had successfully transformed the D Company into a major international crime conglomerate that now topped the list in drug trafficking through all of Southeast Asia. In fact, plans to eliminate Dawood's former partner-in-crime, Chhota Rajan, had come about because Rajan had expanded his operations in Southeast Asia, and had now become a pain in the neck for Dawood.

This was also the first time I found out that Dawood was supplying militant outfits with arms. According to a senior Thai official, Dawood had allegedly been contracted to air-drop arms meant for the Liberation Tigers of Tamil Eelam (LTTE), which at the time had seized control of the Elephant Pass – the gateway to the Jaffna Peninsula in northern Sri Lanka – in December 1999. This consignment fell into Indian waters by mistake and was intercepted by authorities. This was a scoop as Dawood was being linked to the LTTE for the very first time! I shared my information with Indian intelligence officials posted in Bangkok and asked one of them about it. He said he was new to the posting and did not know much about the Elephant Pass operation, but he did confirm that Dawood was involved in counterfeit rackets and drug trafficking, and was supported by international spy agencies and not just the ISI. He also cautioned me that I had stepped on a 'live wire'; this meant that I was under surveillance and was being followed. This was a bit too much for me, and I informed one of my senior editors who suggested that I stick to the brief and be more careful in a foreign country.

I was, however, curious to know the exact motive behind the D Company's botched-up attack on Rajan. The Thai Police believed that one of the causes could be a stake in a major arms smuggling and supply racket. Both Thai and American intelligence officials I met felt that the two gangs were competing for an important consignment, and the attempt on Rajan was to keep him out of the game as he had previously sabotaged a fake currency racket involving the D Company. The shoot-out, it seems, had followed a failed attempt at a negotiated settlement.

Another source in Bangkok asked me if I would like to meet one of his American friends who wanted to 'discuss' Dawood with me. I agreed to meet him but was surprised at the choice of venue: a clothing store in a Bangkok mall. I arrived at the given time and was led to a dingy room at the back of the store. My source and his American friend were already there, and we discussed Dawood and Rajan over cups of lemon tea. The American wanted to know both their stories starting from the early days in Mumbai and, in exchange, he shared information about Indian mobsters and their links with other international crime networks, particularly in Southeast Asia. The conversation confirmed what the intelligence official had indicated to me. Dawood and Rajan were running multinational crime conglomerates that dabbled in drugs, counterfeit currency rackets and arms smuggling. They had moved up the crime ladder and now hobnobbed with international dealers of drugs, currency and arms. It also reaffirmed the commonly held belief that both were protected by intelligence agencies and in the bargain carried out special covert operations assigned by the respective agencies. The two rival mobsters were essentially carrying out a proxy war.

The Thai Police, too, were mystified over Rajan's assassination attempt. A senior Thai Police official told me, 'It was a cakewalk for us. The criminals left behind a lot of evidence.' Whatever the reason for the shooters walking into the police dragnet, the implications of Bangkok emerging as a major conduit for arms smuggling across Asia was not missed by Thai or Indian authorities. Indeed, Indian intelligence officials had been keeping a close watch on the entire Southeast Asian region following the discovery of the failed attempt to air-drop arms for the LTTE.

Here, I had chanced upon some information that had shown me the real side of Dawood and Rajan's crime empire, at least in

Thailand, and I reported this subsequently in my articles in *India Today*. My discoveries raised more questions in my mind and I became determined to find out more about Dawood's footprint in the region. But when I returned home I was summoned by the Mumbai Crime Branch. I was told by a senior official there that my investigations into the attack on Chhota Rajan and its motives had impacted North Block. The same evening, Chhota Shakeel called me to blow his own trumpet about the operation in Bangkok and about his aide Munna Zingada's interview published in *India Today*.[17] I asked Shakeel what I had failed to confirm in Bangkok: 'There are reports that you met Rajan in Bangkok's Hotel Tara to negotiate terms for an arms and ammunition deal,' I told him. Shakeel admitted to staying at the Tara during all his Bangkok visits as Munna always booked a room for him there, but he denied meeting Rajan. The next thing on my mind was the report about the D Company supplying arms to the LTTE. Shakeel laughed when I told him this and said, 'Ridiculous! What proof do you have? Give me at least one instance where our men were caught supplying arms. I don't think so. I have to check. You see, Dawood Bhai's name is so popular that it is convenient for anyone to name us for all wrongdoings in Southeast Asia.' When I probed him further about a counterfeit case involving fake US dollars in Thailand unearthed by a Federal Bureau of Investigation (FBI) raid, Shakeel didn't deny it outright but said that the counterfeit operations were Aslam Bhatti's (a fellow gang member) department.[18]

My investigations into the Bangkok attack disclosed a different side to the multinational crime empires of the two dons. I knew what I had was still a very sketchy picture and merely a glimpse into the D Company's ever-expanding circle of influence in Southeast Asia. I began delving further into Dawood and Rajan's gang equations, their business engagements and their crimes on international soil with a new-found understanding. I discovered that Rajan was giving the D Company a hard time in Thailand and Malaysia as he was exploiting his old network and sources, which were primary to the D Company's functioning in these territories. Both sides had invisible state support, which had become even more evident after the attack on Rajan. Rajan's subsequent appearance in the Southern Bangkok Criminal Court in Thailand was viewed as a simple case of the law taking its course, but in reality he was buying time before he recovered his health; his presence in the court was by design. There was speculation that Rajan was being protected by Indian authorities, who were informed of his movements, although then Indian ambassador to Thailand, R.K. Rai, denied it in a conversation with me. My theory was further strengthened when I heard of Rajan's dramatic escape from the hospital where he was recuperating. His rival Chhota Shakeel, too, had flaunted his connections in 'higher places' in Thailand to me and had even offered me a chance to listen in on his conversation about Rajan with a senior Thai Police official. The conclusions to be drawn from this were quite obvious.

Coming face-to-face with Dawood at his daughter's wedding was a defining moment for me. When I saw the partially bald, portly man with a drooping thick moustache, it was hard to imagine he was one of the most dangerous people in the world. His presence at his daughter's wedding, despite the lookout notice out for him, was a telling example of his reach and influence in Dubai. Riaz Jallianwala had claimed that Dawood had connections with the royal family in the UAE as well. It did not matter if the media was reporting about his absence at the venue. Dawood had already managed to make a statement: he was very much in his comfort zone right under the noses of Indian and Interpol officials, who were keeping a watch on his whereabouts. After all, Dubai had been his second home for over a decade, and it was here that he had made powerful friends who had been instrumental in shaping his career as one of the most notorious gangsters in the world.

At the wedding, Javed Miandad repeatedly mentioned that Dawood and his family loved Mumbai and missed the charm and feel of the city terribly. The topic had cropped up because I had said I was from Mumbai. This statement made me wonder why Dawood had been part of the diabolical murder of innocents in the city he loved so much. His side of the story would later be explained indirectly to me, during my conversation with Fayaz, my escort at the wedding, who suggested, as was rumoured, that Dawood could have been taken advantage of by Indian and Pakistani smugglers now based in Dubai, since all of them had links with the ISI, which helped them thrive and share profits in the bargain.

I thought this was a plausible theory. The narcotics department of the Mumbai Police had knowledge of Dawood's frequent visits to Pakistan and his alliances with the Pakistani drug cartels. Dawood, too, had admitted to his frequent visits to Pakistan in the early 1980s in his 1994 interview to *India Today.*

Indian official records suggest that in the early 1980s, Dawood went to Dubai to smuggle gold into India. With the easing of gold import rules in 1992, gold prices crashed and its smuggling became a losing enterprise. This did not affect Dawood much as he had already switched to the more lucrative business of drug trafficking using the same network and routes. Only after he started enjoying huge profit margins from the narcotics business did his Pakistani friends, who were known to have close ties with the ISI, nudge him to do something more. It is said that the terms of the bargain were well laid out by the ISI, which controlled the illegal shipping routes from the Persian Gulf to India's western coast. Apart from a share in profits, the ISI generally demanded that smugglers operating on these routes should also transport weapons and explosives into India in return for the use of Pakistan's waters.

According to a source in Intelligence who handled the Pakistan–Afghanistan desk for over a decade, one of the fall-outs of the Soviet invasion of Afghanistan was that the narcotics business turned out to be big for wheeler-dealers with money and political power – including top political leaders. The government of Pakistan and its military, with the connivance of tribal leaders and unscrupulous smugglers, converted narco-trafficking into a means to raise funds for Pakistan's covert military operations. It was in early 1991, when Nawaz Sharif was the prime minister of Pakistan, that Pakistan Army chief General Aslam Beg and Director General of the ISI Lt. General Asad Durrani were said to have mooted the idea to the prime minister that the Pakistani Army needed more money for covert operations, which they wanted to raise through secret and large-scale drug deals manipulated by them. Thus began the involvement of the Pakistan government and the ISI in selling heroin from Afghanistan and using the profits to pay for the country's clandestine operations.

Geographically, the area covering Pakistan, Afghanistan and Iran is popularly known as the 'Golden Crescent' because this area is one of the largest opium-producing narco hubs in the world. The manner in which hundreds of mobile laboratories, working round-the-clock to refine opium into fine heroin, mushroomed in the frontier region after the Soviets invaded Afghanistan is itself an eye-opener. It is believed that many high- to low-ranking officers in the Pakistani Army and Air Force have been involved in the racket and used military transport and aircraft to carry the precious cargo to Karachi and beyond.

Once Dawood became close to Pakistani smugglers Yusuf Godhrawala and Taufiq Jallianwala in Dubai and began smuggling, bullion at first and narcotics later, into India and other neighbouring countries such as Nepal, Bangladesh, Myanmar and

Sri Lanka, the two are said to have introduced him to some high-ranking ISI officials. Impressed with his Pakistani friends' high-level links and smooth operations under their protection, Dawood reportedly agreed to invest in their businesses – mostly because there were no risks involved, either of getting caught or of being punished. Once he began to enjoy the perks of his business with the Pakistani smugglers and the ISI, Godhrawala and Jallianwala reportedly approached Dawood with the ISI's proposition to secure his help to protect Muslims in India against the backdrop of the Babri Masjid demolition in December 1992.

By most accounts, Dawood initially resisted the pressure, but the 1992–93 riots that followed the demolition of the ancient Babri Masjid made him more susceptible to be convinced otherwise.The subsequent riots in Mumbai saw hundreds of Muslims being systematically attacked by Hindu goons and their businesses destroyed. Members of his gang, including his brother Anees Ibrahim and his associate Tiger Memon, are believed to have demanded retaliation as Muslim leaders from Mumbai had called out for help. It is believed that strategically the ISI was a step ahead of Dawood as it had always believed in building several parallel networks even within the D Company. The operation was ready to be carried out with or without the don as the groundwork had been successfully completed with the help of the gang's strong Mumbai network. Tiger Memon took the lead before the scheduled time in April and executed the blasts on 12 March 1993.

Dawood claimed in his 1994 *India Today* interview that he watched Mumbai, the city he claimed to love so much, rock with each successive blast, from Dubai that day. He was flooded with phone calls from Sindhis, Muslims and Gujaratis from Mumbai.[19] He claimed to have been shocked beyond words at the sequence of events, and at his name cropping up in the investigations. When the car that was used to plant the bomb was found, he was relieved at the thought that the evidence would prove his non-involvement and there would be no further reason for him to be afraid. In his interview with *India Today*, Dawood repeatedly claimed that he had nothing to do with the blasts. His pitch was that he had become a victim of the politics between Sharad Pawar and S.B. Chavan.[20] 'When the press started hollering that Pawar had links with me, the chief minister ordered the police to involve me in the case. But Chavan wants – now that I have already been maligned – to establish my involvement in the case and then prove that I had links with Pawar. This will provide him with all the ammunition to dislodge Pawar easily. So they're both trying to frame me for their own vested interests,' he said in the interview. Dawood also claimed to have discussed the case with an officer from the Mumbai Police, who told him, 'It is my firm belief that you are not involved in this case. If I want to say anything today, I will have to resign first. And if I don't resign, they will suspend me.'[21]

The clinching evidence against Dawood and the others accused of conspiring to plot the blasts and aiding and abetting terrorism under TADA came from Dawood Phanse aka Taklya in 1993. Taklya was convicted for attending a meeting in Dubai convened by Dawood Ibrahim to plan the conspiracy, and later organizing the landing of arms and ammunition on the Shekhadi coast in Raigadh district on 3 and 7 February 1993.[22] In his interview to *India Today* after the blasts,[23] Dawood Ibrahim had clearly banked on the assumption that the occurrence of the 'meeting' would not stand good in a court of law. The TADA Court not only accepted the charge that the meeting took place, but it also convicted Phanse for being part of the conspiracy. According to Phanse's testimony in Hindi, which has been upheld by Judge P.D. Kode, he claimed, *'Tiger Memon mujhe Dubai mein Dawood Bhai ke ghar le gaya. Main unko pehchana kyunki unka photo maine papers mein dekha tha.* (Tiger Memon took me to Dawood Ibrahim's home in Dubai. I recognized Dawood because I had seen his picture in newspapers.)' Phanse also said, '*Dawood Bhai ne kahaa Tiger jo bolega voh maal* landing *karne ka. Apne ko Babri Masjid girayi hai uska badla lena hai.* (Dawood told me to listen to whatever Tiger says and help land the goods. We have to take revenge for the demolition of Babri Masjid.)' Phanse told the court that after the meeting he was driven back to the hotel by Dawood Ibrahim in his Mercedes and that he and Sharif Abdul Gafoor Parkar helped Memon smuggle the RDX as per Dawood's instruction. Phanse also revealed that they had bribed customs officers to look the other way.

Accepting Dawood's role in the blasts, the TADA Court observed, 'A resident of Dubai formulated a conspiracy to commit a terrorist act in the city of Mumbai. In pursuance of the said object, Dawood Ibrahim agreed to send arms and ammunitions from abroad.'[24]

To add to this, Dawood's denial of knowing the ISI was soon proved wrong. Former director of R&AW, B. Raman, wrote in his memoir, *The Kaoboys of R&AW: Down Memory Lane*, 'The ISI had shifted the perpetrators of the Mumbai blasts to Bangkok and kept them in a hotel for some time in order to prevent detection of their presence in Karachi by US authorities... The R&AW also separately learnt from its sources that under pressure from Dubai authorities to quit Dubai, Dawood Ibrahim had shifted his office and residence to Karachi. He was living there as a Pakistani citizen.'[25]

Ever since the Pakistan government denied that they were sheltering him, Dawood has become a huge asset for the ISI. In 2005, *U.S. News* stated that the ISI had made Dawood an offer: 'If he relocated to Pakistan's port city of Karachi and kept working with the ISI, it would guarantee him control of the nation's coastal smuggling routes. For 21 years now, Dawood has called Pakistan home, where he is believed to own shopping malls, luxury homes, and shipping and trucking lines that smuggle arms and fake currency into India and heroin into Europe.'[26]

After the UN notified Dawood as a global terrorist, the Pakistani intelligence establishment has been under intense pressure and is uneasy about the persistent media reports about the don's presence in Pakistan. In September 2000, the Pakistani monthly magazine *Newsline* ran, for the first time, a detailed story claiming that Dawood was in Karachi and living under the ISI's protection.[27] It also published photos of Dawood's residence and other commercial establishments owned by him as proof. The article revealed that Dawood lived like a king in Karachi with his wife and his children. His home in the elite Clifton area was a palatial house spread over 6,000 square yards boasting of a pool, tennis courts, snooker room and a private hi-tech gym. While in Karachi, he wore designer clothes and sported a ₹5 lakh Patek Phillipe watch, drove a top-of-the-line Mercedes and other luxury four-wheel drives, and showered money on starlets and prostitutes. Like the *U.S. News* article, this one too claimed that he had acquired a large number of properties in Karachi, including malls, business plazas and residential plots in plush colonies.

Dawood's lifestyle, as described in the article, matched his old habits as witnessed in Mumbai and later in Dubai. When I spoke to Ghulam Hasnain, who wrote the *Newsline* article, he said that the story had drawn an extremely harsh reaction from Pakistani authorities. He had been chased and followed by the ISI. The President of Pakistan at the time, Pervez Musharraf, had even called a meeting with the editors of several Pakistani media establishments and described the story as 'an indiscretion that had seriously damaged Pakistan's national interests'.[28]

Another Pakistani journalist, Amir Mir, has written about Dawood's presence in Karachi, his influence in Pakistan's power circles (including the Pakistani Army), and his links with jihadi militant outfits like Lashkar-e-Taiba, Harkat-ul-Ansar and others. In his book, *The Talibanisation of Pakistan: From 9/11 to 26/11 and Beyond*,[29] Mir stated that despite being a Barelvi Muslim Dawood is considered close to the Lashkar-e-Taiba leadership, which is influenced by the Deobandi sect. The two sects do not see eye-to-eye as they are diagonally opposite in their beliefs, and yet the LeT–Dawood nexus exists – a purely tactical arrangement orchestrated by the ISI

Mir goes on to write about Dawood's alleged involvement in American journalist Daniel Pearl's kidnapping and murder. The compound where Pearl was held captive belonged to Dawood's close business partner, Saud Memon. Pearl, who was based in Mumbai then, was investigating the 'shoe bomber' Richard Reid when he was kidnapped, but Mir alleges that Pearl was also working on another story on Dawood's whereabouts. 'It was Saud Memon who, in January 2002, drove...Daniel Pearl into a compound that he owned. It was here that Pearl's throat was slit. Memon subsequently disappeared from Karachi,' he writes.[30]

During a conversation I had with Chhota Shakeel that year he invited me to visit Karachi and said he would receive me at the airport in person and that I would not have any immigration or visa issues. I informed my editor, Prabhu Chawla,who promptly rejected the idea, saying, 'It's a huge risk and we should not take any chances, particularly after Daniel Pearl's killing.'

That was also the first time Shakeel admitted to me that they had been living in Pakistan. I had called Shakeel after General Musharraf had, at the historic 2001 Agra summit, denied Dawood and his associates were living in Pakistan. I asked Shakeel if the President was correct, and whether they had moved out of Pakistan and shifted to a different country, as a theory doing the rounds then suggested. Shakeel simply said,'*Hum to kahin hatey hi nahin*! (We have not gone anywhere!)' I then asked him whether there was any truth to President Musharraf's assertion that Dawood and Shakeel were no longer in Karachi. In response, Shakeel laughed and said, '*Aap Sadar-saab ko galat saabit karna chahti hain*? (Are you trying to prove the President wrong)?'

When I insisted that I wanted to know the truth, he simply said that the issue was between the two countries and not between us.

Later, Pakistani officials admitted to Dawood's presence in Karachi and even accepted that he was active in Pakistan and owned a number of commercial plazas in the city. Then provincial minister for internal affairs, Aftab Sheikh, told the Pakistani newspaper *Jang* in 2003 that Dawood owned the ten-storeyed Kawish Crown Plaza mall in Clifton, which had witnessed two bomb explosions between July and September that year. 'Daud (spelt thus in Pakistan) has a network from Mumbai to Karachi and is working in both countries,' Sheikh reportedly said.[31] He further said that Dawood, Anees and their gang members had invested in prime properties in Karachi and were major players in the Karachi Stock Exchange. The minister's words were echoed by the inspector-general of Sindh Police at the time, Syed Kamal Shah, who revealed to the same newspaper that according to his investigations, he found that the Kawish building was actually owned by Dawood Ibrahim and not Ahmed Jamal as had been mentioned.[32]

Dawood's rise to global notoriety, particularly after he was designated a 'global terrorist supporter' and among the ten topmost narcotics kingpins in the world by the US and the UN, intrigued me. As Mir has commented in his book, the US's notification of Dawood as a global terrorist operating from Pakistan had created ripples in the latter's intelligence circles, which had, until then, cared little about the security implications of harbouring a don who was a wanted man in their ever-hostile neighbour, India. Not only did the US action change Indo–US relations, but it also brought Washington into conflict with Islamabad, its ally in the war against terror, for the latter's alleged covert support to terrorists. This leverage was later used by the US to kill Osama bin Laden on Pakistani soil in a secret operation. While the notification had far-reaching consequences on a larger scale, it did not bring about a huge change in Dawood's position. His chartbuster infamy continued and, in fact, he further strengthened his Pakistani connections in July 2005 when he got his daughter Mahrukh married to Junaid, the son of Javed Miandad, who due to his stature still had immense influence in the Pakistan Cricket Board, considered a powerful organization within Pakistan. That Dawood's ties in Pakistan have remained strong over the years was evident at his second daughter's wedding in 2011 in Karachi, which was attended by top officials of the Pakistani Army and intelligence. This continued to puzzle me until I read about his alleged connections with al-Qaeda chief Osama bin Laden and Afghanistan. When I dug deeper, I also found allegations of Dawood's connections with the larger money-laundering network and their links with financial institutions across the world.

Southeast Asian analyst Ramtanu Maitra wrote in an article for the Washington-based *Executive Intelligence Review*,[33] a weekly news magazine, that Dawood's ambition to become a powerful figure took a turn after he met Osama bin Laden in Afghanistan, where the latter had fled in 1996 following his expulsion from Sudan and Saudi Arabia, barring his return to those countries. According to Maitra, once in Afghanistan, bin Laden set about expanding heroin trafficking in the country to generate enough cash to arm the Taliban against future invaders and protect the al-Qaeda, and to tap into the wide international demand for heroin. To set up his network, bin Laden brought in Dawood, whose syndicate was under the ISI's control. In Maitra's assessment, Dawood was a necessary cog in bin Laden's terror designs.

In Afghanistan, one of bin Laden's first moves was to link his *jihadi* group with the cash-generating and money-laundering international underworld. He took control of the Afghan national airlines, Ariana Airlines. Soon, Ariana Airlines shifted from carrying passengers to carrying cargo. 'The planes would come back from the UAE loaded with weapons,' Julie Sirrs, an Afghanistan specialist at the US Defense Intelligence Agency during the Clinton administration, was quoted as saying in the *Los Angeles Times*. 'They were mostly Soviet weapons, small arms – Kalashnikovs and RPG-7s.'[34]

While the weapons came from Dubai and later from Sharjah, it was reported that when the planes returned to Dubai they allegedly carried opium from Afghanistan. As Maitra's report states, Dawood worked as a facilitator in the drugs–money–arms nexus in Sharjah under his Pakistani, Saudi and MI6 protectors, and continues to be one of the major transporters of drugs from Afghanistan to Dubai. According to Maitra, 'Drugs come into Dubai by means of Dawood's "mules"...in containers which carry equipment sent to Dubai for "repair" from Kandahar and elsewhere in southern Afghanistan.'[35] In Dubai, Dawood's men and the al-Qaeda would take control of the drugs, leverage the drug trafficking network, and purchase weapons using the money they earned from it. In Sharjah, the al-Qaeda's benefactor was the notorious Russian mafioso and gun-runner Victor Bout, who had developed contacts with the Taliban in August 1995. According to several reports,[36] intelligence agencies suspected that Bout's arms supplies were transported on an airline, Flying Dolphin, operated by one of Bout's business associates, which ran scheduled flights from the UAE into Taliban-ruled Afghanistan between October 2000 and January 2001. Flying Dolphin was owned by Sheikh Abdullah bin Zayed bin Saqr al-Nayhan, a former UAE ambassador to the US and a member of the ruling family in Abu Dhabi, who has been described by the UN as a 'close business associate of Bout'. According to a December 2000 UN report, Zayed's company is registered in Liberia, but its operations office was in Dubai.

Dawood's role as a facilitator of international money laundering was highlighted in 2013 when Firstpost.com/CNN-IBN broke the story about Dawood's cash being traced to the Nassau branch of Bank of Baroda in the Bahamas.[37] Highly placed Indian government sources told the news website that Bank of Baroda's Nassau branch saw successive wire transfers of several hundred thousand dollars from at least three Dubai-based currency exchanges – the al-Zarouni Exchange, the Dubai Exchange and the al-Dirham Exchange – which are suspected to be proceeds from organized crime. Though the bank denied the report in a statement signed by the bank's chairman and managing director, it admitted that the Nassau branch had been maintaining the account of the Dubai Exchange, among others, for several years.[38]

According to my sources in the Indian government, Dawood's extensive network within the international finance system is one of the reasons why the Indian government feels the US has not been transparent about Dawood. The government believes putting him on the UN list as a narcotics kingpin and notifying him as a global terrorist was a compulsion as he had become a vital link in funding terror, just as they did with David Coleman Headley, one of the accused in the 26/11 Mumbai attacks, a US Drug Enforcement Agency agent gone rogue. My sources have emphasized that Indian authorities are sceptical about US assistance and believe that the US will not act on Dawood even if they are fully aware of his activities and movements across the subcontinent unless they directly harm US interests. This silence has continued into the current US Presidency.

Under Prime Minister Modi, the Indian government has renewed its efforts to bring Dawood to justice in India with help from the US.[39] My sources tell me that the recent Indian attention on Dawood has made the ISI wary, and the agency, which considers the don a strategic asset, has done everything possible to confuse India about his whereabouts. Knowing that India is capable of tracking his movements closely, in the past year the ISI has shifted Dawood around the country at least a dozen times.

Even though a recent *Hindustan Times* report highlighted the fact that Dawood's family regularly travelled between Karachi and Dubai,[40] Dawood is believed to be holed up in Karachi. Riaz Jallianwala told me during our conversation that Dawood hardly budged out of his Clifton home as the situation was getting too hot for him. The Clifton home belongs to Jallianwala, but was given to Dawood on his arrival in Karachi from Dubai in 1994. Furthermore, Jallianwala said he believes that even though Dawood frequently travelled between Karachi and Dubai in 2013 for business purposes, some ill-timed investments caused him to lose 300 million dirhams, which upset his connections among the upper echelons of Dubai's rulers. Dawood is powerful enough to have recovered his losses, Jallianwala mentioned, but 'he has not returned to Dubai' ever since. The word in the circles has been that Dawood had breached his 'brief and limits'. In the underworld, breaching the code is the ultimate crime, punishable only by death.

When I was informed by Riaz that Dawood was not stepping out of his house because he feared for his life, I realized I needed to verify this crucial piece of information. My sources in the agency confirmed that Dawood was holed up in a safe house on the Islamabad–Muree road, in a hilly region about 20 km outside the capital city of Islamabad. In the wake of the arrest of his rival Chhota Rajan in Bali on 25 October, elite army commandos are said to have been deployed in the area for his security. Rajan's arrest could well suggest that Dawood's elimination is near at hand.

A retired R&AW officer who handled the Pakistan–Afghanistan desk for many years once told me that, like the Kashmir issue, Dawood Ibrahim will be a major bone of contention between the two countries. I had always felt there was a chance of him returning to India, but that was until Yakub Memon was hanged in July 2015. Shakeel had told me in the 2006 interview I did with him that they would come back if their cases had a certain trial limit. I had conveyed as much to the higher authorities. But silence prevailed. Yakub's hanging seems to have drawn an end to Dawood's hopes of ever coming back home. Shakeel sounded agitated when I spoke to him after the hanging. 'Dawood Bhai would have met a similar end had his plan to come back to India materialized,' he said. I wondered if he had already conceded defeat.

Perhaps his worries were not out of context; of all the past and present governments at the centre in India, the Modi government seems to be the most serious about tackling Dawood's network once and for all. I am reasonably convinced that the don must be feeling the heat as well.

The Second-most Wanted Man in India

CHHOTA SHAKEEL WAS NOT SOUNDING as enthusiastic as he usually did when we spoke; he was agitated, even upset, over a story aired on Star News. In April 2007, our show on Star News, 'Company mein daraar? (A rift in the D Company?)', had enquired whether Dawood Ibrahim and Chhota Shakeel had indeed parted ways, with Shakeel setting up his own organization and splitting the D Company vertically down the middle, as reported by the Anti-Terrorist Squad (ATS) of the Mumbai Police. Chhota Shakeel had, predictably, called me to deny the split. But more than that he was upset by how he had been portrayed in the story and claimed that the Mumbai Police was misleading the media. 'I would never part ways with Bhai. Always remember this!' he asserted.

Shakeel is the one gangster I have professionally interacted with since 1994. It has become routine for me to receive a call from him from wherever he has been hiding after a story related to him is aired.

On this occasion, he sounded aggravated. He asked me, '*Yeh Sayeed Ansari kaun hai? Uska number de aap*! (Who is this Sayeed Ansari? Please give me his number!)' Ansari was the anchor of our show.

I tried to pacify Shakeel, but he didn't listen.

'I need to tell Ansari how to address me on your channel. Your channel is a respectable one, and yet you use such nonsense language to describe me!'

I told him Ansari was an anchor, and he read the news from a script that was put before him. 'The scriptwriter is a different person and I will check with him if you tell me what is wrong,' I said, trying to calm him down.

He retorted, '*Galli ka chor, mawali aur shirt ke button khule... yeh sab bhasha aap ke channel ko shobha deti hai kya*? (A petty thief, a rowdy who roams about with his shirt buttons open... Is this language befitting of your channel?)' Shakeel had never objected to the media calling him a dreaded underworld don or a 'Bhai', but he certainly didn't like to be described as a petty thief and a *mawali*. I assured him that I would look into the matter. I subsequently informed the producer who had written Shakeel's profile and asked him to remove the 'objectionable' words. After all, the objections had been raised by a dreaded don himself!

As luck would have it, the same version of the profile got aired a few weeks later in a different context. And, of course, Shakeel called again. I remembered he had told me once that he had a media-monitoring unit working 24/7, which recorded everything that was said about the D Company and its members across the world. This time, he reprimanded me. 'I spared the wrongdoers as you assured me that the story would be rectified. If you don't reveal the names of who did the story, I have my ways of finding out. And then it will be you who will have to call me. This is a serious matter!' By the end of our conversation, though, Shakeel noted in a lighter vein, '*Yeh jumma ke jumme, nayi Dawood–Shakeel ki film banti hai.* News channels *ki* TRP *bhi* Bhai *se chalti hai, samjhe na*! (There's a new film on Dawood and Shakeel every Friday. Even news channels are getting their TRPs because of Bhai!) But barring a few, it's all fiction so why would we mind it!'

Nevertheless, it was indeed a serious matter. Dawood and the D Company were big draws for news channels in 2007. I immediately informed all concerned department heads about Shakeel's call, evoking the funniest reactions. One colleague said he would not take any overseas calls, while another said he would ask his secretary to handle it and avoid the situation. Eventually, the two 'objectionable lines' were deleted from the profile.

This was not the first time Shakeel had objected to a news story. In October 2000, once I had returned from Bangkok after covering the bloody attack on Chhota Rajan and the subsequent case on Shakeel's associates who were caught by the Thai Police (as narrated in a later chapter), Shakeel had called me one evening after reading the story, 'War of the Dons', which I had filed from Bangkok for *India Today*. He was happy that his crony Munna Zingada had given a '*kadak*' (solid) (his words) interview to me in the presence of the Thai Police, but he was hell-bent on convincing me that Rajan had escaped by jumping from his balcony into a trash-bin. I refused to buy his version and told him that the truth was different. He went a step further and asked me for my fax number and said he would send me the legal version of the story Rajan had narrated. A day later, I received a copy of an official statement, which quoted Rajan's trash-bin escape theory produced in the Bangkok court. The fax had been sent from a fax machine in a five-star hotel in Karachi.

Just to further confirm what I already knew, I asked him in my interview why he had been in Bangkok between 11 and 13 September. 'How did you know?' he asked in response. Then he went on to provide some more details about their plan to kill Chhota Rajan in Bangkok, a conversation I have detailed in the chapter titled 'Bedlam in Bangkok' later in the book.

When I wrote my story, however, it was based on the information given to me by my source in Bangkok and related how Rajan had been given safe passage and had escaped to Cambodia across the Thai border in a car. Shakeel called me when the story got published in the web edition of *India Today* in November 2000. I had been given wrong information, he insisted. He claimed that a high-ranking police source in Bangkok had told him that Rajan had been shifted to another government hospital for safety purposes. He admonished me, saying, 'How can a journalist like you write wrong stories? You should have been more responsible and verified the facts before publishing it!' The news of Chhota Rajan's dramatic escape from the Samitivej Hospital broke in the next couple of days and proved my story to be right.

In May 2002, Shakeel was back on the phone, arguing with me. His associates on a motorcycle had shot at rival gangster Ejaz alias Aju Ahmed Lakdawala's car in Bangkok earlier that month. After his split with Rajan, Lakdawala had targeted Bollywood personalities with extortion calls, including producer Lawrence D'Souza, director Sohail Khan and actor Akshay Kumar. A newsflash had informed the world that Lakdawala was dead. My sources confirmed that Lakdawala had indeed been shot in Bobei Market in Bangkok while returning from dinner with his wife on Sunday night; two motorcyclists, who seemed to be of Indian origin, had fired three shots at him from close range, seriously wounding him in the neck, arm and torso.

The attack on Lakdawala had already made the news, and some news channels, including Aaj Tak, had announced, 'Lakdawala shot dead in Bangkok by Dawood gang.' Uday Shankar, who was managing editor of Aaj Tak then, asked me if I could confirm the news for the channel. I was working at *India Today*, and called my source in Bangkok, who informed me that Lakdawala was in a critical condition, but still alive. I informed Uday that contrary to the news headline that had run on Aaj Tak, Lakdawala was alive. This meant that the channel would have to do a U-turn on the news, so Uday asked me to wait till he discussed it further with Aroon Purie and Prabhu Chawla, my editors at *India Today*.

Uday had to take a crucial call on when to disclose the news and change the headline. It was a risky move to go against what had already been relayed. I was asked to reconfirm with official sources once again. This time, I was put in touch with a police official in Bangkok who confirmed that Lakdawala was alive but in critical condition. Uday told me I should be the one to break the news about Lakdawala surviving the attack on Aaj Tak, which I did.

Shakeel's call to me was to contest my information about Lakdawala surviving the attack. He said it was not possible as Lakdawala had been shot from close range. He claimed that Lakdawala was killed to avenge the murder of a D Company ally, Sharad Shetty. However, I stood by my information and story. I told him that Lakdawala was badly wounded but not dead and, rather boldly, I mentioned that Bangkok had been unlucky for him as his second operation in the city had also failed. He said he had spoken to Lakdawala's wife on the phone, who had been crying. I told him that it was natural she would have been crying, as her husband had been attacked and was critically injured. It did not necessarily mean that he was dead. By this time, the Bangkok Police had provided protection to Lakdawala's family, who had been receiving death threats since the shoot-out.

From then on, although Shakeel called often to argue with me about my stories, he never questioned my credibility, not even when I testified in court and identified his voice on tape, which became prime evidence in proving that the Bollywood film *Chori Chori Chupke Chupke* had been financed by the underworld. The full details of how this came about and my experiences of being summoned to court as a state witness are narrated in the chapter titled 'Interlude' later in the book.

When the revelations of this particular case were made public, I had spoken to Shakeel about the D Company financing Bollywood movies. Whereas in an earlier interview he had flatly denied that the D Company had anything to do with financing movies, this time he said, 'Times change. When the other two gangs (Chhota Rajan and Abu Salem) are making money openly from the film world, why not us?'

The case ultimately resulted in the conviction of Bollywood producer Bharat Shah and director Nazim Rizvi for being associated with Shakeel. The Mumbai Police had intercepted their calls, and the voices on the tapes were matched with the voices on the tapes of my interviews with Shakeel. The voice samples were clinically verified in a laboratory in London as well as a government lab in India. In the interview, Shakeel mentioned that the D Company had already invested in at least 20 films before *Chori Chori Chupke Chupke*. 'Instead of extorting money from film personalities, we thought we'd do business with them. And doing business is not a crime,' he had stated.

After I testified, the Mumbai Police generously offered me protection as they expected a backlash from the D Company after the court's verdict. I politely refused as I had given my testimony in court as a professional doing her job. I had stuck to the truth in court and, whatever the consequences, I firmly believed what has to happen would inevitably happen. At this point I was upset with the Mumbai Police because by testifying I had lost access to Shakeel and, perhaps, more important for a journalist, his trust.

After the verdict, Shakeel remained silent for about four years, until one evening I received a call from him. I was on my way back to office after winding up a show recording with make-up artist Cory Walia in Bandra.

At the sound of his familiar voice when he said 'hello', I expressed amusement and laughed. He laughed as well. The ice was finally broken. I am sure he had checked up on me and my responses in the court before calling me. If he had the slightest doubt about anything to do with my role in the case I would possibly have been killed, or worse.

Over the years I have interviewed Shakeel many times on a range of developments and issues.

The first time I had called Shakeel was in 1994. I was getting more and more interested in the workings of the underworld at that point, and someone had passed on his number to me. I thought of checking whether it was the correct number and made the call one afternoon. A male voice at the other end asked me to call in the evening. 'Bhai is sleeping,' the man informed me. Reasonably sure that the number was the correct one, I called once more in the evening. The same person who had taken the call in the afternoon asked me to leave my name, number and the name of the publication I worked for.

The next evening, I received a call on my office landline. It was Shakeel. He introduced himself formally. His tone was mild yet very authoritative: '*Main Shakeel Bhai bol raha hoon. Farmaiyen, Sheela-ji*? (This is Shakeel. What can I do for you, Sheela-ji?)' He told me he had done a routine background check on me before calling, and I guess I passed the primary checks. A short conversation at the time turned into a quarter-column news story, and it opened the doors of possibility for me. I had gained access to the Dawood gang, that too on the first attempt.

My first major interview with Shakeel was in 1999, in connection with a Sessions Court judge in Mumbai. It was based on a tip-off that turned out to be the tip of the iceberg that would lead to shocking revelations. Earlier that year, ACP A.B. Pote of the Mumbai Police was told by an informant that an associate of Shakeel regularly called up a Mumbai cell number. The ACP's investigations revealed that the gangster was in contact with a serving additional Sessions Court judge, J.W. Singh, who had agreed to go easy on cases involving members of the D Company in return for favours. According to the Mumbai Police's taped transcripts of the conversation between the two, Singh asked Shakeel to help him recover ₹40 lakh from an associate. On 25 March 1999, Liyaqat Ali Sheikh, a Mumbai advocate, was at Singh's residence when Sheikh received a call from Shakeel in Karachi. The conversation proceeded as follows:

Sheikh: *Salaam Alaikum.*

Chhota Shakeel: *Walaikum Salaam, Mian. Bolo.* (Tell me.)

Sheikh: I am talking from Judge-saab's residence; please talk to him. He is our special friend.

Singh: *Salaam Alaikum.*

Shakeel: *Salaam...salaam, boliye.* (Greetings; tell me.)

Singh: I have got to recover some money from somebody. His name is Dara.

Shakeel: How much?

Singh: Around ₹40 lakh. It's mine, my son's and son-in-law's together. *Purey* family *ka mamla hai.* (It's a family matter.)[1]

In the same conversation Shakeel also asked Judge Singh to look into the matter of police 'encounter killings'.

'The police does not care about the law,' Shakeel told the judge, and Singh replied, '*Yeh anyaya hai, atyachaar hai.* (This is injustice, an atrocity.)'

Shakeel: Tell me what should be done about these police officers?

Singh: You are a wise man.

Shakeel: I know I am. *Lekin phir aap log hi chillatey hain.* (But when I act, you people make a big noise.)

Singh: No, we don't say anything.[2]

Singh was ultimately booked under the MCOCA, the Prevention of Corruption Act and the Indian Penal Code, and arrested on 20 March 2000. However, Judge Abhay Thipsay of a special MCOCA Court acquitted the judge by way of benefit of doubt in August 2002. The state of Maharashtra appealed against his acquittal, which was eventually dismissed by the Mumbai High Court.

My interview with Shakeel was on this matter. Though the interview could not finally be printed because the case was still subjudice, something Shakeel said during the interview still stays with me: 'The Company helps all those who reach out to them, and deserve it, *samjhe na*.' He has a habit of ending his statements with '*samjhe na*?', as though to ensure that the nuances of what he has just said have been comprehended.

With the D Company regularly indulging in betting and match-fixing along with their bookies across the cricketing world, Shakeel found in the late 1990s that the D Company had new rivals in the betting syndicate. In a match between Pakistan and England in Sharjah during the Coca-Cola Cup in Sharjah in 1999, the Company lost money to the tune of ₹17 crore. 'Bhai has always won whenever he has put in money,' a source close to the D company told me at the time, 'but on April 12 he smelt a rat...' The new syndicate in Mumbai that was competing with the D Company was run by a Gujarati–Marwari clique of diamond merchants, mill owners and traders, and it had allegedly paid the Pakistani team to lose.

One of the few existing photos of Chhota Shakeel.
TV grab courtesy ABP News.

After the match, Dawood 'instigated an inquiry by the Pakistan Cricket Board,' a D Company source told me, and asked bookies to cancel all bets placed on the match. Shakeel himself asked 19 of Mumbai's top bookies not to make or accept payments. His target was known bookie Shobhan Mehta, whom they suspected of having fixed the match. Mehta refused to follow Shakeel's instructions after the match, insisting he would honour all bets made on the match. A police officer told me then, 'Mehta defied Shakeel because the stakes were too high and the punters were so reputed that non-payment would have destroyed him. It was a no-win situation.'

Trouble recurred in winter 1999, after a Zimbabwe–Sri Lanka match, when the D Company lost ₹7 crore, and Vinod Chembur, its man in Mumbai, went bust. Then, when India lost to New Zealand in Rajkot and the D Company lost another ₹13 crore on the match, Shakeel called an emergency meeting of all the big bookies at Mumbai's Kamat Club in Goregaon. While the bookies gathered in the large business centre at the resort, Shakeel was on the speaker phone, threatening all of them to comply with his diktat. '*Deal fok karo aur nuksan bharo.* (Cancel the deals and pay up the money we lost.)' Mehta reached late for the meeting, and after a 'final warning' from Shakeel he asked the police for protection.

In an interview at the time, I asked Shakeel whether the D Company had really lost that much money on a cricket match. 'More than money, the issue was cheating,' he said. 'We asked parties in Mumbai to deposit ₹80 crore as they were responsible for fixing [the match]. We've warned them enough; now we will kill them.' Shakeel specifically mentioned Mehta's role in the match-fixing incidents, saying, 'Shobhan Mehta is the ringleader. The media knows about his connections to star players. Why is he hiding?' Shakeel said Mehta had been given police protection because of their threat.

With Shobhan Mehta going incommunicado, his father, Subodh Mehta, stepped out to take up their side of the story. I asked him in an interview I did in May 2000 for my article in *India Today* why the D gang had accused his son of match-fixing. 'Because we refuse to surrender,' he answered. 'Most of the bookies honour Shobhan's word, which makes his position too strong for the D gang. They have even given a contract to kill Shobhan so that they can control the Mumbai betting business.' But Shobhan had also been accused of fixing Pakistani players at Sharjah and of links with Indian and South African players, I told him. Subhodh denied it flatly and explained, 'At times we get involved indirectly when punters bet because they have information about fixing. In such cases we can't refuse our regular clients but also don't encourage them.' The rest of my interview with him progressed as follows:

Me: Shobhan's association with Tendulkar has come under scrutiny. Were you invited to his wedding?

Mehta: Knowing Sachin or his in-laws is not a crime.

Me: Which teams do you suspect of fixing?

Mehta: Asian teams are considered susceptible. Middlemen having access to team managers, key players. But naming them is to invite death.

Me: Can Indian players be fixed?

Mehta: Why not? We have been hearing names in the betting circuit for the past four years. The same names face serious charges today. It started in the north, mainly Delhi.

Me: Aren't you part of the same business?

Mehta: We're bookies, not fixers. But bookies get involved directly or indirectly when the match is fixed. And nothing is possible without the underworld. They want to share your profit. Pakistani bookie Hanif Cadbury refused to part with his profit and he was killed last year in South Africa.

On the morning of 19 April 2009, a Sunday, I was asked by my channel to telephone Chhota Shakeel to confirm the headline 'Dawood's brother was abducted, shot', published in the *Indian Express* that morning. I found out that the Kaskar family had relayed the information that Dawood's brother Noor-ul-Haq alias Noora had died on 31 March 2009 after suffering a massive cardiac arrest. Other accounts suggested the cause of his death to be cancer complicated by kidney failure. However, the news report claimed, '51-year-old Noora was abducted two days before his death and a ransom demand of $50 million was made... Noora's body was dropped off near Dawood Ibrahim's house in Karachi. As many as seven bullets are believed to have been fired into his head and his body bore signs of extreme torture.' Noora, who had composed a song for a Bollywood movie, reportedly wanted to be known as a lyricist and had been exploring ways to face charges and possibly work around the legal system so he could re-establish himself in Mumbai.

When I called Shakeel, however, he maintained that Noora had died of natural causes. His response when I confronted him with the contradictory news report and the agency's information was, '*Aap ko mein woh doctor jisne Noora ko treat kiya hai uska number deta hun, aap khud pooch lijiye.* (I will give you the number of the doctor who treated Noora, you can confirm it with him yourself). I replied, 'Which doctor on earth would contradict what you want to convey?' Shakeel insisted that I believe him as he had always been 'very honest' with me.

Star News eventually broadcast both versions of the story, and my international sources later confirmed that Noora had been killed brutally due to local political vendetta and gang wars. The local gangs in Karachi, it turned out, were upset about Dawood's growing influence in the country and the unofficial patronage provided to him by the officials. It is believed that the well-known underworld gang of Sardar Rehman Dakait that operates out of the Lyari Town area of Karachi was behind the abduction, and that the gang had been commissioned to send a message to Dawood.

All through my conversations with Shakeel, I was aware that his numbers were officially traced by multiple security agencies and every conversation with him would be recorded, monitored and judged for their content. Shakeel was well aware of this too, and he conveyed his version of a story rather deliberately every time we interacted. I was a medium of communication with the people he needed to reach, and perhaps he trusted me for my professional approach whenever he chose to speak with me.

This has been evident in most of my conversations with Shakeel, and when he called me after a break of four years, things were no different. This time he asked me if I knew a prominent politician, once also a cabinet minister, who had shown keen interest in bringing Shakeel's clan back to India to be tried under the Indian justice system. He asked me if I would talk to the politicians in Delhi about their interest in getting members of the D Company back to India. I told him the politician was not part of the ruling government at the time and he would not have the power to bring them back. This was after the Indian government's successful secret operation to get Dawood's younger brother Iqbal Kaskar deported to India from Dubai in 2003 (more about this in the next chapter). His deportation was followed by the deportation of ten others related to the Shakeel and Dawood clans from the UAE to Mumbai. In November 2006 the government of the UAE had begun a major crackdown on the D Company by rounding up several of its members in a major clean-up operation. This was after Raju Bookie, a major player who fixed cricket matches in the subcontinent, was murdered in Dubai. Raju is said to have fallen out of Dawood's favour. Of the 30 members of the Company who were rounded up in Dubai, 10 were deported to India. Among those deported were Arif, alias Bhai Jaan; Chhota Shakeel's brother-in-law, Zamaar Haji; Anjum Kherwani; Salim Qureshi and Qayum, all wanted in India in connection with the 1993 blasts.

This was the first time that Shakeel sounded to me like he was at the end of his tether. He said all of them were ready to face the law and prove the facts – their facts. He emphasized that they were ready to return to India provided the Indian government assured them of a certain legal deadline: he wanted the trials of all their cases to be completed within six months. I told him I would convey what he had said to the appropriate authorities. At the end of the conversation, he said all of them missed Mumbai and India.

This conversation was very different from the rest of the conversations I had had with him. His voice was low and he sounded sentimental. The very fact that he was checking on a possibility of returning to Mumbai and if I had the right connections in the right places to convey this message astounded me. Having interacted with him over the years and knowing what I did of the underworld I knew that none of them would say such things lightly and Shakeel certainly would not be having this conversation if his mentor, Dawood, did not sanction it. Besides, they knew they were conveying their message to the concerned agencies while talking to me.

Even though I knew that the conversation had already been heard by all concerned agencies, I made an attempt to convey it to the authorities. This was not the first time the D Company had made such an effort. They had made several failed attempts in the past to return to India, most notably through the renowned lawyer Ram Jethmalani. I was given a patient hearing by the authorities, and no questions were asked. They seemed to be aware of all the facts. Then I was politely told that a very strong political will was needed to bring the gangsters back, and I heard nothing further on this thereafter.

The frequency of Shakeel's calls has reduced over the years, but he continues to maintain his relations with a few media professionals, including me. He exchanges greetings on festivals like Diwali, Eid and New Year. I am still optimistic and waiting for the day when he will finally fulfil the promise he made me two decades ago and I will get to hear Dawood Ibrahim's story straight from the don's mouth.

Shakeel Shaikh, alias Chhota Shakeel, was born to Shaikh Mohiddin Shaikh in the same neighbourhood as his mentor

Dawood Ibrahim, at No. 11, 78, Temkar Street, Nagpada, in south Mumbai.

Like his mentor, Shakeel too studied in Ahmed Sailor High School at Nagpada, and discontinued his education after the tenth standard. Dawood, five years older than him, was his hero, from his schooldays and he was captivated by the older boy's courage, style and attitude to live life king-size. In the early 1990s, Shakeel joined Dawood in Dubai, where the latter had already become a don and was living a lavish life hobnobbing with film stars, cricketers and other celebrities. There were two Shakeels in Dawood's gang at the time, so the one who was taller was called Lambu Shakeel, and since he was shorter Shakeel Shaikh became known as Chhota Shakeel.

Shakeel came to the forefront within the D Company and outside it after Dawood's right-hand man at the time, Chhota Rajan, escaped from Dubai following the 1993 Mumbai serial blasts. Since that is a story detailed in another chapter of this book (see 'Bedlam in Bangkok'), it will suffice to say here that Rajan fell out with Dawood after a series of incidents that led him to suspect that Dawood was trying to sideline him and replace him with Chhota Shakeel, and that plans were afoot to get Rajan out of the way. When he found his suspicions confirmed, Rajan managed to escape from Dubai.

Rajan's exit was a turning point for Shakeel's career in crime. After Rajan's exit Dawood needed loyal hands other than his own brothers by his side. By then Shakeel had gained major ground in the D Company and had emerged a loyal soldier. At the time the Indian government was also in the process of inking an extradition treaty with the UAE, and Dawood knew he would have to leave Dubai. In Pakistan, the ISI saw an opportunity in Dawood's criminal skills and widespread network in India's financial capital and other states and offered him an olive branch, an offer to settle him and his clan in Pakistan. This was a great boost to Dawood's ego: the top authorities in Pakistan had recognized his 'power', given him special attention and offered him security. Shakeel, who had followed in Dawood's footsteps from the Temkar *mohalla* in Mumbai to Dubai, chose to go to Karachi with him. He had no compulsion to do so, as he was not involved in the 1993 blasts, and could have remained comfortably in Dubai, but his choice to accompany his boss earned him Dawood's respect and attention. He had proved his loyalty to his mentor, and was subsequently rewarded with a prominent position in the D Company.

In Karachi, from 1994 onwards, Shakeel began to oversee all operations of the D Company through his associates in Mumbai and other parts of the country as well as coordinate the Company's global network – ordering assassinations, arranging the delivery of weapons and money to shooters, threatening victims for extortion and providing legal help to those of their gang who were arrested. As an eye-wash and to create the illusion that the D Company still functioned from Dubai, he used mobile phones registered in Dubai to conduct his affairs across the world.

Once he took over, Shakeel asserted his might with full support from his mentor. He decentralized the management of the organization, delegating work and authority to others below him. Aslam Bhatti, for instance, was asked to handle the gold and counterfeit products business, while Sharad Shetty handled cricket and betting on horses, and was made responsible for dealing with the Udipi-Shetty hoteliers and builders in Mumbai. Sunil Sawant, aka Sautya, was made in-charge of the supply of weapons and contract-based crimes. The money-laundering, films and the real estate businesses were overseen by Shakeel himself, under the guidance and keen supervision of his mentor.

Chhota Shakeel's popularity among his gang members reportedly derives from his communication abilities. He is known to respect his seniors while managing to get work done by his juniors. He flexes his muscles when required while also being a messiah-like figure for the thousands working in his transnational crime syndicate, providing legal help to the imprisoned men and money to the concerned families upon the arrest or death of any of his foot soldiers. Despite being entrenched in crime, he remains a devout believer and patron of the Makhdoom Shah Dargah in Mahim, and is, in fact, known as 'Hajibaba' for his spiritual activities. It is said that much like Dawood, he never forgets his friends and rarely forgives his enemies.

Over the last two decades, Shakeel has become the most-'heard' gangster in the Indian media. Acting as the official spokesperson for the D Company, he has audaciously called journalists and others to brag about his operations and eliminate rivals, mediate between two warring parties or business disputes, deal with builders and hoteliers, and coerce film stars into acting in films funded by his gang. Since the MCOCA laws were enacted in 1999, the Mumbai Police's interception of underworld calls has put many don-friendly personalities in trouble, particularly those who had business connections with Shakeel, including Bollywood personalities, builders, judges, bookies, businessmen, hoteliers, politicians and even police officials themselves. Shakeel's calls have meant greater trouble for those refusing to toe the line drawn by the Company, for that has only led to people losing their lives to violent attacks by the D Company's gangsters.

Between 1995 and 2000, police records highlight Shakeel's role in a number of murders, including the ones of builders like Pradip Brijlal Jain and Om Prakash Kukreja; hoteliers like Harish Vallabhdas; readymade garments trader Hussain Muluk alias Haji Mukhtiar; Gulshan Kumar of the T-Series music company; Ramesh Gunga, a notorious gangster turned film producer; politicians like Jitendra Dabholkar, who was the main architect in the formation of Akhil Bharatiya Sena (ABS), a political outfit floated by Arun Gawli; Bharat Madhukar Mhatre, the Secretary of the ABS; Dharmadas Rohitbhai Solanki, leader of

Shramik Congress and president of ABS; Sudhakar Kashiram Lone, an active member of ABS from Byculla; Parvez Mohd. Ali Ansari alias Gama, a travel agent from Agripada; noted gangster Bhatiya Ismail Kasim Sayyed alias Munna Dadhi; and the well-known defence lawyer Kishorkumar Ramdas Sutrale.

Among these the killing that perhaps grabbed the most headlines and instilled dread in Mumbai's film industry was the murder of Gulshan Kumar, head of the T-Series music company. Kumar was allegedly murdered at the behest of music director Nadeem of the famous Nadeem–Shravan duo, who felt that Kumar had not been publicizing his music properly. He allegedly entered into a conspiracy with Ramesh Taurani of Tips music company and approached Dawood for help. Abu Salem, who at the time worked for Anees Ibrahim, threatened Kumar of dire consequences if he failed to oblige Nadeem. And when Kumar did not pay heed to his threats, Salem decided to eliminate him. It is said that Salem went ahead with the assassination unilaterally, and faced the consequences of Dawood's and Anees's ire, following which he broke away from the gang to set up his own operations.

On 12 August 1997, at about 10.15 a.m., when Gulshan Kumar was visiting a temple near his residence to offer prayers, three assailants armed with sophisticated firearms shot him dead near the back gate of Dhoop-Chhaon Housing Society at Four Bungalows in Andheri, Mumbai. When the CID took over the investigation, they arrested a group of gangsters of Chhota Shakeel's gang. Interrogation of the accused unfolded the conspiracy hatched by Salem, Nadeem and Taurani, which led to Taurani's arrest. Taurani was acquitted in April 2002 along with 18 others by the Sessions Court for want of evidence. Nadeem could not be arrested as he had fled the country and, at present, has taken asylum in London. Efforts of the Mumbai Police to extradite him have failed so far.[3]

The gang wars reached their peak in the 1990s with the D Company driving fear into the hearts of its rivals with the attempted assassinations of Chhota Rajan and Arun Gawli, and of nearly half-a-dozen Shiv Sena members, including the former mayor of Mumbai Milind Vaidya, who was the target of two unsuccessful attempts. Sources indicate that Shakeel and the ISI had allegedly hatched a conspiracy to attack Shiv Sena office-bearers, and that Shakeel had told his gang members that they could attack Shiv Sena members in any part of Maharashtra. In the ensuing spree of killings, Shiv Sena *shakha pramukhs* (division heads) Vivek Gajanan Kelkar, Shivaji Sopan Chavan, Ram Laxman Agale, and former *shakha pramukh* Mahadeo, aka Baban Atmaram Surve, were assassinated under Chhota Shakeel's orders during 1999–2001. In April 2001, Agale, another division head, was shot in Sakinaka while out with his minor daughter; the shooter shot him point blank in the head while he was purchasing medicines, and Agale was declared dead on arrival at the hospital.

The two assassination attempts on Milind Vaidya were part of a conspiracy intended to create communal disturbances in Mumbai. On 17 December 1998, while Vaidya was travelling in his Tata Safari, Shakeel's gangsters attacked the vehicle and shot him through the window. Though injured, Vaidya survived. Although the first attempt had failed, Shakeel was on the lookout for another opportunity, and in March 1999 unknown assailants in a Maruti 800 fired indiscriminately on Vaidya and his friends at Mahim and escaped from the scene. Three of his friends died, while Vaidya and six others were seriously injured.

Shakeel's emergence as the second-most powerful gangster in the D Company, leaving all of Dawood's brothers behind in the power race, has struck many observers as something of significance. Remarkably, he has managed to hold on to this position for the past two decades, though it has not been easy for him. Shakeel's rise in the empire has not gone down well with Dawood's younger brother Anees Ibrahim, who always considered himself heir-apparent to the business. The Mumbai underworld is abuzz with stories of rivalry and one-upmanship between the two. For instance, while Shakeel was recruiting uneducated and jobless youth from Muslim localities in south Mumbai for the gang and successfully using them for his operations, including executing murders in Mumbai, Anees set up a parallel network that has given rise to gangsters like Abu Salem. Nevertheless, Shakeel's recruits – such as Firoz Konkani, who initiated the second round of riots in Mumbai after the Babri Masjid demolition, and Munna Zingada, who played a key role in the attack on Chhota Rajan in Bangkok – have remained loyal to him and the D Company, while Anees's protégé Abu Salem left him to start a separate operation. When I pointedly asked Shakeel about this in an interview, he denied the existence of any bad blood between himself and Anees, calling it a 'simple difference of opinion' that finally got resolved as a result of Dawood's intervention. Sources in the Mumbai Police indicate that Dawood resolved the issue by separating businesses – both legitimate and illegitimate – for each of his brothers.

Chhota Shakeel is known to be a manager par excellence. Under his management, the D Company continues to be a criminal empire functioning successfully through fear and coercion, even though none of its leaders are based in India. His power and his mandate to manage the vast transnational criminal empire worth $6.7 billion comes from the implicit trust and faith his mentor has put in him. This characteristic has caught the eye of the US authorities who have placed him second only to his boss under the most-wanted global terrorists' list. His personal life, too, has begun to resemble his boss's. Like Dawood's brothers, Shakeel's younger brother, Anwar, has also followed him into his crime business in Dubai. From the bits and pieces of information that Shakeel has revealed to me about his children in various interviews, it is clear that he wants them to stay away from the dark world of crime. He has sent his daughters to the UK for their education – one of them is a doctor while the other has a degree in business management – while his son is pursuing his studies under Shakeel's vigilant eyes. His elder daughter, Zoya, has recently been married in Karachi to a doctor based in the US.

Against the backdrop of Dawood's alleged by-pass heart surgery and ill-health, the obvious question that crops up is: Who will be holding the fort after Dawood? The power struggle between the don's brother Anees Ibrahim and his lieutenant Chhota Shakeel has continued over many years, but it is now being said that Shakeel's skills of management, diplomacy and running operations are preferred by the Company's business associates in the crime world over the dynastic claim to Dawood's throne by his brother Anees. Shakeel, it seems, is most likely to step into his mentor's shoes when the time is right.

The Younger Brother

'BADA BHAI HAI TO SHAADI-EID *ke mauke par milna hota tha*,' Iqbal Hassan Ibrahim Kaskar told me outside the special MCOCA Court in Mumbai in April 2006, in response to my question about the last time he had met his brother Dawood Ibrahim. According to him, they met only during family get-togethers or on functions like Eid. A portly man with a stubble, he looked visibly tired, perhaps because he was observing the Ramzan fast, or it could be from waiting for the post-lunch hearing in the Sara–Sahara shopping complex case, for which the special court had been convened. Iqbal was one of the prime accused in the case of the unauthorized construction of the twin malls.

My instinctive reaction was one of disbelief; how was it possible that he met his brother only occasionally? Iqbal explained that 'Bhai' cared for them and made sure his younger siblings lived in financial comfort, but nothing beyond. He helped them become financially independent and all the Kaskar brothers had legitimate shops and other business establishments.

'*White ka business hai* (It's all legal),' he asserted.

I asked him what it was like when the Kaskar clan met. He said that like all traditional Muslim families, men and women of the Kaskar household, too, celebrated functions separately. The clan hierarchy – from the oldest to the youngest – was strictly maintained, and younger brothers or junior gang members could not speak loudly or drink and smoke in front of their elders.

Later, Samira Jumani, Abu Salem's first wife, would confirm the protocol at D Company functions and share with me her not-so-pleasant experiences at these get-togethers. She said the women in the Kaskar family followed the same male hierarchy in the *zenana*, and Dawood's wife Mehjabeen was at the top in terms of status, followed by Anees Ibrahim's wife, and then other family or gang members' wives depending on the seniority or status of their husbands within the D Company.

Iqbal Kaskar outside the court. Photo courtesy Mahendra Parikh.

Iqbal told me that Dawood Bhai believed in maintaining *tehzeeb* and led by example. 'So courteous is he that even when he wants to drink a glass of water, he requests his servant politely, "*Miyan, ek glass paani pilaoge*? (Would you please get me a glass of water?)",' he said. Iqbal emphasized that Dawood kept his family away from the business, and this was true of his rivals as well. He said that Dawood's elder brother Shabbir's murder in 1981 had been a lesson for his family. Iqbal further added, '*Dhande mein* family *nahi aana chahiye.* (Families should not be involved in this "business".)'

The day I met him, he was outside the second-floor courtroom where the special MCOCA Court had been convened on the premises of the sessions court, with a policeman guarding him, waiting for his case to come up. He didn't need to be persuaded to talk to me and answered my questions quite readily. He seemed quite agitated and upset. The lengthy court trial process he had never thought he would have to go through seemed to have got to him.

'Why did you leave your comfortable life in Dubai and choose to come to Mumbai? Didn't you know that you would be jailed on arrival?' I asked him.

'I knew there would be trouble and I would go to jail, but not for so long. My lawyer had told me that I didn't have any case against me and I would be free from legal hassles in a few days. But it has been three years and I have no idea how long I will stay in jail!' Iqbal grumbled.

By then he had already been acquitted in a case pertaining to the murder of customs informant Ravindra Singh for want of evidence in August 2003. Singh was gunned down in 1999 and the police had arrested six persons in connection with the murder while declaring eight more, including Iqbal, as absconders.

Iqbal Kaskar was deported to India on 19 February 2003 by the UAE government, honouring requests from Indian authorities after he was arrested in January 2003 from his villa near the Dubai airport in connection with the murder of Sharad Shetty, a friend-turned-foe of Dawood. Two other Kaskar brothers – Noora and Mustaquin – were also arrested on the charges related to the same murder. An Indian-born hotelier and a gangster known to have links with the D Company, Shetty had been murdered on 19 January that year.[1] Shortly afterwards, the Dubai Police arrested 30 suspects, ten of whom were already marked as wanted in India. Besides Iqbal, Mustaquin and Noora were also arrested. The Indian government was quick to react, pressuring UAE authorities to send Iqbal home. He was the only Kaskar brother to have retained his Indian passport in Dubai, since his wife and children were still in Mumbai and, as my sources in the Mumbai Police told me, held Indian passports. Iqbal knew that once he accepted Pakistani travel documents like his brothers it would be impossible for him to return home to his family, and they would be stuck in India or in Dubai.

Back in Mumbai, the police had been monitoring Dawood Ibrahim's family after Dawood and Anees were named as accused in the 1993 blasts case. While the others had already accepted Pakistani travel documents, Iqbal had been locked in a legal battle with the Indian government ever since the Dubai Consulate impounded his passport in 2001. He was seeking passports for himself and his family members, and his argument was that his family should not be punished for his brothers' alleged crimes.

Along with Iqbal, gangster Ejaz Pathan had also been deported to India. Pathan was a former D Company member and one of the main accused in the 1993 blasts case. Sometime in 2001, Dawood's right-hand man Chhota Shakeel accused Pathan of having links with the rival Babloo Srivastava–Chhota Rajan gang; and after he was almost gunned down in an attack, Pathan, then living in Karachi, had escaped to Dubai.

When Iqbal and Pathan were extradited, the Deputy Prime

Minister at the time, L.K. Advani, described it as a 'setback for Pakistan-backed terrorism'.[2] But R.S. Sharma, then Mumbai's Police Commissioner, was cautious and viewed the entire episode with scepticism, which he expressed during a meeting I had with him at his office. There was enough ground for cynicism. Far from indicating the D Company's decline in Dubai, the duo's deportation seemed to be a strategic move that would prove advantageous for the Company. Pathan's deportation, sources said, had been 'influenced' by the D Company so that its enemies would face the heat in India. There was little doubt that with their presence on the ground in India a new chapter in the ongoing power struggle between gangs would begin. Pathan was subsequently tried in the special TADA Court in Mumbai for his part in the 1993 blasts.

Iqbal's return had a more complicated explanation. It was revealed that when the Dubai Police reached his house to arrest him, a female relative pretended he wasn't home. After placing a guard at the gate, the police returned the following day. The 24-hour interval was all the time Iqbal needed to call Dawood in Karachi and discuss with him the implications of his arrest. Since Iqbal had already declared himself an Indian citizen, he knew he was likely to be deported. Still, getting a Pakistani passport, forged or otherwise, at such short notice would not have been a problem. It seems in hindsight, therefore, that the decision to persist with an Indian identity was a well-thought-out one, both for Iqbal as well as Dawood.

In a post-9/11 scenario, Crime Branch officials believed, the D Company had to curtail its activities as it was under increased scrutiny and pressure from UAE authorities. In fact, many of its men were being deported to India from the Gulf under pressure from the USA. It was a bad time for his underworld operations in general. It was then that Dawood, along with Iqbal, is believed to have begun investing in property and men to revitalize the gang. The deportations of Lambu Shakeel, Dawood's close confidant, in January 2003, and of Iqbal himself were viewed by the Crime Branch as chances taken by Dawood to strengthen the D Company's network in Mumbai. The Mumbai Police believed that the D Company may have calculated that Iqbal's criminal record was less serious when compared to that of his brother and his punishment for them would also be limited. After being arrested in connection with a murder in Mumbai's Agripada area in 1983, he had been granted bail. If the other murder cases could also be weakened – perhaps with prosecution witnesses being 'nudged' into turning hostile – Iqbal Kaskar could be out on bail and even acquitted and could become a 'free and respectable' Mumbai citizen once again. This would allow the D Company to expand into some legitimate businesses in the city.

Senior officials at Mumbai Police's Crime Branch believed that Iqbal's wish to return to Mumbai must have been allowed after factoring in all risks as Dawood is known to be very protective of his family and siblings. One of the main apprehensions would certainly have been the possibility of Iqbal getting entangled in a fresh case and therefore being kept in jail for a long time.

But as fate would have it, the cookie did not quite crumble the way the Kaskars had wished it to. The Mumbai Police had been preparing to clip Iqbal's wings and, thus, send his plan of pursuing a dream life in Mumbai crashing. Even after his arrest at Mumbai Airport, Iqbal didn't realize that his worst fears had come true and that he was done for a long period of time.

The Mumbai Police had decided to nip in the bud the D Company's audacious plan to revive operations in the city. The state of Maharashtra now had a new and stringent law (MCOCA) to deal with organized crime. The police presented transcripts of 65 conversations from 141 calls intercepted between 22 November 2002 and 26 January 2003 in the MCOCA Court. Iqbal, along with his associates Ghulam Nabi Tanvar, Altaf Patani and Ashraf Rehman, alias Lallubhai Builder, was charged with aiding and abetting the unlawful acquisition of property worth ₹30 crore, including the Sara–Sahara shopping complexes on Mohammad Road in upmarket south Mumbai. The property originally belonged to the central government (CPWD) and was illegally converted into a private mall with the connivance of Brihanmumbai Municipal Corporation (BMC) officials at the behest of Iqbal and his aides in Mumbai.[3]

Mumbai Police claimed that they had enough evidence to prove that Iqbal had been leading an 'organized crime syndicate' on behalf of his brother even before returning to India. This gang, the police said, had forced residents in the south Mumbai neighbourhood to sell their property at dirt-cheap prices to make way for the illegal shopping complex to be built on more than 2,700 sq. yards. Ironically, the mall was situated very close to the Mumbai Police headquarters. Those allegedly threatened included low-income residents who had indeed sold off their small huts to Iqbal by 1997. These former owners, the police said, gathered courage after six years to give evidence. The other suspects included four BMC officials, who allegedly connived with the accused to illegally allow the Sara–Sahara shopping complex to come up. Most witnesses said they had wanted up to ₹5 lakh per hut, but were threatened into accepting ₹75,000 to ₹1.2 lakh for each hut. One man who ran a garage broke down in court, saying he was forced to sell his property worth ₹45 lakh for only ₹33 lakh.

Another part of the case was related to the dubious sale of an ice factory adjacent to the Sara–Sahara property. The prosecution claimed that Kaskar's men forced the factory owner to sell it at ₹4.58 crore, far less than the amount of ₹12.51 crore agreed on earlier. The prosecution said the buyers routinely threatened the residents in the name of Dawood Ibrahim and his lieutenant, Chhota Shakeel.

Being chargesheeted under the MCOCA Court meant Iqbal would get no bail for at least 15 months. If convicted, he could face up to ten years in jail. A senior Crime Branch official who had interrogated Iqbal in jail told me that Iqbal was often found crying in jail as he found his situation to be hopeless. The public prosecutor, Rohini Salian, was known to be tough and had had successful convictions under the MCOCA. She argued that the Sara–Sahara acquisition clearly pointed to the D Company extending its nexus to builders with official connivance. The prosecution's case was based on the confession of a woman named Parveen, who said that she had been forcibly evicted from her house from the Sara-Sahara land and 104 other prosecution witnesses along with that of four court witnesses who testified that their land had been forcibly taken away. Several frontmen were identified for Iqbal, who owned and controlled the properties. Sherif Abdul Sheikh and Rehman Abdul Gaffer Sheikh ran Iqbal's share of the Royal Touch Mall which had been illegally constructed on the land in question. The police also suspected that Iqbal had illegally built at least a dozen more buildings in wards C (parts of south Mumbai) and P (in the Malad to Goregaon area) with the connivance of BMC officials.

Ultimately, in 2007, the special court acquitted Iqbal and five others, including four BMC officials, of all charges in the Sara–Sahara case. But it convicted three of Dawood's associates – Abdul Rehman Shaikh, his associate Abdul Sattar Radhanpura and Tariq Parveen who had been deported from Dubai – and sentenced them to prison terms ranging from five to seven years. They were also directed to pay fines ranging from ₹10.05–14.05 lakh.[4] All three, who had already spent four years in custody, were found guilty of illegal construction and forcing tenants to vacate their shanties so that the malls could come up. Tariq Parveen, out on bail after his conviction in the Sara–Sahara case, was arrested once again in January 2015 in a 16-year-old case of waging war against the nation. The BMC officials were acquitted for lack of any evidence to show that the officers gained pecuniary benefits from the transactions. The state of Maharashtra immediately filed an appeal, which was admitted by the Mumbai High Court, but the decision on the case is still pending.

In 2012, Iqbal filed an application requesting the court to expedite his hearing, saying that whenever he or his children applied for a passport it was refused on grounds of the case.

Not only was Iqbal the only one among the Kaskar brothers who chose to retain his Indian identity, he had also fought a long legal battle to get his family's Indian passports re-issued. His other brothers had followed Dawood to Karachi and preferred to become Pakistani nationals. Dawood's brothers went to him in Dubai in the early 1990s itself, as he had already become a rich man and wanted his brothers to have stable financial lives. Iqbal had set up an electronics shop in Dubai in the 1990s and settled there with his family. Since he was the brother of a man notified as a terrorist, his passport had not been renewed. After Dawood and Anees were named as the main accused in the 1993 blasts, the other younger brothers Noora, Qayum and Mustaquin followed their elder brothers to Karachi.

In April 2014 the Mumbai High Court directed the Regional Passport Office (RPO) in Mumbai to decide on the aforementioned application for fresh passports. Iqbal had also sought permission from the court to travel to Saudi Arabia for a period of four weeks, for the Haj. The court held that if the passport office granted Iqbal a passport, he could approach the court seeking permission to travel abroad.

Though he had been acquitted in the Sara–Sahara case, the punishing remarks on Iqbal's family members' passports, even though they held no criminal records, prohibited them from travelling anywhere except between the UAE and India. His wife Rizwana had moved the court and appealed to the Ministry of External Affairs to remove the remarks on her and her four children's passports citing educational reasons, as the children were unable to go abroad for higher studies to countries other than Dubai. They also faced hassles because of the legal constraints. Apparently keen on aeronautics, they had missed out on a once-in-a-lifetime opportunity to take part in a NASA space camp in April 2011. The petition cited the case of Chhota Rajan's brother Deepak Nikhalje, whose passport had borne a similar remark. However, Nikhalje was able to have it deleted, and Rizwana wanted to avail of the same relief.

Just as Iqbal's deportation was seen as a strategy to test the Indian waters once again on part of the Kaskar clan, his decision to persist with an Indian identity was also seen to be a considered one. The Mumbai Police had smelt a rat as soon as Lambu Shakeel had landed in Mumbai in January 2003. When notorious D Company gangsters Mustafa Manjnoon Dossa, Anil Parab, Raju Sharma and splinter gang member Ejaz Pathan also arrived in the country after being deported from Dubai, the police were alerted about the D Company's nefarious plans to resettle in Mumbai.

Interestingly, apart from accumulating prime properties in Mumbai, Iqbal is said to have told the police during interrogation that the D Company planned to set people up with a parallel career in politics. Since then, Lambu Shakeel aka Shakeel Ahmed has formally joined the Samajwadi Party in Mumbai. Defending his admission to the party, Maharashtra Samajwadi Party Secretary Abu Azmi said, 'He is not a criminal unless proven guilty.' Iqbal followed suit and tried to contest the 2004 Assembly elections as an independent candidate from the Umarkhadi constituency of South Mumbai while still in jail, but had to later withdraw his nomination as his name did not figure on electoral lists and Dawood, too, had advised him to stay away from politics.

When I met Iqbal Kaskar, however, the verdict on the Sara–Sahara case was yet to come, and he was deep in a legal soup. I asked him why he hadn't opted to go to Pakistan like his other brothers had. His response was that he was an Indian and had always retained his Indian passport. 'I wanted to come home, and Mumbai is home,' he said. I told him that the Mumbai Police believed he had been sent home to handle the D Company's business from Mumbai. 'What was the need to come to India in that case?' he retorted, leaving it unsaid that he could have worked with Dawood from anywhere in the world. However, one cannot ignore the fact that he had a thriving electronics business in Dubai and was worried about his trading licence there, which, if discovered, Indian authorities would promptly ask the UAE authorities to cancel. He asked me not to write anything about his business in my story as it would be noticed by the court or the police and his licence to do business in Dubai could be cancelled.

I pointed out to him that Dawood was said to have had many influential friends, including politicians, in Mumbai and India. 'Won't they help you?' I asked him. He lowered his voice and nodded in agreement. 'Many have come home and we have clicked photos with all of them – including some top guys.' I proposed a story on these photographs, and he was quick to respond, 'No way! I will be killed in jail if it's revealed!'

I changed tack and asked him if he had returned home to pursue a political career. He said his name did not figure on the voters' list, which is why he could not contest any elections. 'But many well-wishers, including Bhai (Dawood), have advised me against entering active politics,' he said, adding, 'I was told to live peacefully and go on with life instead of inviting more trouble.'

I finally finished off my interview by asking him if his other brothers, including Dawood, would ever return to Mumbai. He thought for a while before saying, 'Mumbai is greatly missed by the family. Changes in our circumstances have put a lot at stake. But who knows about the future?'

And so it remains.

The irony of being Iqbal Kaskar is that if his older brother's name worked as a magical key that opened new avenues for him in his real estate and other businesses in Mumbai, it also kept him under the watchful eyes of the law since being extradited to Mumbai. Also, while being Dawood's brother brought a natural aura of awe and fear towards him, it also made him a sitting duck for Dawood's rivals. Iqbal told me that 'Bhai' had cautioned him that he would be a soft target for his rivals, the 'department' (the police) and the 'agency' (IB). Even though Nagpada in Bhendi Bazaar was considered Dawood's den, Iqbal had watertight security arrangements made for him by Dawood.

Dawood's fears came true on the night of 17 May 2011, when two armed shooters on a bike fired at least five rounds at the bodyguard guarding the entrance below Dambarwala Building at Pakmodia Street in Bhendi Bazaar. Pakmodia Street is thickly populated by Bohra Muslims. Most families live in rickety old buildings and among them tales abound of the activities of the gangster Dawood, who spent his childhood and youth in the four-storey structure now called Dambarwala Building. Pakmodia Street is very much Kaskar territory, a law unto itself. No one can venture there without being scrutinized. The residents of the street question and stop every stranger who passes through. So much so that if they find the individual suspicious, he is subjected to a thorough security check that would put airport security checks to shame.

The Dambarwala Building served both as residence and office to Iqbal. Even though the shooters had direct access to Iqbal's apartment on the first floor, they did not make any attempts to storm it after gunning down his bodyguard, Arif Abu Bakr Zaveri. Only a flight of stairs separated Iqbal from the shooters, yet they chose to escape. In the mayhem that followed, the two shooters tried to dart through the narrow bylanes, but were apprehended in the crowded street by a mob that had gathered at the sound of the gunshots. After being beaten up by the crowd, they were handed over to the police.

Iqbal later told the court, while deposing as a witness in the case, that he was resting in his house at the time of the incident. He heard people shouting and was later informed that there had been a firing. When he came down from his house, he saw bloodstains on the stairs and an empty cartridge.[5] The involvement of a Nepali shooter raised further doubts on whether the shooting was the handiwork of those protecting and using Chhota Rajan's network for covert operations in India and the subcontinent, according to him. He said that the Chhota Rajan gang had trained a large number of unemployed youth in Nepal as sharpshooters since the mid-1990s. Rajan's Nepal wing had also pulled off a major operation by killing Dawood's key associate and Nepali Member of Parliament Mirza Dilshad Beg in 1998.[6]

After the attack, Dawood didn't retaliate, as was expected by the Mumbai Police. Perhaps, the D Company thought that the attack was a ploy to provoke the don or to lure him out of his hideout. Later, a senior IPS officer from Mumbai told me that the shooting might have been carried out to send a clear message to Dawood that Iqbal was spared for now, but he could always be attacked.

When I spoke to Chhota Shakeel later and asked him about the attack, he told me that Rajan had broken the unwritten protocol of not attacking each others' families, and their gang would avenge the attack and hunt him down. Soon afterwards, the Mumbai Police arrested seven individuals in connection with the case. While the case is still being heard at the special MCOCA Court at Arthur Road Jail, according to the Mumbai Police, Rashad Abdul Rashid Sheikh, one of the seven arrested, has called two witnesses to the jail through his brother and threatened them of dire consequences if they deposed against him. These witnesses had seen Sheikh taking stock of the weapons that were used in the crime. The witnesses informed the court in July 2015, and the court ordered the police to provide security to the two.

Meanwhile, Chhota Shakeel allegedly sent two shooters, Mohammad Mahir Ashraf Kalbe Siddiqui and Akhtar Jamal Khan, to bump off D.K. Rao, a gangster loyal to Rajan who was also among the seven arrested, and another Rajan loyalist Ashok Satardekar as a retaliatory attack. Rao is lodged in Nasik Jail after the attempted hit on Iqbal, and he was to be killed when he was brought to court. Satardekar, secretary of the Sahyadri Krida Mandal in Tilak Nagar (one of the biggest Ganpati mandals in the city which is allegedly funded by Rajan), was to be killed in Chembur. He was among those arrested for the murder of noted trade union leader Datta Samant in 1997. However, the police arrested the two shooters after a tip-off and the operation proved a failure. With Chhota Rajan's imminent arrival in Mumbai the dynamics of the Mumbai underworld are bound to change. The don's presence might just prove to be a booster shot for his dwindling gang. In fact, the Mumbai Police are preparing themselves for what they suspect will come true – the trio of Hindu dons (Rajan, Gawli and Ashwin Naik) re-grouping to build up a formidable front against Dawood and his clan.

Iqbal's travails with the law continued beyond the Sara–Sahara case and the attempted hit on him. In February 2015, he was arrested once more, this time for allegedly attempting to extort ₹3 lakh from Salim Shaikh, a real estate agent in Byculla, and assaulting him. In his complaint to the police, Shaikh stated that he had received a phone call on 30 January 2015 saying Iqbal Kaskar wanted to meet him. When he did not acknowledge the request, Shabbir Sheikh, the co-accused in the case, picked up the victim and took him to Iqbal's house, where he demanded ₹3 lakh from him. When Salim refused, the two men hit him and threatened to kill him if he did not pay up within seven days.[7]

The Mumbai Police, in its remand application to the court, stated that they wanted to check if Dawood Ibrahim was himself involved in the case and whether Iqbal had acted at his behest. Iqbal's family advocate, Shyam Keshwani, contended that the charges were fabricated by the police and no money or property was retrieved from Iqbal. The court granted him bail, but the local police sought preventive action against Iqbal so that he would not commit a similar crime again. Chapter proceedings were initiated against Iqbal, and he was served a show-cause notice. A chapter proceeding is a unique procedure in Indian law that allows an ACP to perform the role of a special executive magistrate, and proceedings are held under Section 110 of the IPC as security for good behaviour from habitual offenders. When an executive magistrate receives information that there is a person who is a habitual offender within his local jurisdiction, the magistrate may require such a person to show cause as to why he should not be ordered to execute a bond, with sureties, for his good behaviour for a period not exceeding three years. In Iqbal Kaskar's case, if he did not execute the bond, a DCP could take over and extern him from the area. In simple words, a process had been initiated to keep Iqbal Kaskar away from Mumbai for three years.[8]

When I spoke to Chhota Shakeel in July 2015, he told me that the D Company had stayed away from any killings in Mumbai for the last six years. Though he said that they had honoured 'the deal' by not killing a single person, he refrained from mentioning who he had made the deal with. When I asked him if the deal had changed after the new state government, he didn't respond. I wondered if the safety of Iqbal Kaskar and his family was negotiated with someone more powerful and whether the 'deal' had also been honoured by both sides.

Yet another salvo was fired in the long-drawn-out war between the D Company and Indian authorities when the Narendra Modi government, working under the ambit of the Smuggling and

Foreign Exchange Manipulators Act 1976, sent Iqbal a notice in June 2015 stating that his current apartment building, Dambarwala Building on Pakmodia Street, had been forfeited. The government, in the notice, alleged that Dawood had bought the building with his illegitimate income, and Iqbal was asked to hand over the property within 30 days. Iqbal took the battle to the Mumbai High Court and sought the court's intervention. In his writ petition, he claimed that he and his late mother owned the building and that it had nothing to do with his brother. In his defence, he also stated that the Income Tax department knew that he and his late mother Aminabi Hasan Ibrahim Kaskar had bought the building for ₹60,000 and that the department had not disputed the purchase of the property at all.[9]

Iqbal Kaskar's latest brush with the law has initiated a long-drawn battle with the BJP-led state government, which is a part of the larger war between Dawood Ibrahim and Indian authorities. So far, Dawood has managed to stay away from Indian authorities, but his brother Iqbal's errant ways with the law are unlikely to be taken lightly by the Maharashtra state government and the central government, particularly when it is widely perceived that Chhota Rajan could be an antidote to Dawood and his gang in Mumbai and even in Pakistan.

The Don Who Loved Mumbai

ON 12 OCTOBER 2011, I read a newsflash that Muhammed Iqbal Memon – also known as Iqbal Mirchi due to his family's traditional business dealings in red chillies and spices – had been arrested in London for threatening his business associate.

I had come very close to interviewing him in July 2005 while I was in Dubai to cover the *walima* of Dawood Ibrahim's daughter. At the time, his sons' passports had been restricted, and the case was pending in the Supreme Court of India. Asif and Junaid, his sons, had been denied Indian passports since their father was a wanted fugitive, but Mirchi was contesting it. His argument was that his family should not be punished for his alleged crimes. In Mumbai, I had got word that he would like to meet me. I was ready to meet him or his sons in Dubai, but at his hotel I got a message that they would meet me at some other time.

Once considered Dawood Ibrahim's right-hand man, Iqbal Mirchi had successfully thwarted attempts by the Indian authorities to extradite him, but had lost his Indian passport and his freedom to travel outside Britain.[1] Mirchi lived a very glamorous and colourful life in a six-bedroom palatial mansion in Horn Church, a posh locality in northeast London, for almost two decades. He had traversed a vast criminal landscape, from being a petty dockyard pilferer to a landing and distribution agent for smuggled goods in Mumbai to eventually being ranked among the top 50 global drug barons by the UN in 2005.

Now, as the news of the arrest filtered in, I immediately thought of meeting him and convincing him to appear for an interview on television – it would be his first. I knew that his older son, Asif Memon, used to run the Imperial Suites Hotel in Dubai. I called the hotel reception and took his email address from them. I also left my number with them along with a note for Asif, in the hope that he might return my call. I did not expect him to respond and when he finally did two days later, I could not be thankful enough. It was extraordinary! Asif asked me to send him a list of questions that I intended to ask his father in what he insisted had to be a formal TV interview. The only condition Iqbal Mirchi had was that the channel would air an uncut version of his interview without adding any interpretations or opinions. We agreed to his conditions on email, and he invited me to London thereafter.

This was a big deal. The interview would be Iqbal Mirchi's first-ever appearance in the public sphere in the last two decades, ever since he had been declared a fugitive by Indian authorities. All that the world had seen till then was an old black-and-white photo of him from his Mumbai Police dossier, used over and over again by the media for their stories on the underworld. On top of that, I was going to meet one of the world's most wanted men, notified by the UN as a senior figure in the D Company, a criminal outfit that was said to rival the Italian mafia in its global clout and crime syndicate operations.

Then, suddenly, on the eve of my flight to London on 3 November 2011, Asif called me to say that the meeting would have to be called off. Even though he did not rule out the possibility of an interview sometime in the future, I was extremely anxious. I knew that Mirchi was having second thoughts about appearing on camera as he was risking his identity as a businessman in London.

He was unsure of the impact that his appearance on camera would have on his personal life and his family in general. But I did not want to lose this chance.

I decided to be straightforward about it and told Asif that we would be losing a good amount of money with all the cancellations at the last moment – not just the tickets for the cameraman and myself, but also a week-long booking at a hotel which had already been paid for. Asif said he would need to consult his father and, fortunately, this time around the response was positive. He said that his father would meet me first before taking a call about appearing on camera.

When we landed at Heathrow, my phone rang as soon as I switched it on. It was Asif checking on us. He had called to find out whether we had reached without any hassles, and then he invited us – my cameraman Maan Bahadur Singh and me – for dinner the next evening. He asked us to be ready by 8 p.m. and said that he would pick us up from our hotel on Kensington High Street.

The next day, at the designated time, Asif arrived in a black Mercedes with his wife, two children and his younger brother, Junaid. He apologized politely for the delay – traffic congestion, he said – and took us to an Oriental restaurant in Essex, an hour-long ride away from the hotel. Asif had been in constant touch with me since we landed, and I knew that Mirchi would not cancel the meeting, but I would have to be prepared to convince him to come on camera. Facing a news camera is not easy on the nerves for many. Nonetheless, I had prepared myself for a marathon question-and-answer session with him and his family; there was some certainty about that coming through.

A table for seven had already been reserved at the restaurant. The staff was warm and familiar with Asif and the others of the family, indicating that they were regular customers. The food was lavish – from oysters to Oriental vegetarian delicacies. The Mirchi family declared they were big foodies. Junaid, the younger son, said what his father craved most here in the UK was the pomfret fish masala so typical of Mumbai. He revealed that when he had finally got his Indian passport and travelled to Mumbai, the first thing he did was eat his father's favourite dish in a Mumbai restaurant.

Everybody seemed to be in a pleasant mood, and it felt as if we were in the midst of a family celebration. I was observing them when I realized that both Asif and Junaid were watching me closely. Just then, the entire family stood up and the kids ran towards an elderly man in a blue V-neck sweater and beige pants with grey hair and a moustache. Iqbal Mirchi had arrived. Both the men got up to touch their father's feet, while he asked us if we were comfortable and liked the food. For the first time since we had arrived in London, Maan looked a little relieved. He whispered to me that the man standing in front of us, allegedly a narcotics kingpin and a fugitive, looked more like a jovial grandfather than a hardened criminal. The gangster's polite and soft-spoken approach was working – at least on my colleague. However, to me he appeared to be a restless man, someone who craved social dignity, which no money could buy him.

In subsequent conversations, I would discover that Iqbal Mirchi was willing to go to any length to put his notorious past behind him and get rid of the label of being a drug lord. He seemed to be extremely vulnerable, someone who was distraught at discovering his receding power. Perhaps he knew that his 'utility' was on the decline in the eyes of his mentors and masters.

When dinner got over, Asif drove us to their home, a plush house in an exclusive part of London. It looked like Mirchi had mastered the art of distancing himself from the criminal empire he was said to be controlling. We arrived at a huge iron gate that had sensors and closed-circuit cameras both inside and outside it. As we drove up to it, the gate opened from the inside to reveal a typically large English bungalow – a detached six-bedroom house that had an indoor swimming pool. Two luxury cars stood in the driveway, and a spiral wooden staircase went up to the first-floor bedrooms from the lobby. Mirchi led us into a living room that looked more Arabic than English in its style. The room had dark wooden floors and walls, and was furnished with two cream leather sofas and Persian carpets. He told me later that it was his second wife's wish to live in a house with an indoor swimming pool, a party area and a sprawling garden in the backyard. His second wife was a starlet of yesteryears, Heena Kausar, daughter of the legendary filmmaker K. Asif of *Mughal-e-Azam* fame.

Over a dessert of pistachio and rose-flavoured kulfi, Mirchi contested all the allegations against him. He began with his recent London arrest and called it a family matter. Mirchi had been arrested by the London Metropolitan Police and charged with threatening to kill 41-year-old Nadeem A. Kader, who was from Essex. The UK's Crown Prosecution Service dropped all charges against him later, because the evidence was not enough to provide a realistic prospect of conviction. 'We knew the Kader family and I was thinking of marrying Junaid to his daughter. But he had financial issues, and this culminated in a false allegation of (me issuing) a threat to his life. The police called me in for questioning but let me off,' he said.

He reacted strongly when I mentioned the charges of drug smuggling against him in India, and the Interpol red-corner notice on him since 1994 followed by his subsequent interrogation by the London Police. 'Everything they (the police) say about me is total *bakwaas*,' he insisted. Flanked by his second wife Heena, and Asif and Junaid on either side, Mirchi said, 'A senior police officer (from the Mumbai Police) told me that my name would be attached to false charges unless I paid millions in bribes. I refused and moved to Dubai. They put these charges against me in my absence and claimed I had absconded. That mud has stuck to my name ever since.'

The author with Iqbal Mirchi. TV grab courtesy Star News.

Iqbal Mirchi's house in London. TV grab courtesy Star News.

Mirchi began his criminal career as a small-time thief on Mumbai's docks in the 1970s. In the social surroundings in which he grew up, he was most inspired by the crime lord of south Bombay in the 1960s, Abdul Karim Khan Pathan, aka Karim Lala. The Peshawari Pathan was Mirchi's hero; at six feet six inches, his well-built Pashtun physique and thick trademark moustache made him awe-inspiring. He was wealthy, powerful and helpful, and had successfully created an impression of being a messiah for the poor people living in his neighbourhood. He gave them a sense of security, and provided a parallel system of justice with speedy solutions for those who sought it from him at his weekly *janta darbar*s held at his residence every Sunday. Young Mirchi started attending Lala's weekly *darbar* regularly and observed Lala with great adulation. What impressed him the most was the way Lala would sit on a throne-like chair and exude the authority of an emperor, delivering *farman*s (orders) after listening to the disputing parties.

Organized crime first came to Mumbai (then Bombay) in the late 1950s, with ethnic Pashtuns, largely immigrants from Afghanistan, taking the lead in establishing the first criminal groups. The Afghans' physical attributes gave them an image of being a belligerent group in general, and lack of education and professional skills pushed them towards being more engaged in physical labour. Mumbai's textile industrialists and rich traders put them to use as muscle-men for *vasooli* or to guard their business interests. In fact, at one point, it was rare to find a Mumbai industrialist, trader or financier who had not hired criminals to lean on defaulters. Karim Lala had emerged as the leader among the growing Afghan community in the dark alleys of south Mumbai's Muslim ghettos. Lala realized soon enough that he did not need to work for the rich traders and could start his own gang instead, which he did in the late 1950s, forming a core group around the Dongri area. After what was then 'Bombay state' imposed Prohibition in the state in 1948, which was extended to the rest of Maharashtra right upto 1969, smuggling and illicit sale of cheap liquor became rampant. Lala grabbed the chance and started liquor dens where one could also gamble.

The next big opportunity for Mumbai's outlaws came with the Gold Control Act of 1968. Importing of gold had already been banned in India post independence through the Foreign Exchange Regulation Act 1947, and the government exercised control on the production of gold within the country as it was thought to be the best possible protection against upheavals, both political and economic. The gold policy of independent India was centred around the idea of discouraging people from purchasing gold, reducing domestic demand, regulating the supply of the metal, curbing illegal incomes and conserving foreign exchange. The 1968 Act further tightened controls on the metal, putting severe restrictions on its import and export, despite failing to curb the domestic demand for gold jewellery.

Unsurprisingly, there was a boom in the grey market for gold as there was no dearth of jewellers in Zaveri Bazar looking for cheaper ways to procure the metal by any means to earn profit. Gold now began to be smuggled in. Sporadic attempts were made to smuggle it in through air or sea routes, but this would not satisfy the high demand for the metal. Grey market operators found a solution for their problem in Mastan Haider Mirza aka Haji Mastan, a dockyard coolie turned petty dock thief. He not only had the knowledge of safe passages to land gold consignments along the coastal areas of Maharashtra but also had a deep desire to become rich at any cost. Soon, through his smuggling operations, Mastan became a vital link between the demand and supply of gold.

Mastan's story was a familiar tale of struggle: as a boy from a poor family of Tamil Nadu, Mastan came to Mumbai looking for work. Working as a porter at the docks, he turned to pilfering goods from the parked containers. He learnt the tricks of the trade fast enough to become a 'landing agent', someone who had to arrange safe passage for illegal goods by establishing links with the port or customs officials and bribing them. Mastan specialized in supplying smuggled goods to traders at Musafir Khana, at the time a hub of smuggled goods in south Mumbai. Money started flowing in and he began roping in more porters and carriers to handle his operations, effectively forming the first ever organized gang in Bombay. The clever and enterprising Mastan understood the business and established direct contacts with agents in Gulf countries to bring in gold. One such old-time facilitator residing in Null Bazaar area, who had worked with Mastan, told me that to this day hawala money finances gold smuggling operations. The smuggler's investment is negligible as he borrows from the hawala operator to buy the gold. If the consignment is large, the smuggler or financier seeks out a facilitator; if not, he arranges for carriers himself. Indian gold smugglers can be found in all Gulf countries, but most of them work through agents based in Dubai.

It is not a coincidence that most smugglers, hawala operators and the bullion market operated from the same stretch of south to central Mumbai. In the 1960s, Mastan ruled the area from the docks to Crawford Market, while Dongri was earmarked as Karim Lala's domain. The Tamil-dominated pockets of Matunga-Sion-Koliwada and Dharavi were marked as self-styled benevolent gangster Varadarajan Mudaliar's territories, the last of the big three dons of the era. Mudaliar aka Varadabhai had also begun his career by stealing from the docks, and by the 1960s had emerged as the sole bootlegger from north to central Mumbai. His illegal distilleries were the main source of illicit liquor in Mumbai, and he also ran gambling dens in Dharavi.

Inter-gang rivalry was unheard of at the time because territorial integrity was upheld by the three dons. Sure, there were occasional altercations, but there was no large-scale war. The dons believed in making money and sharing the spoils with the people involved in the game, and realized that violence resulting from gangs battling for supremacy would prove detrimental to their business. They considered themselves heroes, and never thought of themselves as the bad guys. They visited social functions and behaved like patrons in gatherings. They had their own system of justice and held weekly courts to resolve civil and social issues – including family disputes. For the next generation, those like Mirchi, these dons were the heroes.

At one time Karim Lala's blue-eyed boy, Mirchi became emotional when he spoke about his former mentor. He said, 'He was a father figure in my life. He was very generous and good at heart.' The first, and the most important, lesson Mirchi was taught by his mentor was that he had to befriend cops to be successful in the *do numbri* (illegal) business, and the easiest way to do that was to pass on information about various illegal activities taking place in the docks – apart from his own, of course. Many officers were happy with this weekly under-the-table arrangement, while more corrupt officials demanded a fixed percentage from any profits earned by smugglers on a subversive 'dock-job'. As a bargain, cops never came knocking at his doors. This was the accepted underhand practice at the time, which is why very few criminal cases were registered and there remains even less on record from this era with the exception of a few news items.

By the late 1960s, the port had become crowded with many experienced smugglers carrying out their illicit businesses. They had formed a cartel that prevented new entrants into the scene. Cut-throat competition existed even among the cartel members. In this setting, Mirchi found a way to be successful through 'official channels'. He started spending a lot of time at the Mumbai Port Trust police station, sharing inside information about his competitors with officials and helping corrupt policemen to dispose of seized goods from the back door. Expensive goods seized in official raids by the police eventually made their way into the grey market via Mirchi at lower prices. As a bargain, Mirchi had to share a bigger chunk of his profits with these corrupt officials. Soon, he became a vital link between corrupt officials and manipulative traders in the illegal bullion, textile, commodities and electronics markets. Police records reveal that he did not believe he was committing any crime as he was simply helping the police. In his mind, the latter had breached official rules, and he was a mere facilitator, for which he received his commission. With the police on his side, there was hardly any risk of getting busted, which in turn made his patrons in the textile and yarn trade, commodity trading and bullion dealers more comfortable in dealing with him. There were other benefits from this arrangement, too. It was a duty-free channel, profit margins were huge, and there were no tax liabilities – a win-win situation all around. As Mirchi put it, 'I was just a small cog in the well-oiled "*do numbri*" business circuit thriving around the Mumbai's port area.'

The trading cartels tapped into the uneducated, unskilled yet ambitious group of dock workers to carry out their operations. Once the goods landed on a given berth and reached their allotted shed, they were ferried out discreetly, and the goods were then declared 'missing' or 'stolen'. The importer would then filc a missing goods complaint or one of theft and receive the insurance sum for the value lost, while the goods would be delivered to the original importer or the owner as planned. Thus, the owner had his cake and ate it too. While everyone in the chain would get a fee for the job carried out, the landing and delivery agents often got a pre-decided commission as part of the profits. Some senior landing agents had developed direct links with traders. Their parallel networks knew that there were many traders who would simply buy looted cargo at half the price after it was declared 'damaged'.

Uneducated but street-smart, Mirchi worked hard to find people besides his mentor willing to teach him the ropes in the business in exchange for assistance in their businesses in and around the Mumbai port area. His brother being a customs official and his proximity to police officials boosted his confidence. In his time at the port he learnt how various goods like silver, gold, textiles, yarn and electronic items were valued and tested, and how they could be imported and sold in the local market. It didn't make any business sense for him to join any of the existing gangs or to start out on his own. Either way, it would be a risky proposition, one full of liabilities. Instead, Mirchi chose to build professional alliances with most of the gangs operating in Mumbai at the time. This 'fraternity' approach to business worked for him. He told me he looked up to the senior dons like Lala, Mastan and Varadarajan for 'professional guidance', but that his motto in life was to 'be your own boss'. Fraternizing with the organizations working in the port area helped him, as he was not perceived as a strong competitor, a foe or a close friend. This helped Mirchi to stay away from violent skirmishes and to carry on with his activities quietly but steadily. Originally a native of Gujarat whose family had settled in Bhendi Bazaar, Mirchi went on to become a powerful member of the smugglers' cartel. Mirchi had always dreamt of becoming a world-famous *seth* (merchant) some day. His dreams had finally come true with a twist.

Often slipping into memories of a different Mumbai during our conversations, he said that the old gangs of Mumbai were driven by money. Like his seniors and other contemporary smugglers of that era, Mirchi maintained his stance that they smuggled simply to earn money. 'It was a smooth ride for smugglers as there were no murders or shoot-outs,' he elaborated.

Mirchi recalled a particular December night from this era, when he had arranged a birthday party for a textile tycoon from Mumbai. Otherwise wary of being seen in public, the textile tycoon had agreed to come to Mirchi's party at his night club, Fisherman's Wharf, for 15 minutes as a gesture of goodwill. The only night club at the time that had waitresses, Fisherman's Wharf was closed for the public that night. Although he had an official sanction to run cabaret shows and had paid the cops in the area, Mirchi was nervous because he had organized a strip-show for a few specially invited elite guests for the first time, with the performers being flown in from Dubai.

The textile magnate arrived in his white Mercedes at the stroke of the midnight, and almost immediately scantily clad waitresses brought him an ice-cream cake shaped like a pair of breasts. Mirchi continued to be nervous; he just couldn't take his eyes off the door because he hated the idea of going to jail. Finally, when the tycoon excitedly said, '*Paisa vasool*', Mirchi heaved a sigh of relief. The return gift from the tycoon was as generous as Mirchi's gift had been – a 10 per cent commission on the total value of every smuggled container of yarn besides the regular fees. His chubby face with his grey mane and moustache lit up when he shared this little secret with me, claiming his club was the first in Mumbai to organize private strip shows for the *crème de la crème* of the city.

During our conversation, Mirchi admitted that he had met Dawood Ibrahim in Dubai. Both of them hailed from Nagpada, but that had not proven to be a point of connect earlier. 'There was some contact but I have never worked for him. It was a social interaction and we often bumped into each other at social functions,' Mirchi said, denying any business links with Dawood.

According to Mirchi, his problems began soon after the 1993 Mumbai bomb blasts when his name appeared as the brother of

Tiger Memon – one of the main accused in the serial blasts. While it was clarified later that Iqbal Memon Mirchi was not related to the Memon brothers – Tiger, Ayub, Yakub, Essa and Yusuf – all co-accused in the blasts case, in any way, Mirchi complained to me that the media had never bothered to rectify and clear his name as an accused along with Dawood Ibrahim. I was aware that his name had come up as a suspect in the blasts case as a result of mistaken identity and the Mumbai Police had already cleared his name; I told him that I would rectify it in the story I did of the interview. I remember how relief flooded his face when I said this.

It was 1 a.m. already and Maan and I decided it was time to leave for our hotel. As a parting shot, Mirchi told me that he would like to show me some important documents and talk to me in detail before he agreed to a television interview. His hesitation was perfectly understandable. The Central Bureau of Investigation (CBI) had declared Mirchi an absconder in 1994 and an Interpol red-corner notice was subsequently issued in his name the same year. When he was arrested in London in 1995, Joginder Singh, former CBI director, said that an investigation was carried out on Mirchi's activities between 1995 and 1999, but the magistrate in London turned down the CBI's request for his extradition for want of substantive evidence to prove his crimes in India. Yet, although his tone was not very promising, at least he had mentioned the interview himself. To me, it was not at all a bad beginning.

I was a bit apprehensive about taking a cab at 1 a.m. to our hotel in Kensington, but Mirchi assured us that we would be safe. Asif told me while walking us to the gate that his family usually went to bed by 8 p.m., and it was very unusual for his father to stay awake so late. He knew the cabbie outside and asked him not to charge us. I had noticed right through the evening that Mirchi had been observing us closely and had been trying to gauge what I was about. He was a seasoned and shrewd man, and I was quite sure that he had met us with his family to test us; the entire family would certainly have screened us as well. I knew that I had to pass a psychological screening to get any further with the interview, but at the back of my mind I had a feeling that I had passed the preliminary round. It was a cold night, but the thought that Iqbal Mirchi would grant me his first TV interview actually warmed me.

The next afternoon Asif called to ask if I was at the hotel and said his father would like to meet me in half an hour. I was ecstatic, and waited for Mirchi in the cafeteria, where he arrived with some files. Over cups of latte and some biscotti, he showed me legal documents and case files. Although the British Home Office had granted him permission to remain in the UK indefinitely in 2001, his name had been added to the list of narcotics kingpins issued by the US State Department the very next year. Earlier that year (2002), his name had cropped up during the trial of Hemant Lakhani, a Briton accused of smuggling a shoulder-launched missile into the US; Lakhani was declared to be an associate of the 'drug lord and terror suspect' Mirchi, and his name was inserted on the list. Mirchi sounded frustrated when he said, 'I have spent 15 years in London. Do I look like a man on the run?' There was no doubt that Mirchi was an Indian fugitive and a UN-notified narco-kingpin, yet he really did not appear to be a man on the run.

He then showed me a letter he had written to the US State Department, expressing outrage at his name being included in the international drug kingpins list. 'I have never made any secret of where I am,' the letter said. 'The British police, the Indian police, the American police – all have my address because I have written to them and told them. If I am a kingpin and they want to arrest me, they know exactly where to find me.'[2]

When the Indian government had put together a list of cases and asked for Mirchi's extradition, he was arrested by the British police and produced before the Bow Street magistrate's court in London to face extradition proceedings to India. He now showed me a file containing the Bow Street magistrate's judgement and the London Police's closure notice. Mirchi had hired one of Britain's top lawyers to fight the extradition bid, James Lewis, whose sharp arguments ensured that he stayed put in the UK. The magistrate had not only dismissed the extradition plea of the Mumbai Crime Branch but Mirchi was also awarded £95,000 in damages.

The obvious question then was why Mirchi had not faced the law but had chosen to escape from it. 'I now realize that I made a mistake,' he told me. 'I should not have fought the extradition. I should have stood trial. I would have cleared my name and would have been free to go about my business. I have offered to return to India but have asked for a guarantee that I will be given judicial protection.'

Mirchi was aware that returning home would mean being imprisoned, but in his mind it would not be for long. He seemed to believe that there was no definitive proof that could put him in prison for a long duration. This erroneous belief made him consider surrendering before a magistrate in India on the guarantee that he would be given judicial protection. When Mirchi's request to have a security official escort him from the airport to the court was rejected by the magistrate, he dropped his plans as he feared he would be killed by the cops in an encounter.

I took the chance at this point and suggested to him that this was reason enough for him to come on camera and express himself openly about his wish to return. I could see that he was ready but he was trying to gauge my response to his story. He asked me several questions on professionalism in my news channel and how I had maintained my credibility through the years. When I told him plainly about my job, he looked satisfied with my answers. It was weird getting interviewed when I had come here as the interviewer, but these were not normal circumstances nor was he a normal subject.

I walked him to his BMW and he introduced me to his trusted

Austrian associate-cum-driver. According to Mirchi, his main business in London was to acquire old properties stuck in litigation. He said he was 'lucky' that he could always get out of the legal maze and get full ownership of the property with clean titles in the end. His penchant for properties was known from the old days. Most of his wealth had found its way into real estate, like the sprawling piece of land he owned in Worli, where he still owns a house on the seafront opposite the famous Haji Ali Dargah, and a cluster of buildings around it. Mirchi claimed to have sold one of the buildings he owned on Dr Annie Besant Road in Worli to a former senior minister from Maharashtra who was in the UPA government. Around 2008–09, his second wife Heena had moved the Mumbai High Court seeking the lifting of a sealing order on the two flats she owned in Milton Apartments in Juhu. Between 2010 and 2011, litigation issues on his land in Panvel (near Mumbai), and his palatial villa in the upscale Nadir Colony in Bhopal, regularly made headlines.

After Mirchi fled to Dubai, he went legit with hotels – one of which was Imperial Suites, which was run by Asif – and other businesses in Dubai and the UK. He owned a restaurant called Dockmaster's House at Canary Wharf in London, and a few other commercial properties, including hotels. This made him one among the rich and elite Asians in London. Yet, he told me in a hushed voice, as if sharing a secret, 'I don't have *gora* friends despite living here for 15 years. I could never trust them. You can never be sure of their intentions – *aastin ke saanp hote hain yeh.* (They will betray you.) If this interview goes on air successfully, I will give your channel a huge scoop on that.' This is one grudge he held – that in London he did not get the respect he thought he had earned. He felt very acutely the discrimination towards the Indian or the South Asian business community here. He realized that his knowledge of the criminal world in Asia and the Gulf, and his sources and networks that he had created over three decades, were not enough and he would have to pay the price of being given asylum in a foreign country. He told me he was getting older, and he wanted his children out of any mess.

Before getting into his car to leave, he turned to me and said, 'Can you guess why David Headley came to London and whom he did business with here? Wasn't he involved with counterfeit bills and the illegal arms business? Who was facilitating his business in India and Pakistan? No one has looked at this UK angle. You might get a good lead into the Headley story.'

His questions were intriguing. They confused me. Was he taking a chance or playing a game with me? But this much had been made clear in his conversations with me – that he wanted to go ahead with the interview.

Sure enough, the next evening he asked me to visit him at home, saying that he wanted to discuss something important. We met again on Thursday evening at his place, where he announced that his legal counsel Shyam Keshwani was on a British Airways flight from Mumbai to London, arriving with all the documentary evidence that would verify Mirchi's claims, though the lawyer had not been informed about my presence and the interview. Mirchi also said he wanted me to meet his relative Sibghatullah Qadri, who was his legal adviser in London. Barrister Qadri's younger brother's daughter was married to Asif. Qadri was pretty well-known in London and was considered to be close to the former prime minister of Pakistan, Benazir Bhutto. Born in India, Qadri had migrated to Pakistan in 1950 and gone on to become the first British Muslim on the Queen's Counsel in 1989. He was also known as a leading authority on immigration and race relations.

Clearly, Mirchi had decided to go public, and I knew it was a big decision on his part. He was taking a calculated risk and did not want to leave anything to chance. I readied myself for more scrutiny and intensive interrogation.

The next day I reached Mirchi's house at 7 p.m. to find Keshwani there with a bag full of documents. Keshwani was surprised to see me but immediately sensed the situation at hand and went with the flow. Mirchi asked him to show me all the important documents that suggested he had actually been entrapped by a former narcotics department official. Keshwani was a seasoned criminal advocate and played his role to the hilt to convince his wealthy client that he was there for his good. After all, he had been flown in on a business-class ticket and put up in a plush hotel. Keshwani tried his best to convince me with his version of the story that Mirchi was actually a victim and not an accused.

The story went thus: The money Mirchi earned from his illicit activities during the smugglers' era had been invested in properties, including the Fisherman's Wharf night club. But Mirchi's success had not gone unnoticed by the Enforcement Directorate. Soon, the customs department levied a ₹5 lakh penalty on him, a huge sum in the early 1980s.

Here, Mirchi interrupted Keshwani's narrative and coaxed him to tell me the story about the latter having been part of the negotiations between Mirchi and a senior Mumbai Narcotics Bureau official, who had demanded a huge amount to settle the case against Mirchi. When Mirchi refused the demands made by the officer, his troubles began. He had to escape to Dubai, and in doing so he crossed the line of no return. Efforts had been made many times to play down his past with the pitch being that Mirchi was simply a businessman with legitimate business interests in London and the Middle East, but this time the argument just did not work.

The following day was Eid, and as Mirchi would be busy with his family for the festival, we scheduled the recording for the coming Monday. Keshwani left after we wrapped up the confirmation, and Mirchi took me around his house as I waited for my cab to arrive. I noticed two big Persian cats wearing gold chains with a huge pendant that had 'Memon' etched on them. On the ground floor, the indoor pool stood warm and inviting in contrast to the ice-cold weather outside; the kitchen was huge too, with a dining area that had a table for a dozen people; and there was a cosy office, too. Outside, in the backyard, was a large barbeque area and an English-style garden with white benches.

While showing me around, Mirchi suddenly lowered his voice and took out a small piece of paper from his pocket, from which he read out a cell phone number and asked me to write it down. The number belonged to an influential Kolkata-based Marwari trader and wheeler-dealer. Mirchi then posed a question: What did I think of the currency notes that got distributed for votes during various elections in India? From where did so much cash come? It was a tough question, and I looked suitably confused. He gave me a clue: 'You can buy a lakh worth of currency for just 20,000 or 25,000 real cash.' This was a most intriguing piece of information, and as he caught me thinking it over he changed the topic quickly to a safer subject, proclaiming that he was a happy man to have such obedient and god-fearing children. He went on to tell me that he had settled Asif in Dubai because he wanted to inculcate Islamic family values in his grandchildren by having them study in more conservative schools. Junaid had studied business management from a reputed British university and was getting ready to take over Mirchi's UK business. Mirchi's only daughter, Nadiya, was married to Javed Malik, solicitor and former Pakistani ambassador-at-large. The official dossier on Mirchi states that it was Dawood who had arranged the marriage between Nadiya and Javed, which had brought the families closer. After her marriage, Nadiya is said to have stayed in Dubai with her husband to help her brother to run their four hotels and construction business.

The next week, on Monday, the entrance passage to Mirchi's mansion became our mini-studio. We fixed two cameras and lights for the interview. Mirchi, probably facing a camera for the first time in his life, looked nervous. A large audience had gathered to cheer him on, among them his family and both his lawyers. A regular commentator on legal and ethnic minority issues on British and Pakistani channels, Qadri gave him tips, asking him to look straight into the camera and hold his chin up while talking. Keshwani also encouraged him by saying that it was merely a recording and not a live event, so he would get a second chance to correct himself if he said something wrong at any point during the recording.

Asif and Junaid sat on the spiral staircase, recording the whole event in their handycams, while Heena watched us from the first-floor gallery overlooking the entrance. Junaid had a copy of my questions as reference. It was clear that none of them wanted to leave anything to chance, and their presence was a sort of soft warning to us to toe the line.

The interview began, and I asked him wide-ranging questions on his legal issues, his troubles with the authorities in India, whether he knew Dawood Ibrahim or not, on his alleged involvement in the 1993 blasts, and his fondness and longing for Mumbai. He seemed to miss the city quite a bit. He had grown up there, he said, and the city gave him a sense of 'security and comfort'. He answered my questions quite openly and without hesitating. A selection from the interview follows:

> **Me:** When did you leave India? When did you realize you would never go back to Mumbai?
>
> **Mirchi:** Since the time my name figured in the Mumbai serial blasts case. I immediately wrote a letter to the [Mumbai] Police commissioner informing him that I was living in

Dubai and was not a fugitive. I had left my address for correspondence – just in case he had any issues against me in connection with the 1993 blasts. The terrorism charges were dropped later and replaced with a charge relating to murder (of a former manager of Mirchi's who was shot dead in Mumbai soon after quitting his job). I have never made any secret of where I am.

Me: You have been notified by the UN as one of the top drug barons in the world and there is an Interpol red-corner notice against you, both considered very grave charges. There is no smoke without fire. Don't the two charges weaken your credibility?

Mirchi: I have no involvement in organized crime or terrorism and I am being persecuted by some vindictive officers in India. The same officers were suspended and left their jobs, but they ended up being posted at the UN and managed to put me on the list of criminals. I have written to the US State Department asking them to substantiate charges against me or clear my name from the narcotics kingpin list.

Me: What is your connection with Dawood Ibrahim? There have been reports that suggest you are involved in the narcotics business with him.

Mirchi: I knew his father and we used to meet once in a while. I came to know him through his father. We used to live in the same area in Mumbai. There was no relationship or friendship with him. I had never done any business with him in India. They were connected with people from the world of glamour in Dubai. But I had no connection. If you or anyone else gets any proof of my involvement with him, I am ready for any punishment.

Me: How did you come to know him and when did you meet him for the first time?

Mirchi: I had met him when he was a kid. I might have met him two or three times in Mumbai and a few times in Dubai. The last time I met him was in Dubai for 10–15 minutes at a party thrown by filmmaker Feroz Khan, when he was shooting his film *Yalgaar* there.

Me: Your name also figured in the 1993 Mumbai blasts case along with the main accused, the Memon brothers. What was the connection there?

Mirchi: I am not related to Tiger Memon at all. The Memon community is one of the largest Muslim communities, and I was dragged in because of my surname. We had a thriving hotel business in Dubai with five successful hotels. I persistently fought to clear my name from the blasts case, and finally the Mumbai Police realized my innocence and dropped my name.

Me: When you left Mumbai for Dubai, your children were young, and now you have become a grandfather. How do you feel when your children or grandchildren are called names because of criminal charges against you?

Mirchi: I get emotional when it comes to my children and grandchildren. I am worried about their well-being and security. It's not a good feeling when my alleged criminal past affects them in any manner socially. I wish to stand trial and clear my name for them. I am old and have lived my life, but I don't want them to carry the burden of the criminal accusations against me. They should be able to live with dignity in society.

Me: Why didn't you stand trial in India? What stopped you from doing so?

Mirchi: When you are young, you don't think about future repercussions. I now realize that I made a mistake. I should not have fought the extradition; instead, I should have stood trial. I would have cleared my name in the case and would be free to go about my business. I have offered to return to India but have asked for a guarantee that I would be given judicial protection. The Indian government has refused my request so I have to stay put here. My lawyers feel that I might get implicated in new false cases.

We finished recording the interview at around 2.30 p.m. and Mirchi asked us to lunch with his family and the others who were present. He recommended Qadri's *nihari*, and said we must taste it. The barrister praised Mirchi's culinary skills as well. According to him, Mirchi was not only a gourmand but also a good chef, and it was his nose for good food that had contributed to the success of his hotels.

After lunch, we wanted some candid shots of Mirchi, so we asked him to walk in his garden with me. Though he agreed, Asif insisted we could not record any further. We took some shots as Mirchi walked around his backyard holding his granddaughter's hands. He kept repeating that he wanted to go back home to Mumbai. He could not imagine going to an Indian jail at the age of 63, he said, and wondered aloud whether at that age his body would be able to withstand the harsh life in prison. His advocate Keshwani had already warned him that his return would not be as smooth and easy as he seemed to think it would be as he would have to face the law in India. He shared some more juicy tidbits about the crime world and its Indian connections, after which we packed up and left for our hotel.

Over the next two days, Asif called on us daily. The evening before we left for India, he once again invited us for dinner at an Indian restaurant with his family. Mirchi didn't join us this time, but while chatting with his wife Heena I learnt some more about their lives – about Mirchi's interest in Bollywood and her brother Akbar Asif's plans to revive *Mughal-e-Azam* in colour. I later found out about Akbar Asif's alleged proximity to the Dawood Ibrahim family and the common link with the Memons.

After we aired the interview on 16 November 2011, Mirchi called us. He sounded overwhelmed. A former CBI director had emphasized on our show that if Mirchi wanted to surrender before a court in India, as he had told us in the interview, this should have been pursued by the agency. We, as a channel, conveyed it to the agency bosses then. Ironically, the rhetoric of the agency to bring back India's most-wanted criminals and terrorist fugitives to face justice didn't stand in Mirchi's case. He began cooperating with Indian agencies, and his leads helped the Intelligence Bureau bust a counterfeit nexus before the Uttar Pradesh Assembly elections in 2012, but no mention was made of his return to India.

After the interview, Mirchi periodically checked in on me to see if there was any progress. Six months later, he had an open-heart surgery and got Asif to tell me about it. I had by this time given up on his case and his return to India. I think he knew it as well. Yet, he was hoping against hope. Perhaps he had seen his own end, or maybe he had fallen out with his mentors.

Back home in Mumbai, a police source told me that it would be impossible to bring Mirchi back as he had entangled himself in Indian Premier League (IPL) cricket wheeling and dealing through the back-door funding of an IPL team. Mirchi had entered into a memorandum of understanding with a London-based businessman who had enough Bollywood connections to invest in a team. But he now suspected that the businessman was taking him for a ride as far as sharing the profits from betting and fixing deals were concerned. Mirchi insisted that one more MoU should be signed in India with his younger son Junaid as a fallback. If, as he suspected, the businessman tried to act smart with him then he was in a position to leak information about the businessman being involved in betting on IPL matches since 2008, which would invite legal trouble for the businessman. A reputed Mumbai solicitor's firm was thus called in to solemnize a new partnership deed between Junaid and an Indian family member of the businessman.

Since April 2008 Mirchi's partners in the cricket betting racket, who were also the frontmen for many white-collar businessmen and other individuals in India, had complained to Mirchi's mentors that he was playing a double game. A telephonic interception by the Mumbai Police revealed that Mirchi had allegedly been contracted to kill a top industrialist for ₹3 crore, but when he didn't honour his contract there had been a squabble over the contract money. Finally, his name came under the scanner once again when the IPL match-fixing and betting scandal broke out in May 2013 in Delhi and Mumbai.

On 14 August 2013, I heard about Mirchi's fatal cardiac arrest, one day after he had suffered it in London.[3] I called Asif to verify the news and get more details. He confirmed the news and said that he had been in Istanbul, holidaying with his family when it had happened. Mirchi, apparently, had not been keeping well after his heart surgery, and on that fatal morning, after months of staying indoors, he had gone out for a short walk. He had experienced a pain in his chest and sat down on a bench on the road near his house, where he had died. Alone.

His close relatives told me that his death seemed natural, yet UK authorities took longer than usual to hand the body over to his family, that too after a detailed examination procedure. An intelligence official revealed to me that his open-heart surgery had not gone well, and that his health issues had their own implications. Mirchi was allegedly being monitored, and the plug had been pulled as he had crossed a line he was not supposed to.

A man who started off as a *naan-chap* (a mutton and beef delicacy) maker in the bylanes of Null Bazaar before turning to a life of crime in the dockyards of Mumbai, Iqbal Mirchi was one of the last living members of the era of Mumbai's smugglers, when loosely organized crime groups ruled the bylanes of the city in the 1960s and the 1970s. I guess he had a premonition about his fate, and knew he would never return to the city he loved. (A retired Mumbai Police officer once told me that Mirchi used to love driving from Mumbai to Pune.) Despite living outside India and being marked by both intelligence agencies and rival groups, Iqbal Mirchi always remembered the city he had left behind. As he told me, 'Mumbai is home. I have grown up there and it always gave me a sense of security and comfort. I love every bit about the city and miss it a lot.'

The Don Who Fell in Love

WHEN THE MUMBAI POLICE SUBJECTED noted criminal Abu Salem, who had been extradited from Lisbon, Portugal,[1] to a number of tests (a lie-detector test, brain-mapping and narco-analysis) in the last week of December 2005, it was simply a way for police investigators to collect material to strengthen their case against him. I got a copy of the test report in March 2006, and was not surprised by the contents. In fact, the report only confirmed what I had already known since 1993. But as a TV journalist, I needed visuals to report it effectively.

My sources had told me that the CD with the visuals of the narco-analysis test would reach me soon. But at the time 'breaking news' was a huge phenomenon in the broadcast universe, particularly in the Hindi one. The pressure to be the first to report something was mind-boggling. Salem's revelations were sensational, and an editorial call was taken to run a special show even if it got aired without his truth-serum visuals. Though television is an instant medium, the work behind the scenes is laborious. We, therefore, got to work right away, and began shooting anchor-links at 11 p.m. After shooting through the night till 6 a.m., we finally finished an hour-long show, '*Kya Woh Sach Bol Raha Hai*? (Is He Telling the Truth?)', for that evening's prime-time.

The show was based on the report that a drugged-out Salem had made several startling revelations that had thrown Bollywood and the Mumbai Police into a tizzy. He had alleged that Bollywood producer Subhash Ghai had paid Dawood Ibrahim's brother, Anees, anything between ₹20 lakh and ₹25 lakh as extortion money. Producers Rakesh Roshan and J.P. Dutta, he said, had not paid even a dime, which they had been accused of doing earlier.[2]

Narco-analysis tests have their own share of critics, as they are invasive procedures used to extract information from a suspect. A narco-test can be conducted only once the police acquires permissions for it from both the court and the subject. Although every state in India has a forensic laboratory, narco-tests are conducted only in one of the five government specialized forensic laboratories in Bengaluru, Ahmedabad, Hyderabad, Delhi and Chandigarh, and the entire process is videotaped. One gram of sodium pentothal is diluted and injected into the subject along with a 10 per cent solution of dextrose, after which the subject slowly descends into a sort of hypnotic trance. Though narco-analysis is not admissible as evidence in a court of law, the information gathered during such a test can be used to corroborate existing evidence or details gathered at a crime scene. The Mumbai High Court had upheld the legality of the use of brain fingerprinting, lie detector and narco-analysis after a special court in Pune allowed the police to conduct scientific tests on Abdul Karim Telgi, the prime accused in the multi-crore counterfeit stamp-paper scam in 2004.

Salem's narco-analysis transcript had him naming D Company honchos Chhota Shakeel and Anees Ibrahim in almost every murder and extortion case in which Salem was suspected to have played a part. The two were named in builder Omprakash Kukreja's murder in 1995 ('Shakeel made the plan and Anees supplied the weapons from Bhendi Bazaar,' according to Salem);

it was Anees who allegedly gave the *supari* (contract killing) orders for Subhash Ghai and director Ram Gopal Verma. Anees was named once again in the murder of music baron Gulshan Kumar, while Salem denied that music director Nadeem Khan (who had been suspected of being involved in the murder) had anything to do with the killing. Salem said that Anees had made him call builders to extort money, but gave him very little for his efforts. '*Kabhi das-panch haat de deta tha.* (He would sometimes give me 5 to 10 per cent of the money.)' Salem also held UP gangster-turned-politician Babloo Srivastava responsible for Chhota Rajan-aide Vikram Wahi's murder in 1997, and Chhota Rajan for killing producer Mukesh Duggal in 1997 and Nepalese member of Parliament Mirza Dilshad Beg in 1998 'because he was a Dawood man'.

Abu Salem being escorted to the court. Photo courtesy Mahendra Parikh.

The Mumbai Police had earlier held that Aziz Bilakhia, Salem's immediate boss, used to report to Anees Ibrahim and was responsible for bringing the arms and ammunition from Gujarat before the 1993 Mumbai blasts. He was also responsible for distributing them to a number of people, including actor Sanjay Dutt. In his narco-analysis test, Salem said, 'Aziz Bilakhia gave me a car to bring gold from Bhiwandi. Baba Musa Chauhan, Sameer Hingora and Sanjay Dutt were also there. Aziz's vehicle was full of weapons, and everyone took a weapon.'

Salem revealed that he was living in fear that Dawood Ibrahim, Anees Ibrahim, Chhota Shakeel and Chhota Rajan were out to finish him. Dawood, he said, was angry with him for giving the CBI information about the 1993 blasts. Salim Kurla, who had allegedly played a key role in bringing into India the explosives meant for the blasts, and 'Hegiway' were named by him as key personnel in the blasts. When asked in the course of the narco-tests who Hegiway was, Salem said he was the man who had been sent to kill builder Pradeep Jain in 1995. Salem alleged that Jain was murdered because he had abused Anees Ibrahim over the phone in a drunken state. 'Builder Virendra Kumar Jhamb (another accused in the case) may also be involved. Jhamb was interested in the land. I had called Pradeep's brother, Ashok Jain, two or three times and threatened him. Salim Chiplun collected the money from the Jains. Anees Ibrahim called Mehdi Hasan (Salem's former driver) and Salim Haddi (killed in an encounter) to Dubai and gave them the job of eliminating Pradeep,' Salem said. The Supreme Court in 2002 had convicted three of the accused in the case, while Salem had been absconding.

The Mumbai Police rubbished some of Salem's revelations, though. According to them, builder Pradeep Jain was murdered by Salem for refusing to sell his prime property in Andheri at a throwaway price. Their version of the events was strengthened by

Pradeep Jain's brother, Sunil, on my show. Sunil Jain said, 'Abu Salem and his men killed my brother, and not Anees Ibrahim. Salem threatened us many times. Salim Haddi was nowhere in the picture.'

When asked if he knew any policemen, Salem said he knew Mumbai Police encounter specialist Pradeep Sharma, who he alleged was in the narcotics business along with Anees Ibrahim, and was being assisted by some other police officers. Pradeep Sharma, however, refuted all charges and said, 'I destroyed Abu Salem's gang. When the CBI brought him to India, he told them, "Please don't send me to Khandiwali police. Pradeep Sharma will kill me." This speaks for itself.'[3]

Immediately after his extradition from Portugal, Salem in his confessional statement had told the police that he had stacked away crores in his Swiss bank account and several other banks in other countries. Mumbai Police had taken detailed records of the various bank accounts from him. But during the narco-tests Salem backtracked and said he did not own a single bank account and his nephew was paying his legal fees after selling his shop and house in Lucknow.

On the personal front, Salem revealed that one of his aliases was Arsalan Moizin. He spoke about his fascination with the film world, and how he had bought a theatre in Chicago called Discipline. Quite dramatically, he admitted he was guilty of only one count: loving Monica Bedi. In his words, '*Humne sirf pyar kiya tha*! (I had only loved!)'

In my long conversation with Salem's wife Samira Jumani in the US in November 2005, which is detailed later in the chapter, she had called him 'Arsalan' throughout. She had also confirmed to me his love for the movies and the theatre in Chicago, and how she had entertained some big Bollywood stars at home.

Salem had stated in his narco-analysis test that actress Manisha Koirala had asked him to get her secretary, Ajit Deewani, and film producer Mukesh Duggal killed. Koirala refuted the charges and Mumbai Police Commissioner Satyapal Singh himself gave a clean chit to Koirala. Singh said on my show that it was Salem who had threatened both Duggal and Deewani over the phone. I knew, in fact, that Salem's paramour, Monica Bedi, was close to Duggal, who had been planning to launch her in his film. Samira Jumani had also told me that Monica Bedi had come to their home in Dubai as Duggal's girlfriend.

When the programme was aired, many questioned the veracity of the story and Salem's claims.[4] Some raised doubts about the validity of the narco-analysis report itself. For a while, it became a question of credibility. Then, once we received the video of the test, all that Salem had said and we had reported was there for all to witness. The world had seen and heard Salem in person on our channel.

The events and their reportage by the channel had far-reaching consequences. A day after the tapes were aired, prosecutor Raja Thakre submitted an application to the court which said, 'The telecast of Abu Salem's narco-analysis leads to disclosure of names and other details of witnesses. If such an eventuality occurs in this case, it may have adverse repercussions either on the prosecution's case or even lead to prejudging the accused.' Special Judge Mridula Bhatkar upheld the submission and directed that no audio or video recording, clipping or transcript related to any accused should be telecast till the trial gets over.

In November 2005, I was in New York with my family when a source called to tell me that Abu Salem and Monica Bedi were on their way to India on a specially chartered flight from Lisbon, where the two had been arrested in 2002. A Portuguese court had cleared the way for their extradition to India in February 2004.

I called my Lisbon sources to verify the story, and they confirmed it as well.

I checked with other reliable agency sources in India and the Mumbai Police. They confirmed that Salem and Bedi were expected to land in India within the next few hours, but the port of landing had been kept secret. I broke the news on television that night from New York and remained on the phone the entire night, reporting details and other follow-ups. It was an exhausting experience for my family as they had to go through the night-long torture of listening to my 'phonos' – television jargon for news relayed live over the phone.

A TV grab showing Abu Salem being escorted to court after his extradition.

Then I remembered that Salem's first wife, Samira, had been living in the US. I called my source in India and an address was given to me with a phone number, although I was told that the information was a decade old and would probably be of no use. I did not lose hope, though. It would be interesting to meet Samira and get her side of the story. I called the number given to me, and a male voice at the other end identified himself as a relative of Samira. The man sounded upset that Samira's name had been dragged into the media coverage of Salem's arrest and extradition. Bingo! If the number was correct, the address might be too, I thought.

There was no question of getting an appointment over the phone, so it was a matter of taking a chance. I decided I would simply land up at her door and request her to speak to us, and immediately booked a flight to Atlanta.

In Atlanta, I called for a cab very early in the morning, as I had been told that it would take us (the camera person, Prasil, and me) an hour to reach our destination. The address we had been given was vague and when we reached there we realized it was a huge town-house colony, like the suburbs of any other American city. We searched for the house whose number we had been given and found it, but my elation proved momentary. There was a big lock on the door. I had already booked a return flight for the evening, so time of the essence.

The house had big French windows, so I went around it, trying to get a look inside, but there seemed to be no one there. It was too early in the morning to knock on a neighbour's door. In desperation, I walked all the way to the other side of the house and found a man cleaning his car. I almost ran up to him and asked if he knew the people who lived here or their possible whereabouts. He shrugged his shoulders and said he did not. I was disappointed. My office had already spent quite a bit getting us here, and it didn't look like this story would materialize. It was a stressful thought.

I resolved to find Samira come what may, and walked a bit further in the adjoining lane to find someone who could help. A woman was walking her dog in the lane. I asked her if she knew the owners of the house. Her answer was negative. I shamelessly persisted and asked if she knew any Indians in the colony. Suddenly, as if she had remembered something important, she said, 'I think her sister is supposed to be staying in a nearby colony. You may check there.' I could not thank her enough for giving me some hope!

I sprinted towards our cab that had been kept waiting. Knowing which colony to go to was a good omen, but how would I find her sister's house in a neighbourhood that stretched over a few kilometres? I suddenly remembered that my brother's colony in the US had a maintenance office, so there was a possibility that this colony could have one, too. Prasil mentioned that it too early for anyone to be there, but I thought every housing colony in the US had a maintenance office for round-the-clock emergency services and we could try our luck there. The cabbie helped us find the central maintenance office of the colony and, fotunately for us, it was open!

There were a few men in the office, and I told them that I had come all the way from New York to meet a person named Samira Jumani but she was not at the address I had been given and her neighbours had guided me to this colony. I requested them to help me find her sister's house. One of them looked up the register and told me that there was no person by that name in the colony, but there was an Indian family and I could check with them.

The name I was given sounded familiar; the person I had spoken to on the phone from New York had the same name. I asked the cabbie to stop at a little distance from the house, where I got off and walked the rest of the way. When I rang the bell, the door was opened by a young boy. I asked for Samira and he immediately closed the door in my face. This confirmed my hunch that I was at the right address. I waited outside for some time. Five minutes later, an old lady in her late 50s, wearing a typical Indian maxi gown, came out and told me, 'She doesn't want to talk to the media. You should have taken an appointment before coming here. Go back!' I tried giving my reasons, but she shut the door on me once again.

I became more determined to reach Samira. I stood outside and began a brief monologue in a voice loud enough for the people in the house to hear. It looked ridiculous, and some neighbours came out to see what was happening. I dreaded the thought of someone calling the cops, but I stayed put. After 20 minutes, the door was flung open once again. A fair and chubby lady in a tracksuit looked at me and said sternly, 'You will not leave, so come in!' This could only be Samira.

I thanked my stars and went in behind her. It was a small yet cosy home. The old lady was Samira's mother, and the two spoke with each other in Gujarati and Kutchi. As I understand both languages, I told them that I was Gujarati too. I saw relief on their faces. They kept insisting that they wanted to stay away from the Salem case. My pitch was that I was offering them a platform to clear Samira's name of any wrongdoing mentioned in the Indian media. Cases had been filed against her, Abu Salem and Monica Bedi for allegedly using the fictitious names Rubina Baig, Danish Baig and Fauzia Usman respectively to acquire Indian passports.

After much persuasion, Samira finally seemed convinced. She agreed to talk about the subject, yet refused to come on camera. I told her that my cameraperson was waiting outside in the cab, and she graciously told me that I could release the cab and she would drop us to the airport in the evening. I paid the cabbie while Prasil came inside with the luggage. She sat down on a sofa and I sat on the carpet across her with my notebook and pen.

Sabina Arsalan Ali Ahmed Azmi, also known as Samira Jumani, began her story still a little agitated, insisting that what was known to the world was not the truth. She seemed to be scared of her husband even though he was in jail in India and claimed that Salem was capable of harming her from inside the jail. It seemed the boy who had first opened the door was Aamir, her (and Abu Salem's) only child. While on the run, Salem regularly called his son Aamir and dotingly called him 'Papa', she said, and added that she was worried about how Aamir would react when he found out about his father's bloody past.

For the next five hours, Samira told me all about being married to Salem and being on the run – from Mumbai to Dubai, Sharjah to New Jersey, Chicago and finally Atlanta.[4] As Samira began her story, she took me back to a time when she was still a teenager living in Jogeshwari, a north Mumbai suburb, with her middle-class Kutchi parents and brother.

Originally from Sarai Mir in Uttar Pradesh, Arsalan Ali Ahmed Azmi, or Abu Salem, was a small-time vendor at the Arsa Market in Andheri, and lived at the nearby Quba building. Salem's father was an advocate by profession, but after he died in a road accident, Salem could not complete his education. He started a small mechanic shop in his home town to support his family but, soon after, he moved to Delhi, where he drove a taxi. After some time, Salem returned to Mumbai, where he worked as a driver and hawker.

Samira used to shop with her friends at the Arsa shopping centre, which is where she first met Salem. Salem liked Samira, and expressed his interest in her. Like any teenage girl, she liked the attention but was not aware of his background and intentions. The initial infatuation took a turn for the serious when she refused to meet him as her parents did not approve of their relationship. He did not take her rejection kindly, and began stalking her. At the time, she was studying in the twelfth standard at Bhavan's Art College; he would wait for her outside the college, then follow her home. This went on for a whole year, until she turned 17, when Salem coerced her into marrying him.

On 5 July 1991, Samira went to college where Salem was waiting in a white Maruti 800. She got into the car and he took her to a *qazi* in Bhendi Bazaar. He had already organized two witnesses, and the *nikah* was solemnized. Samira said she was sad despite the wedding because she knew her parents would never approve of her marriage. She wrote them a letter asking for their forgiveness and told them that she had been forced into the marriage, because Salem had threatened to kill her family if she refused. Her father went to the police and lodged a complaint against Salem for kidnapping a minor, and Salem was arrested, but medical tests proved Samira was not a minor.

When Salem was released from police custody, he banned Samira from meeting her parents or any other relatives. From Andheri, they shifted to a dingy house in Jogeshwari. Samira claimed she had been physically abused and mentally tortured by the short-tempered Salem since their *nikah*. He did not like her Kutchi-Gujarati way of cooking, and would swear at her and physically abuse her if she retorted. He would leave in the morning and return home late at night. She thought he was attending to his shop, but she later found out that he was involved in bigger rackets for his boss, the Mahim-based trader Aziz Bilakhia, aka Tingu, so named because he was a short man. Samira insisted that she and Salem would have had a good life had Salem not worked with Tingu, who had introduced Salem to the D Company. Salem worked as a driver and assistant to Bilakhia, who was friends with Anees Ibrahim Kaskar, Dawood's younger brother.

Samira would not have found out about Salem's criminal activities if Salem had not allowed her to go to Tingu's house in Mahim. In fact, she was only allowed to interact with Tingu's wife, Hamida. It was there that she heard Dawood Ibrahim's name for the first time. She realized Tingu was connected to Dawood and Anees Ibrahim. While her husband Salem was working with Tingu, he in turn was reporting to his bosses in Dubai.

The day that changed her life forever was 12 March 1993, when Mumbai was rattled by 13 blasts. On that fateful day, Salem had asked her to be ready by 1 p.m. and meet him at the Santacruz station, from where, he had said, they would go to Tingu's house to see his newborn child. While she was getting ready, Salem called her and ordered her to go to her parents' house in Jogeshwari immediately and stay there for three to four days. She was surprised by this, because he had banned her from going there or even mentioning their names. Nevertheless, she left for her parents' house and stayed there for two days. After that, Salem ordered her to go to her sister's house without informing her parents. She spent a night at her sister's place, and in the morning he again called to order her to leave her sister's house immediately and roam around on the streets till 3 p.m., when she had to call him from a PCO on a given number. A *burqa*-clad Samira followed his instructions and roamed the streets of Bandra till 3 p.m., and then called him on the number he had given her. It turned out to be a Dubai number.

It was then, four days after the blasts that Salem finally revealed to her that the Mumbai Police was looking for him and that he was in hiding. He instructed her to go to the market where a *burqa*-clad woman would meet her and tell her what to do next. She met the woman who took her to a beauty salon to have her looks changed. Her long hair was cropped short and she was given tickets to fly to Delhi, where Abu Salem finally joined her before they left for Dubai together.

According to the records of the Mumbai Police, Abu Salem had never been arrested prior to the blasts though he was wanted in as many as two dozen criminal cases registered at various police stations in Mumbai alone. Before he fled to Dubai on an Indian passport he had fraudulently obtained from Lucknow in the name of Akil Ahmed Azmi, Salem was also allegedly involved in the abduction of a few businessmen for ransom on the orders of the D Company.

For Samira, Dubai was a completely new place, but not for Salem. He seemed extremely familiar with the city, where they were staying in an apartment in Jumeirah. Official records would later reveal that Salem had set up an automobile company in Dubai called 'Kings of Car Trading', and also organized stage shows on behalf of the D Company where he invited actors to perform. It was at one of these shows that he was introduced to Monica Bedi, who had accompanied producer Mukesh Duggal.

What Salem told her after the blasts kept haunting Samira. She remembered Salem had gone out of Mumbai for four days in January without informing her. She had called Hamida, Tingu's wife, and told her she was extremely worried as she had not heard from him. Hamida informed her husband, who had called Samira and told her that he had sent Salem to Gujarat on some work and he would be home soon. According to her, whenever she asked her husband about the nature of his work, he would either evade her questions or simply snub her. In Dubai, Salem finally revealed to her that he was working for the noted don Dawood Ibrahim and not for Tingu, though their work was similar.

In the course of our conversation, Samira insisted that the real culprits behind the Mumbai blasts had not been arrested and had gone scot-free, and angrily claimed that no agency had bothered to find out the truth behind the blasts. She claimed that the real culprit behind the 1993 blasts was not her husband but his boss, Aziz Bilakhia, who had managed to stay away from the case with the help of corrupt police officials. His name was not even mentioned as a suspect in the case filed by the Mumbai Police. She also claimed that he was supposed to have come to the US on a fake identity and was successfully running a business in New York City. This was a revelation. Bilakhia had flown to Dubai with his family just before 12 March 1993, when the blasts occurred, and had not figured prominently in the Mumbai Police investigation.

In the years that followed, Samira knew that her husband was not in love with her anymore, though it still came as a big jolt to her when he casually told her that every don had a girlfriend, and he would soon have one too. Even his producer-friend Mukesh Duggal had one, he said. Although Duggal used to come home with his wife, Samira recalled that Duggal's wife had occasionally mentioned something about a starlet named Monica Bedi being her husband's new girlfriend. According to his wife, Duggal openly flaunted his affair with Bedi, who was acting in his films.

Although she was in an abusive marriage, Samira could not let go of her status as Salem's wife, and in 1997 she got pregnant. Duggal helped arrange a relative's house in New Jersey for the pregnant Samira to stay in since Salem was on the run at the time. Samira lived in New Jersey for three months and Salem visited her there twice. Duggal and Salem were extremely close, but Dawood Ibrahim did not trust Duggal as he suspected him to be his arch-rival Chhota Rajan's mole. (Duggal was ultimately assassinated in Mumbai in 1997, and Samira told me that though Salem was sad about it, he knew it was all part of his profession.)

Police records indicate that it was after Duggal's murder that Monica Bedi became closer to Salem and they began living together in Sharjah. According to Samira, Salem was so besotted by Bedi that he even asked a three-month-pregnant Samira to abort her baby. She refused. When Samira ultimately delivered a baby boy in New Jersey the same year, her husband was not there by her side but in a jail in Dubai, arrested on charges of financial fraud.

When Samira returned to Dubai with her newborn child, things had changed, she said. Salem was in jail and looked subdued and scared when she met him. Salem's arrest in December 1997 is said to have been engineered by Anees Ibrahim. Although Anees Ibrahim and Salem eventually fell out, Salem was once his trusted lieutenant. In 1994, Salem is believed to have supervised the assassinations of Maharashtra BJP leaders Ramdas Naik and Prem Singh. For the next three years he remained a key figure in Anees Ibrahim's operations, working from safehouses in Nairobi, Lagos, Bahrain and Dubai under false identities. Police records indicate that Salem was also named in a number of other murders, such as those of Kamruddin Khan, a watchman hired by Shah Builders at Malad in 1994; Santosh Pandurang Patole at Kandivali in 1994; film producer Javed Riyaz Siddique at D.N. Nagar in 1994; and businessmen Ahmed Ibrahim Batliwala and Abdul Maruf Khan at Mahim in 1996. It was also reported that in mid-1997, Salem went to Pakistan to make arrangements for Dawood's brother Humayun's wedding.

However, things changed when, on 12 August 1997, the Abu Salem group killed Gulshan Kumar, allegedly to help a rival music producer, Nadeem Akhtar Saifi, part of the famous Nadeem–Shravan duo. On 25 September, prosecution witness Arif Lakdawala told Mumbai Sessions Court Judge M.L. Tahilyani that Saifi and Ramesh Taurani of Tips music company had paid him ₹25 lakh, which he had passed on to the killers. Saifi denied the allegations, and has succeeded in blocking India's efforts to extradite him from the UK.

Dawood was furious with Salem for killing Gulshan Kumar without his permission, and Anees Ibrahim was particularly incensed that Abu Salem had more or less taken over his operations in Mumbai's film world. Tariq Parveen, one of Anees Ibrahim's closest aides, is believed to have argued on several occasions in favour of eliminating Salem, his one-time friend. It is said that when Anees Ibrahim summoned him, Salem went into hiding. Anees then lodged a complaint with the financial fraud authorities in Dubai against Salem's automobile firm, which was run by his brothers Salim and Nayeem. He was subsequently picked up by the Dubai Police in connection with the charges.

Upon getting the news of Salem's arrest an Indian Embassy official went to the Dubai Police chief to confirm the details. But he was told that the man arrested was one Akil Ahmed Azmi with only a facial resemblance to Salem. The CBI immediately sent all documents proving that Akil was actually Salem, and that he had been travelling on a fake passport. However, UAE authorities did not match the fingerprints of 'Akil' with those of Salem, and despite Indian authorities sending details on Samira stating that Salem's wife and Akil's wife were also the same person, UAE authorities turned a blind eye. In the meantime, the CBI had moved its first extradition request against Salem, but the UAE authorities chose to ignore the request as well as warnings that Abu Salem was likely to escape the country.

Salem knew that after he was released from prison he would no longer be safe in Dubai.[5] When he was released on bail with a UAE resident acting as guarantor, he hid in Sharjah with Samira and their son, but Anees Ibrahim informed the UAE authorities about his presence there. Before the authorities could initiate any action against him, however, he managed to escape to Africa using a Pakistani passport, leaving Samira and their son behind.

An incensed Anees reached Salem's Sharjah apartment along with his other brothers and some gang members, apparently looking for a certain photograph. When they did not find Salem at home, they misbehaved with Samira and broke things in the house. As related by Samira, when Dawood got to know about the incident, he called Samira. An upset Samira told him that she did not know the whereabouts of her husband, and asked him if they ever informed their wives about their criminal activities or hideouts. Further, she asked Dawood, had his brothers forgotten that women and children were kept out of the gang's business?

To her surprise, Dawood politely expressed regret for the entire episode and apologized on behalf of his brother. After that ugly incident, she said, neither Dawood nor his brothers had ever bothered her.

Salem knew that Anees would not give up on him and would try every trick to hunt him down. He hid in Africa for a few months before going to the US, from where he called Samira and instructed her to leave with their son for her sister's house in Atlanta. Once they reached Atlanta, Salem joined them there. He bought an apartment and an office, from where he ran his global criminal operations. In the US, Samira confirmed, he mostly employed youth from Sri Lanka and Bangladesh.

According to informed sources, after escaping from Anees Ibrahim and splitting from the D Company sometime in 1998, Salem set about asserting his own sphere of influence in earnest. His crime syndicate started to expand in Mumbai and other parts of India, while he was in the US. He often visited Kenya and other African countries to expand his criminal activities.

The most significant crime committed independently by the Abu Salem gang was the abduction of Chiranjeev Vaghani, proprietor of Milton Plastic Industries. On 17 February 2000, Vaghani was kidnapped along with his driver by Abu Salem's men while on his way home in the evening. Both victims were later released after the family allegedly paid ₹5 crore as ransom. Though a case was registered under the MCOCA, both Vaghani and his driver were so scared of Salem that they did not cooperate with the police, with the result that no further progress was made in the case.

Meanwhile, Samira's marriage continued to be troubled. She knew about her husband's affair with Bedi, but whenever she tried to ask him about her, he snubbed her. If she insisted, he would beat her up. After six months of being in Atlanta, he asked her to go to Chicago, where, he said, he had bought her a house.

Reportedly, Salem had also bought a house for Bedi, who wanted to meet Samira. Salem put her off for a while, but not for long. When he was travelling in Europe, a stubborn Bedi went to meet Samira, and the latter's worst nightmare came true. Bedi tried to coerce Samira into divorcing Salem. Samira did not relent and asked Bedi to leave, as she was not willing to give up her rights as his legally wedded wife. Aamir was her only son, and she had his welfare and future on her mind. Samira claimed that in a fit of rage Bedi told her that if she insisted on staying in the marriage she would meet the same fate as Duggal. Bedi's ego was badly hurt at the outcome of her meeting with Samira, and she called Salem and complained about Samira's rude behaviour.

Salem knew that their son was Samira's weakness and he threatened to separate her from him. Samira could not imagine her life without her child. She had learnt to live with Salem's abusive ways and now, to retain her son's custody, Samira had to give in to Salem. Bedi, as Salem dictated, was to live in the same house as them. Bedi then moved into their home in Chicago, where Salem and she treated Samira like a servant. Still, Samira claimed, Bedi did not leave any stone unturned to separate the two. She wanted Samira to divorce Salem at any cost so that she could be his only wife. She began to incite Samira by describing Salem as a hot and passionate lover and sharing other private details with her. Ironically, she often remembered Duggal and compared him with Salem. In her weak moments, Bedi told Samira that Duggal was a better lover than Salem and had given her lead roles in 'A' grade films, while Salem could only manage to get her roles in 'B' grade films. She was concerned that she would not fulfil her dream of being a big-league Bollywood actress with such films. She also admitted that Salem had a violent streak and would hit her if he got upset or angry with her.

Samira's troubles were not limited to her family life; after 9/11, the FBI in its general combing operations found illicit financial deals through a few bank accounts in the name of Arsalan Ali Ahmed Azmi. The FBI traced the accounts to Samira Ali Azmi in Georgia, who was summoned and questioned in detail, and the information given by her was passed on to Indian authorities. Abu Salem already had a red-corner Interpol notice on him and, in the aftermath of 9/11, he was declared a fugitive and a terrorist wanted in the Mumbai serial blasts case.

By this time Salem had begun to operate from European countries, where Bedi and he travelled together as a couple. He had distanced himself from Samira completely, and would occasionally call only to speak to his son Aamir. It was one such call that was traced by US agencies, who informed Interpol and Indian agencies. Salem's satellite phone was traced via GPS to an apartment in a plush Lisbon area, from where he and Bedi were arrested. When Samira got the news that Salem and Bedi had been arrested, she said, she was neither sad nor happy. She was simply relieved that she would no longer have to face living with a violent husband. She sold the house in Chicago and moved back to Atlanta, where her sister was staying with her family, and changed her name to become Sabina. Once her US residency came through, as an American citizen, she got an ex-parte divorce from Salem. She was now a partner in a local departmental store and owned a gas station. She spent her time working in the local Khoja (Aga Khan) Community Service Centre, and Aamir was now studying in a private school. She was perturbed about the case against her in India for travelling on a fake passport. She knew that her return to India was not possible due to the case. Her name had been dragged into the media over the fake passport case, she said, she had been flagged as 'wanted', a tag she wanted desperately to be removed.

Though she was finally free from Salem's shadow, she revealed that she remained cautious and kept tabs on developments in the Salem–Bedi case. She hardly had any links with her in-laws. Despite this, she kept a photograph of Salem's mother, who lived in Sarai Mir village in Uttar Pradesh. She would tell her son, Aamir, to remember his grandmother and respect her.

It was hard to believe that a convent-educated girl from Mumbai had lived such a tormented life with an outlaw and a terrorist, and had not yet thought of escaping. I told her as much. Her reasoning, she explained, was that he would have got to her family living in Mumbai. She had suffered in silence though she had been aware of her husband's dark side. Her mother, who was present while we spoke, began to cry when Samira said this. She told me Samira had never shared her pain with her family because she thought it would make them more miserable. The interview was the first time her mother had heard the full details of what her daughter had gone through.

The CBI, however, believes that Samira enjoyed all the luxuries of Salem's ill-gotten wealth till Bedi arrived in their lives. Till then, she lived as the don's rightful wife and escaped from the law along with him. She enjoyed meeting the celebrities he mingled with, including Bollywood superstars who used to frequent their house. Samira, on the other hand, told me that she hardly attended the lavish parties Salem threw for the stars, perhaps because of Bedi. She remembered the time when a superstar had come to their home while she was still pregnant. The Bollywood star and her husband, she said, had even decided to give their children the same name. Incidentally, the actor's son bears the pre-decided name, but Samira had already decided on the name 'Aamir' for her son and she stuck to her decision.

Meeting Samira gave me an insider's view of a mobster's life. For Samira, being married to a criminal had been like constantly living on the edge. She had learned to live with a threat on her life. She was afraid of Salem's reaction to the interview. She said, 'He might bump me off for revealing his secrets.' It was also very obvious that she had not overcome the humiliation caused by Bedi.

As she spoke, it often seemed as though her hatred for Bedi was more than her fear of death. In the end, she sounded more like a mother with an intense survival instinct for the sake of her child than the defeated wife of a mobster.

When the story, titled '*Biwi* Number One', finally aired in India a few days later, I received six missed calls from Samira. When I returned her call, she sounded stressed and worried about the reactions she had received on the story. She was agitated that we had aired the video of our conversation (though we did not shoot inside her house as per her request, a video was recorded on the way to the airport while she dropped us). She had wanted me to convey Salem's story without mentioning her at all. No words could pacify her. To air the programme as we had had been a tough and painful call for me, too. The irony was that without her in the story, it would not have had any soul or credibility. We had debated this issue in office before the story was planned. One of the senior editors had made a point concerning the identity of the subject and her safety. It was a matter of ethics, but in the end it was also a question of national interest, and the latter had won the argument. Some of the facts pertaining to the D Company and its alleged involvement in the 1993 blasts were crucial.

Samira Jumani's revelations made the CBI sit up and pay attention. Among other things, after further investigations, they filed a supplementary chargesheet against Aziz Bilakhia in the 1993 blasts case and issued a red-corner notice on him. The two biggest national dailies – the *Times of India* and *Hindustan Times* – splashed it across their front pages the next day. My mother came with both newspapers to my room in the morning to find me fast asleep after going to bed at 3 a.m. All I felt once the story was out there was plain relief.

I finally met Abu Salem in a room full of cobwebs on the ground floor of the TADA Court, where the 1993 blast trials were being conducted on the first floor.

Getting an interview with Salem while he was in jail had been a tough task. It not only required permission from the TADA Court, but before I wrote a formal request to Pramod Kode, the designated judge, I also needed to know if Salem was okay with an interview. I called my advocate friend, whom I had known for a decade-and-a-half, and he asked me to meet him at Worli Sea Face Promenade the same evening. There, he suggested that I should go with him to the TADA Court and take a chance with Salem myself. That is how I found myself in the room at the TADA Court, awaiting Salem's answer to a request for an interview.

I had been told to wait in the room located behind the court building during the lunch break, at around 1.30 p.m., after the first session was over. I did as instructed, and in about 15 minutes Salem appeared with his lawyer and a constable. He was wearing an indigo-blue half-sleeved shirt and black trousers. With his gelled hair neatly combed, clean-shaven and a gait that made him flex his biceps even though his hands were cuffed, it seemed as if he was walking the ramp at a fashion show. Salem had always paid attention to how he appeared in public, particularly before the press and he hardly missed a chance to look directly into the lenses of cameras.

He entered the room and sat at the table, with me on a chair across from him and next to his lawyer. He continued to stare at me for a few seconds. My advocate friend, one of the most expensive and successful criminal lawyers in Mumbai, formally introduced him to me. But even before the advocate could complete his sentence, Salem butted in, looking straight into my eyes. 'Did you also meet my son, Aamir? How was he? How does he look?' he asked.

I nodded my head and said, 'I met Aamir very briefly. He is a good-looking child and appeared to be a well-behaved, obedient son. His mother kept him away from us deliberately and he was not part of my conversation with Samira. He stayed in the bedroom during the time I was at his house.'

His hardened expression seemed to ease with my answer. I could imagine why Samira was so scared of him. Her fear that Salem could reach out to her even from jail and have her killed seemed a very real possibility at that moment.

From Salem's question about his son, it was clear that he knew about my interview with Samira. I was not surprised, but I noticed he was concerned about whether his son knew of it or not. Salem appeared to be a sharp observer who had a knack for delivering a threat in a plain tone. He told me coldly, 'Personal and professional lives should be kept separate.' Before I could grasp the meaning behind his menacing tone, he changed his voice and mood in an instant like a chameleon and turned to his advocate to enquire about some legal aspect of his case. I found that he could easily gauge a person's psychology. No wonder he had survived after splitting from Anees Ibrahim and the D Company, I thought.

I asked him what his objections were to *Gangster*, an upcoming movie made by Mahesh Bhatt which was said to be based on Salem's life. He said he respected Bhatt as a filmmaker and he himself had many friends in Bollywood, but Bhatt had portrayed him as a villainous character, distorting his story. I asked him how he knew about what Bhatt had written. He smiled and with a devilish glint in his eye said,' '*Hamare bhi bade mitr hai industry main* (I, too, have friends in the industry).' Indeed, Salem's Bollywood connections had long been known, besides his role in the murders of Gulshan Kumar and Jain. When I asked him who would be a suitable actor to play his character in the film, he named some top stars whom he claimed to know well.

About his arrest, Salem said that the jails in Lisbon were more comfortable and the Portuguese approach to treating the accused was more 'professional'. At Arthur Road Jail he had many enemies in the form of rival gang members to deal with. Despite this, he was confident of pulling all his 'might' and using every resource to come out of jail at the earliest.

Most people with a criminal bent of mind live in denial mode when they get caught, but it was not so with Salem. When he talked about Dawood and his network, he said there was more to the D Company than met the eye. International crime syndicates, he explained, worked with many factions that develop their own networks, and what was considered a crime in India may not be in the same legal category in other countries.

A different side to Salem came to light when he began to talk about Monica Bedi. The expression on his face changed and softened. He said he had got married to Samira at a very early age. His first marriage was more of a 'hormonal' match than an 'emotional' one: merely puppy love. When I asked him about not wanting to have a child and asking Samira to consider an abortion, he said he dreaded the emotional turmoil his child would go through when he would be taunted for his father's alleged crimes. I told him I had spoken with Monica at the Hyderabad Court during the previous Ramzan, and Salem got very curious to know what she had said about him. I told him Bedi had said she regretted her past deeds, at least in court and during our conversation. He became pensive, and said she was his first love, and perhaps his last. When he saw her for the first time at a social event in Dubai, he recalled, he fell for her instantly, and when she reciprocated his feelings he was on cloud nine. He said, 'It was a mature love and I was head-over-heels in love with her. *Jaise ek duje ke liye bane the. Woh bhi meri diwani thi.* (It was as if we were made for each other; she was also smitten by me.)' He said Monica was a smart and intelligent girl and she understood him better than anyone else. But it had hurt him immensely when he heard the stories of her denial – even though he knew it could be a part of her legal strategy.

Later, Advocate Raja Thakare, the CBI lawyer, would tell me that Salem had celebrated his eighth 'wedding' anniversary in jail in his presence. He had read letters and greeting cards that Monica had sent him since 2001 and expressed that he felt 'very lonely'. When Bedi became a contestant on the reality show *Bigg Boss* (Season 2, in 2008), Salem demanded a TV set to watch her in his Arthur Road Jail cell. He sent his first legal notice to her from jail on 7 October 2008, stating that he was deeply hurt and distressed by her statements to the media denying their marriage.[6] In that note, Salem revealed his romantic side by mentioning that he had found peace, solace and comfort when he read Monica's letters and cards sent to him on their marriage anniversaries while in prison in Lisbon.

The second legal notice he sent her read more like a heart-wrenching love letter from a dejected lover. He felt cheated on the love front, he wrote. He could not stand Monica's alleged liaisons with another man (presumably Rahul Mahajan) in the *Bigg Boss* house and was upset at Bedi's comments on the show about on how she would like to get married and settle down when she finds the right man. In the notice, Salem warned her that if she failed to publicly acknowledge her marriage to him, he would be forced to resort to take legal action against her. If she wanted to settle down with somebody else, she would have to divorce him, and because he loved her so much he would not trouble her if she wanted to separate. However, even in later press interviews, Monica stuck to her stand that she had known Salem for many years but had never tied the knot with him.

In our conversation on the TADA Court premises, Salem continued to speak very fondly of Monica. He told me that they had got married in a Los Angeles mosque in November 2000 and had been living as a married couple till they were deported. His version corroborated what Samira had told me about Monica staying with them in Chicago.

Forty minutes later, Salem had to go back to his '*anda*' – an isolated and secure cell in the jail. He said he would think about the proposal for a formal interview and convey his response through his lawyer, who had also been hired, along with another Mumbai-based criminal lawyer, to oversee the remaining legal proceedings in Portugal. The two had visited Lisbon to check for any possible windows for their client's extradition re-appeal and sort out his financial issues, which had come under legal scrutiny in Lisbon. Bedi's father had told me when I met him that she had been carrying about €30,000 on her at the time of her arrest, which had not been returned to them yet.

Photo of Abu Salem and Monica Bedi in Lisbon from official records.

Ever since his arrest, Salem has wanted to return to Portugal by hook or by crook. First, he filed a complaint against the CBI claiming that the organization was violating his extradition conditions. Judge Pramod Kode rejected Salem's claims and said the prosecution had rightly charged him with causing the Mumbai blasts in 1993, and with transporting and distributing arms and ammunition, including those supplied to Sanjay Dutt. Salem then filed a petition in the High Court at Lisbon, alleging violation of the Rule of Speciality (a principle of international law that is included in most extradition treaties, whereby a person who is extradited to a country to stand trial for certain criminal offences may be tried only for those offences and not for any other offences). In a ruling on the petition, the Lisbon Court said that Indian authorities had breached their undertaking on the extradition process. Armed with this judgement, Salem approached the Supreme Court in India seeking dismissal of all proceedings against him. The Supreme Court had stayed the trial after Salem approached the apex court against the TADA Court's order rejecting his plea for the closure of his trial. He simultaneously filed an application in Portugal's Supreme Court against the CBI, again for violating his extradition conditions, and the judgement went in his favour when the Portuguese apex court terminated his extradition to India for the 'violation' of deportation rules by Indian authorities. But the Supreme Court in India dismissed his plea for quashing all proceedings against him, ordering only certain charges to be withdrawn. The court ruled that the gangster should remain in India to face trial. 'The verdict of Portugal's constitutional court is not binding on us,' the apex court said, adding that Abu Salem's extradition was still valid in the eyes of the law in India. The Supreme Court allowed the CBI to drop additional charges slapped on Abu Salem under the TADA and Explosives Substances Act in view of its commitment to the Portuguese government at the time of his extradition that he would not be awarded the death penalty or detained in custody for more than 25 years if found guilty.[7]

However, since Salem could not have his way legally, the Mumbai Police firmly believe he has been trying other means as well to get himself out of the country. Salem was attacked twice in jail – first inside Arthur Road Jail in 2010 and then inside the Taloja Central Jail in Navi Mumbai in 2013. After the first attack, he was moved to Taloja Jail, where a bullet fired from a *katta* (a country pistol) brushed Salem's right hand but did not cause any serious harm. The Mumbai Police have raised serious suspicions about the attacks and believe that they were intended to prove he is not safe in Indian jails.[8]

Salem continues to enjoy a comfortable lifestyle even within the confines of his jail cell, wearing designer clothes and shoes and eating only the best of food including his choice of biryani. One of the most manipulative and shrewd gangsters I have met, his driving force seems to be his survival instinct. Of the 52 cases lodged against him in India, he can only be tried for eight as per the extradition terms with the Portugal government. Salem has already spent ten years in jail (he can be jailed for 25 years only, as per the terms of the extradition treaty), and is now desperate to get out. A control freak, Salem has decided to not leave any stone unturned to become a free man. He seems to have devised a smart legal approach, executed by his advocate Saba Qureshi and her legal team in Lisbon. In addition to moving the Portuguese courts to cancel his extradition on the grounds of torture and use of force on Salem in an Indian jail by Indian authorities, they have also approached the administrative court in Lisbon and have been pressurizing the government there to rescind the extradition. The case is currently pending before the administrative court. The legal team has also approached the European Union Court to pressurize the Portuguese into repatriating Salem, seeking the execution of an order by the Portuguese Constitutional Court cancelling his extradition.

Salem has long tried to outsmart his mafia bosses to become one of the most-wanted gangsters in the world. He has not had any close aides and has never shared his ideas and plans with anyone. Despite having a barely organized gang structure, he has operated in the crime world in an organized way, travelling light and without a steady or loyal force of shooters. Instead, he always hired youth from his native village Sarai Mir in Azamgarh, Uttar Pradesh. They came cheap and he did not have to bother about their safety or maintenance after the job was over.

Salem's fascination with Bollywood since childhood has made him believe that he, too, is a hero in real life. He is known to charm women in a very filmy manner, chasing them like an obsessed lover and making them believe he is a die-hard romantic. He has even romanced a reel-life heroine, presenting himself to her family as the best man for her. A renowned Bollywood director once told me that Salem had sent him a message saying that were a film to be made on his life, he should act in it as himself, as he is better-looking and more talented than any actor in the industry. Salem continues to follow his fitness regime in jail, and even shaves regularly to maintain his looks.

Currently, he is said to be writing his autobiography, presenting himself as a man who rose from the dusty lanes of an Azamgarh village to become an icon for the youth of the region. If the battery of expensive lawyers fighting his case succeeds in setting him free, Salem will surely be ready for his second act. And if a film is indeed made on his life then there is no doubt that he will play himself in it.

The Gangster's Moll

FROM A SMALL VILLAGE IN Punjab to a jail in Portugal, Bollywood starlet and Abu Salem's paramour Monica Bedi has travelled a long way. A proverbial small-town girl with stars in her eyes, Bedi never rose to be a star to reckon with even in her prime. She gained fame only after her romance with gangster Salem became public knowledge and she became known for being an internationally wanted criminal.

In September 2002, Bedi was arrested along with Salem by the Lisbon Police for entering Portugal with forged documents. They served two years in jail before being deported to India on 11 November 2005, after India promised Portugal that Salem would not get a death sentence. The CBI had filed a case against Bedi under Section 420 (cheating), 120B (criminal conspiracy) and Section 12 of the Passport Act for procuring a passport on a fictitious name, and on 29 September 2006, a special CBI court convicted her on charges of passport forgery.

Monica made a surprise comeback when she participated in the reality show *Bigg Boss* in 2008, her first on-screen appearance after being released from prison on bail. She claimed to have joined *Bigg Boss* 'to start life afresh', and then participated in more TV shows such as *Jhalak Dikhla Jaa*, *Raaz Pichhle Janam Ka*, *Desi Girl* and *Saraswatichandra*. She has been working in regional movies, but mainstream Bollywood has maintained its distance from her. The fear that comes with her name is still too daunting for the industry.

Meanwhile, Bedi approached the court in connection with her passport. The RPO issued an affidavit, in response to Monica's petition seeking reissuance of her passport through the Mumbai High Court, saying that it could not issue a passport to Monica if any proceeding pertaining to the offences lodged against her was pending before any criminal court. Later, the Mumbai High Court directed the RPO to process her passport application, on merit and after following all formalities. Bedi's legal battles got over in December 2014 when she was finally issued a new passport as per the court's orders.

In September 2006, just before the CBI Court announced its judgement on her, I had travelled to Hyderabad with the brief to find out who Monica Bedi really was. Was she the forgettable Bollywood starlet from films like *Jodi No. 1* and *Aashiq Mastana*, or was she Sana Malik Kamal, the woman who had converted to Islam to marry Ramil Kamal Malik aka Salem, or was she Fauzia Usman, the name under which she had travelled across the globe on her fake passport?

I was to meet her on the day the judgement was delivered and had spoken to her advocate about meeting her privately for 15 minutes on the premises of the court. He asked me to wait near the prosecution office after the judgement was announced. He was positive about the meeting, but I knew that he was yet to speak to her about it.

That day, the special court at the Namapally Court Complex was packed with journalists. Monica finally came in wearing a cotton *salwar-kameez*. Her hair was neatly clipped. She sat on a bench, her eyes lowered to the ground. I found that jail had mellowed her. I had heard that while imprisoned she had turned to yoga and spirituality for solace. Like her gangster-boyfriend, fitness had become her mantra. Reality seemed to have hit her hard, and her chats with the female staff at the jail were mostly philosophical. She had managed to deglamourize herself. According to my sources in the State Prison for Women, Chanchalguda, Hyderabad, where she had been lodged, Monica had been praying and preparing herself for the judgement.

Monica Bedi's father, Prem Kumar Bedi, who lives in Drammen, 45 km from the Norwegian capital of Oslo, came to India after she was deported in November 2005 and met her three times in prison, but he could not stay till the judgement was delivered. Her uncle, Purushottam Lal Bedi, from Hoshiarpur district in Punjab, had come to assure her that her family was with her. But she knew she had to face the judgement alone.

When the judgement was pronounced by Judge C.V. Subrahmanyam and she was sentenced to five years' rigorous imprisonment, she looked sad but remained composed, as if she was not surprised by the outcome. Another passport forgery case was pending against her in the Bhopal Court, for which she had not got bail, and so would have to be taken to Bhopal to be tried the following month. She knew that this judgement would influence the Bhopal case trial as well. In both the cases, the charge against her was that she had acquired a passport under a fake name. Monica's lawyers contended there was no proof that she had applied for a passport under a fictitious name because it had been issued when she was abroad.

Also present in the court was Pallavi Ashar, Abu Salem's legal counsel. Pallavi and I were on the same flight from Mumbai, and I wasn't surprised to see her there. I was amazed at the realization that Salem cared enough for Monica to send a lady counsel to attend court on the day of her judgement. Originally from Kutch, Gujarat, and married to a Muslim, Khalid Ansari, Pallavi had converted to Islam and changed her name to Almas. As it was the month of Ramzan, Pallavi was observing the *roza*. The court proceedings went on till 6 p.m., and she was carrying water to break the fast in case the proceedings were delayed.

A TV grab showing Monica Bedi being escorted to the court.

Pallavi's presence helped me reach out to Bedi. Familiarity broke the ice between us. I told her I was there to cover Monica's court proceedings and she said she was also there to witness the proceedings. Taking a chance, I asked her if she could help me to meet Bedi and she agreed.

After the judgement had been pronounced, while Monica was waiting for the paperwork formalities to be done with, I went along with Pallavi to meet her. I introduced myself to her and Pallavi endorsed me as a senior journalist covering crime and the mafia from Mumbai. I was curious to see how Monica would respond to Pallavi, knowing that she was Abu Salem's lawyer and worked closely with him, but when they met they seemed comfortable talking to each other. In fact, Pallavi made a call to her boss and Salem's lawyer Ashok Saraogi in her presence. Monica too spoke to Saraogi after Pallavi did, although I suspected that it was Salem on the line with her. Monica seemed to have learnt the art of talking softly on the phone; it was hard for me to hear her conversation even though I was standing merely five feet away. When I asked her later, Monica denied being in touch with Salem, although he seemed to be constantly updated about her case. Pallavi, I guessed, was the trusted link between them.

My conversation with Monica started with a request to clarify the criminal charges that had led to her conviction. She accused the media of being biased in portraying only the dark side of her life. I told her that it might be because she had shunned the media and there had been no access to her for anyone to clarify or portray her side of the story. I tried to convince her that she could use the channel I worked for to clear her stand that she 'was an ambitious but not a bad girl'. She said she was someone who took time to open up, and it was not possible to do so in 15–20 minutes. But she asserted that she really needed people to know that the real Monica Bedi was not a 'bad girl', and certainly not a criminal.

I asked her if she felt she had paid a heavy price for a few mistakes. Did she marry the wrong man? 'I was never married to Abu Salem, I only lived with him for a year,' she clarified. She didn't deny her relationship with Salem, but said she had not been in touch with him since they were arrested. 'I loved him but it isn't the same anymore. I last spoke to him on 18 September 2002, the day we were arrested. I haven't been in touch with him since then. I am not with him anymore and have got nothing to do with him at all.'

Monica said she was not aware of Salem's identity when she met him first, but conceded that his feelings for her were genuine. 'He tried really hard to change and made a lot of effort for my sake. I should get credit for it. He tried his best but his past kept catching up with him.'

When I asked her why she had introduced Salem as Sanjay to her family in Lisbon and said that he was a businessman, and what had compelled her to travel under false names on forged passports, she stared at the floor for a while before saying that she had been forced to flee India out of fear that the police would trap Salem through her. 'He feared that the cops would catch me and torture me to find out his whereabouts,' she said. 'He told me he wanted time to change, so I went with him.'

Monica said her relationship with Salem had started falling apart once they left India and that she tried to escape at least three times. 'When we used to meet for two or three days, he was always on his best behaviour. But we were very different, and our way of thinking was totally apart. He was very possessive of me. And I found this out only after I started living with him.'

I mentioned Samira, and said she had told me Salem had abused Monica as well. She had also said Monica and Salem maintained joint bank accounts and some properties had been transferred to her name. Monica kept quiet at this, then denied Samira's allegations of her having any joint accounts with Salem. 'If I had property in my name, I would have been better off. My legal expenses are paid by my family,' she told me. Later, when I met her father, Prem Bedi, he would hint that someone else had paid all of Monica's legal bills as it was beyond his means to hire an expensive Supreme Court lawyer like K.T.S. Tulsi.

Monica expressed her desire to start life afresh without Salem. Perhaps she knew that it would take very long for Salem to walk out of an Indian jail. She told me, 'I want to leave my painful past behind and want to marry one day and settle down, but only after I find the right guy.'

What Monica did not know was that I was in Lisbon soon after their arrest, and was aware that Salem and she wrote love letters to each other while in jail.[1] CBI documents also suggest that Salem was madly in love with Monica and that the two had admitted they could not imagine their lives without each other. Monica used to call him 'Babu' and he called her 'Gudiya', and she used to get desperate if there was a delay in receiving Salem's letter.

'My love where are you...no letter from you...are you angry with your Gudiya...I know you are angry with your baby,' Monica wrote to him in one such letter, obviously referring to a rough patch in their relationship. 'I want only you, and I can sacrifice anything for a life with you,' another of her letters read, 'only you are my life and identity. I will always be associated with you. Till the time I die, I will be your Gudiya.'

In yet another letter, she threatened to commit suicide: 'After showering so much love on me, don't go away from me. Your wife can't go anywhere. At best I can commit suicide here. If I realize you have changed, I swear, I will die here.'

But after being extradited to India, Monica changed her stance completely. She cut herself off from Salem, at least in public. He became a thing of the past for her, and she continues to maintain this stand today.

Later, Pallavi told me that Salem was upset that she had not recognized their relationship in public and he had made it clear that he still cared deeply about Monica. Salem had, in fact, served her a legal notice saying he was deeply hurt and distressed by her statements denying their marriage, as I have detailed in the previous chapter. In his notice, he claimed that the duo had married in a Los Angeles mosque in November 2000. In November 2008, Salem announced, 'Monica Bedi is my wife', while coming out of a Delhi court. Then the don, who usually deflects media queries, obliged journalists by saying they were husband and wife once again. Salem's claims in public about their alleged relationship contradicted Bedi's attempts to refute their marriage.

The fallout of their relationship had to be borne by Pallavi.

Pallavi and I had again been on the same flight on the way back to Mumbai from Hyderabad after my meeting with Bedi. What I had gathered from her was that Salem trusted her completely and often kept her boss Saraogi out of the scene when he communicated with her. Later, I went to her house at Mahindra Park in Ghatkopar to discuss the case further. In the meeting, Pallavi shed some more light on the Salem–Bedi relationship. She claimed to have attended all of Monica's court proceedings in Hyderabad and Bhopal, and said that she had visited her in jail several times, as Salem was concerned about her imprisonment and her facilities in the prison.

According to Pallavi, after each visit she had to report back to Salem, who was more than keen to know every little detail about his lady-love, from her looks to her mood, and of course the status of the case. He would ask Pallavi what she was wearing when they met and if Bedi needed clothes or money to spend on her daily needs.

In February 2008, I read in the newspapers that Pallavi had allegedly attempted suicide by consuming sleeping pills at her Ghatkopar residence. In her statement to the police, she said she took the step due to mental torture caused by her former employer and advocate Ashok Saraogi, who had she claimed defamed her in the media by talking about her alleged love affair with his client Abu Salem.[2]

It occurred to me that the suicide attempt could have resulted from Salem's complete trust in her and her involvement in his affair with Monica. I had first-hand knowledge of Pallavi's role in legal matters pertaining to Salem and Bedi, and knew that the arrangement suited her boss Saraogi and their important client, Salem. According to my police sources, the issue was about the money and property that Salem allegedly managed through his legal help. Even after she left Saraogi's firm, Salem continued to hound Pallavi for her legal assistance, such was his trust in her.

❖

While Monica Bedi tried hard to get out of jail on bail, top-notch legal counsel K.T.S. Tulsi was representing her in the Supreme Court. I met Prem Bedi, her father, at Tulsi's home-cum-office in Delhi.

In an earlier hearing, Additional Solicitor-General Amrender Sharan, appearing for the CBI, had opposed the bail plea, saying that if Monica Bedi was released on bail she would flee the country as she did not have a permanent residence in India. However, Tulsi disputed CBI's argument by claiming that though her parents were living abroad, her uncle was living in Punjab and their family still had ancestral property in the Hoshiarpur district. To prove that the Bedi family is more Indian than Norwegian, Prem Bedi was called to India. He was visiting Tulsi before the hearing date and this is when we were formally introduced to each other.

Bedi spoke about his humble origins in Chabbewal, a small village in Punjab, where Monica was born in 1975. He was a registered medical practitioner but migrated to Norway to run a garment store business. He also told me that his daughter had written a letter to then Prime Minister Manmohan Singh pleading for bail and denying she had anything to do with Salem's criminal activities.

In the letter which she wrote on 7 November 2004, Bedi had written, 'I am a 29-year-old Indian citizen by birth originating from Hoshiarpur, Punjab. I belong to a respectable Punjabi family. In 1976, my family immigrated to Norway where they set up a trading business. I resided there for 16 years, then returned to India, alone, to start a career in the Indian film industry, where I worked for eight years, starring in around 30 films... In the later period of this career, I was introduced to Arsalan Ali during a stage show in Dubai, supposedly a respected Pakistani businessman. It was a long time after this first encounter that I discovered his real identity was Abu Salem, a married man and father.'

She further wrote that she had nothing to do with Salem's criminal acts and that she should be allowed to return to Norway. She said she would be ostracized from society as nobody wanted to associate themselves with her. She also feared for her life and claimed that the police would torture her to get information out of her. (It was apparent that her plea was baseless. It was an open secret that the mafia had been bankrolling Bollywood films at the time, and she had known Abu Salem was a notorious criminal all along and he could get her into films.)

In my conversation with her father, Prem Bedi, he lamented his daughter's entry into Bollywood. He said that when Monica first moved to Delhi to try her hand at modelling, she was young, naïve and innocent. But when she did not find much work there, she decided to move to Mumbai and enter the world of films. Her bad luck started from there on, and the rest of her story is familiar to anyone who reads the news. Like any worried father, he wanted to know how soon Monica would be out of jail and whether the Supreme Court would grant her bail.

The day we met, Prem Bedi had to meet his sister in Punjabi Bagh, and while we were talking Tulsi's office had been trying to organize a cab for him. He looked hassled as he was told he would have to wait for another hour for the cab to arrive. When I offered him a ride, he happily accepted, and we continued our conversation on the way to his sister's house.

Bedi spoke dejectedly about his dwindling garment business in Norway, saying Monica had some money in the bank and that had helped for a while, but the legal expenses had been quite hefty since her arrest.

I had earlier met and interviewed João Nabais, a top-notch and expensive lawyer who was defending Bedi and Salem in Portugal, for *India Today*. When I mentioned this, Bedi opened up a bit more. He said Nabais was helping them with Monica's frozen bank accounts in Lisbon. When she was arrested in 2002, she had about €30,000 on her, which was seized by the Lisbon Police. The amount was not returned to them despite legal intervention. Till today, Monica Bedi's brother, Bobby, is still fighting for it.[3]

I asked Monica's father about his daughter and Salem's relationship. Bedi said he found out about the relationship only when the two were arrested in 2002. He said Monica had also not known that the man she was involved with was Abu Salem. When I asked him if Monica had ever told him about Salem, or if he had ever met Salem, he said Monica had introduced Salem to the family by another name. 'He was known to us as Sanjay, a Hindu. We didn't know his name was Abu Salem and that he was an accused in the Mumbai blasts case.'

It became evident to me from these details that Bedi knew what she was doing all along. 'Was it possible that Monica knew about him, but didn't tell you?' I enquired. Bedi defended his daughter and emphasized that Monica did not know anything. He said she found out the truth only after moving to Dubai, which was Monica's version too.

According to the investigation report by the Mumbai Police, Bedi had an affair with producer Mukesh Duggal. Things soured between them when Duggal started using her as a liaison between him and his financiers to get films on the floor. While he did cast her in one or two odd films, Duggal was far more abusive than he was helpful. It was at this time that she was introduced to Abu Salem in Dubai during an event. Salem and Duggal knew each other. Salem began calling her under a false name and she fell for him.

Monica had confided in Salem about how Duggal had used and abused her, and the result was that Duggal was allegedly shot and killed by Salem. The incident shocked the industry but soon things were back to how they used to be. The show, as they say, went on. Salem used his influence to get Monica a handful of films but none of them did too well.

Knowingly or not, Monica was involved with a gangster who was wanted for the 1993 blasts. She knew she was in a relationship with a married man and she figured the only way to get what she wanted would be to change her religion and marry Salem. After they got married in Los Angeles, as Salem claimed in his legal notice to her, the two planned to settle in Lisbon, but Anees Ibrahim, Dawood's brother and Salem's enemy, found out that he was in the US. Salem sensed the danger as he knew his former boss's ire and he escaped to Portugal, where he and Bedi were arrested.

I asked Prem Bedi what he thought about the passport forgery case that had been brought against Monica. Bedi denied his daughter's crimes, as I suppose any father would. He said, 'She didn't get the passport made, she never signed the passport. Abu Salem was responsible for everything. She only did what she was told. It was possible she was scared of him. She was so scared that she never told us anything. She may have found this out after reaching Dubai... We only found out once she was arrested in Portugal.'

Bedi remained vague about Salem's claim that the two had married. 'We weren't present for any wedding. She didn't tell us anything either,' he repeated. When I asked him what the family thought of Monica's relationship with Salem when they met him, he said that Monica had told them that he was only a friend. 'We had sensed they were more than friends, but she insisted that he helped her with getting films,' he said.

The Bedi family was hurt, he said, and he was in great emotional turmoil. Though his daughter had fallen for the wrong man, he had to face his family, relatives and larger society. He blamed Salem and tried to convince me (and perhaps himself) that his daughter was innocent. She was not involved with the forgery of the passport, he repeated, and her only fault was that she had travelled on it.

He regretted having met Salem in Portugal. He felt cheated as Salem was polite and courteous to them like any regular man meeting the family of his lady-love. Even after their arrests, when the Bedis met them in Lisbon, it took them time to believe that he was not Sanjay but Abu Salem. Prem Bedi said that when he confronted Salem in Lisbon, he asked him in disbelief if he was indeed Abu Salem. Salem's response was, as Bedi recalled, 'I am being framed.'

'He used to call me Papa,' Bedi told me. 'He said, "Papa, I am innocent."'

It seemed that Salem got him to believe he was innocent and someone more powerful had framed him and used him. Perhaps Prem Bedi believed Salem as such a grave matter led him to question his own judgement as well.

He feared public backlash and hatred for his daughter in India. When he saw all the walls closing in on Monica, he told me, he had gone to meet an astrologer in Delhi with her *janampatri*. When the astrologer told him that his daughter was destined to spend time in jail, Prem Bedi found a good reason to blame her luck on her stars. With a smile on his face, Bedi shared the astrologer's words: 'Monica will bounce back and will be able to put her past behind her. She will soon be a free person, and will return to the entertainment business and earn fame and money again – this time on her own.'

On that hopeful note, I dropped him at his sister's house in Punjabi Bagh.

The stars finally favoured Monica Bedi in 2007, when the Supreme Court granted her bail in the passport forgery case, in which she had been sentenced to five years in prison by the Sessions Court. This was later commuted to three years by the

Monica Bedi at a social event in 2007, after being released by the court. Photo courtesy Mahendra Parikh.

Andhra Pradesh High Court. In November 2010, the apex court upheld her conviction and dismissed her appeal challenging her conviction, but the court also reduced her sentence to the period of imprisonment she had already undergone (two-and-a-half years). The Bhopal Court in Madhya Pradesh, where she faced a similar charge, later acquitted her. She returned to the entertainment business and is now back in various shows on television.

Interlude: Becoming a State Witness

WHEN DETAILS ABOUT THE ALLEGED involvement of the underworld in the making of *Chori Chori Chupke Chupke* were made public in 2001, I filed a cover story on the film's financier Bharat Shah's arrest and his relations with the Mumbai mafia; the story also carried a transcript of the conversation between Chhota Shakeel, Shah and the film's producer Nazim Rizvi, and an interview I had done of Shakeel over the phone. The story that shook the film industry, until then living in denial about the involvement of the underworld in their finances and related affairs, appeared in January 2001. I left for the US for a two-month leave soon after it was published.[1]

In mid-February, I got a call from a senior colleague at the Mumbai office, saying that the Mumbai Police had come to the office with a search warrant issued by the special MCOCA Court, looking for any recordings of Chhota Shakeel's interviews filed by me. My colleagues wanted to know if I had left the keys of my work cabinet at home in Mumbai and whether they could access my apartment to look for it.

Not all of my interviews with Shakeel had been recorded, but there were a couple that had been recorded for my convenience. The don had the habit of talking fast and in exceptionally long sentences, and it was tough to take all of it down during the conversation. Further, a single untrue quote or word could result in consequences I had no desire to face. I had, however, made the mistake of locking some of these tapes in my office cabinet – I regretted this, but it was too late now – and the Mumbai Police took away the few tapes that were there after filing a *panchnama*. Two of my colleagues at the Mumbai bureau signed on the *panchnama* as witnesses.

When I returned in March, Shankar Kamble, then assistant commissioner of police at Mumbai's Crime Branch, sent me a summons. I knew ACP Kamble as I would regularly go to the Crime Branch as part of my work, and when I met him after coming back I told him he need not have sent me an official notice and he could have just picked up his phone and called me. I had, however, failed to read between the lines. By the time I understood what it was that he was asking of me, it was too late and I was in for a long roller-coaster ride. I was made one of the prime witnesses in the *Chori Chori Chupke Chupke* case (*State of Maharashtra vs Bharat Shanti Lal Shah & Ors 2001*) by ace public prosecutor Rohini Salian.[2]

For the first time in my career I realized that every good story comes with a price. I was not sure of the implications my deposition would have, but I was certain that Chhota Shakeel, and my other underworld sources, would never talk to me again. I was angry, but was left with no choice. What troubled me was the fact that I had failed to think about the consequences when I had filed the story. The other thought that struck me strongly was that this was a question on my credibility and integrity. I tried to resist and confronted the officers who had put me in this situation, but to no avail.

One of Bollywood's most influential film financiers, Bharat Shah had been booked under the MCOCA for aiding and abetting Chhota Shakeel's activities in the film industry. The 'activities' mostly revolved around extortion and film financing, with Shah accused of being a respectable front for Shakeel. When he was arrested, 'Bharat-bhai' was one of Bollywood's most powerful men. His arrest was based on the transcript of two separate taped conversations between Shah and Shakeel. The first contained references made by producer Nazim Rizvi of Shah and their dealings in connection with the film *Chori Chori Chupke Chupke*. In the second, Shah had discussed business and *hawala* deals pertaining to the same film. The Mumbai Police had unearthed documentary evidence linking Shah's business with the mafia, which was produced in court to substantiate the charges levelled against the duo. The charges were non-bailable and under the MCOCA, Shah could be kept in custody for close to 18 months. In a rare turnaround, the Supreme Court accepted his ninth bail plea after Shah hired a team of nine high-powered lawyers, including Kapil Sibal and Ram Jethmalani. It had cost him nearly ₹10 crore to get the bail appeal upheld.

As for me, the state wanted me to identify a voice on the tape and confirm whether it belonged to Chhota Shakeel, as I had spoken to him many times before in the course of investigating a story or interviewing him. The brains behind this plan were Salian and D. Sivanandan, then joint police commissioner (Crime) Mumbai Police. Sivanandan and his crack team dealing with the case didn't budge from their decision to put me in the witness dock to identify the don's voice. The Crime Branch was looking at a potential conviction which could be a landmark judgement to curb the underworld–Bollywood financial nexus. My 'normal' conversation with ACP Kamble in his tiny cabin at the Crime Branch then became my 'witness statement' to the Mumbai Police, which was later read out to me in court. I realized that Sivanandan had taken a chance and was relying heavily on my professional credibility and integrity, but I was still apprehensive and unhappy about the situation.

An experienced and intelligent officer, Sivanandan gave me a pep-talk to make me feel better. In turn, I expressed my predicament to Sivanandan. 'What if the dons harm me?' I asked him pointedly. He smiled at me and said, 'Madam Raval, you are a courageous and sincere citizen of this country. Isn't this your moral responsibility? We will provide you protection and you have nothing to fear.'

He repeatedly told me to trust him, but I could not. More than anything else, I began to view my court appearance as the event that would bring about the end of my crime reporting career. When I left his office that day, I felt hugely disappointed. I agreed with his statement that it was my moral responsibility, but I had refused his offer for security. I couldn't imagine myself moving around with armed guards. I wasn't sure how my family would react to it. My father had warned me against my tendency to take undue risks. He had said that not many people like to hear or see the truth once it is out. And most people don't have the appetite for it either. It was a little late in the day to follow my father's advice. I found out much later that some senior officials who respected my professionalism had also resisted the idea of putting me at risk.

It wasn't fear that had made me anxious, though. In fact, I was more upset than afraid as I believed that my access to the D Company would be severed, which would be a big professional loss.

When the trial began, the witness summons was served at my office one afternoon to the security guard. I informed my editor and was asked to speak with our in-house legal counsel, who gave me some tips on how to handle the situation in court. I realized that his presence in the court would not help me much, as this was my battle and I had to fight it on my own.

I chose an in-camera trial procedure for my deposition and cross-examination, which would mean that the public and the press would not be allowed to observe the procedure. The presiding judge, Justice A.P. Bhangale, asked me why I did not want the media to report on my deposition. After all, I was from the media. He suggested that if I assented to media coverage of the court process, it could inspire others to come out and help the system. However, I stuck to my choice of an in-camera trial. As I explained to the judge, this was simply to avoid any misinterpretations. I felt very strongly that I had to avoid any publicity around my deposition process in the media as I was not sure about the kind of questions I would be asked in court, and I also wished to avoid the glaring eyes of those who would dissect my professional skills in public. The court granted my request, and only the accused, their legal help, the concerned police officials and court officials, and the judge were present at the closed-door proceeding.

My deposition lasted for six days, from 11 a.m. to 3 p.m. each day. Both Shah and Rizvi had hired top-notch defence lawyers, Harshad Ponda, Majid Memon, Shiraz Rahemtulla and Shrikant Shivde. When Public Prosecutor Salian read out a statement purportedly made by me, I wondered when I had given such a statement. Then I remembered my conversation with ACP Kamble in his office and realized that was what made up the statement she had read out; this was not a statement I had signed, as I would have under other circumstances. I mentally noted that in criminal cases statements are not given but taken.

After Salian explained to the court the need for me to be a witness in the case, the recordings of my interviews, which were seized from the *India Today* office, were played in court. These were not related to the case but were recorded on different occasions and then published in the magazine. Usually, the witness is made to stand in a wooden box as you typically see in movies. But in my case, Judge Bhangale was considerate and allowed me to sit on a chair for the daily four-hour procedure. I felt acutely awkward as the courtroom, with nearly 60 to 70 people present – the accused, their lawyers, the judge, the court staff and police – listened to my conversations with Chhota Shakeel. Here was another lesson for me to learn: to be precise, clear and careful in my interaction with underworld dons in the future. The deposition was a massive learning process for me. It completely changed my outlook on reporting. From here on, I learnt to factor in all possible perceptions that a story might generate and to handle them patiently and with thought and precision to avoid such episodes in future.

The cross-examination was a unique experience too. Reporting from the court is vastly different from participating in its proceedings as a witness. As a correspondent covering the crime beat, I knew most of the criminal lawyers in Mumbai. I often used quotes from them in my articles. But whatever familiarity I had with the lawyers went out of the window once they began to cross-examine me. They were there to defend their clients, who were facing grave charges, and they had been paid to win the case. The onus was on the public prosecutor to make me identify the person I was talking to, while the job of the defence advocates was to nullify my stand. They were there to destroy all arguments made against their clients. It was clearly an us-versus-them battle, and they used every trick in the book to intimidate and overwhelm me.

Some showed aggression in their body language, while others voiced preconceived opinions about me to extract a desired response. One of the lawyers made sexist remarks from the bench to provoke me, to which I raised an objection to the court and he had to apologize. The questions were a mix of the clever, the crass and the bizarre. I had to be alert and focused all the time. My strategy was to respond to the question and not react. Since it was my first-ever (and hopefully last!) experience as a witness, I was told that all my answers would have to be addressed to the court (in this case, the presiding judge). This was handy, as I realized I could avoid looking at the advocate who was coaxing or provoking me to give an answer that would suit them. I turned my back to them and answered the judge directly, and this helped me to remain calm in a tense situation.

The crux of the matter was that the prosecution wanted to prove that the person I had interviewed over the phone and had identified as Chhota Shakeel was indeed him, and no one else. The defence wanted to contest the prosecution's stand, challenging it on the grounds that I had no way to be sure that the person talking to me was Shakeel himself. I had never met Shakeel; I had only seen his photos in police dossiers. Apart from witness voice identification, the forensic voice matching had already been carried out, and the results had turned out to be positive.

One of the advocates sought my answers in a simple 'yes' or 'no' format, telling me that was how witnesses always answered. When I insisted to the court that all my answers could not be in the yes-or-no format, the judge supported my point. The advocate then started playing mind games in different languages, perhaps wanting to capitalize on the fact that I spoke four languages – English, Hindi, Gujarati and Marathi. Another advocate came prepared, carrying all my *India Today* reports on the Mumbai underworld, reading lines from them and asking me how I had found out about certain situations and why a gangster was comfortable talking to me. As I answered him, his questions continued: How had I got a gangster's number? Had I had verified the information criminals had given me? How did I know that the criminals had not deliberately misled me and the magazine? Essentially, he was nit-picking my stories to throw me off-track. However, Judge Bhangale intervened and said he would like to read the articles, and after reading them he commented that they were all reasonable stories. I knew that was the end of my five-day-long ordeal.

I noticed Shah and Rizvi, seated on the back benches of the court, watching me avidly and listening to every word I uttered. I knew Shah from earlier. He had invited me to his daughter Reshma's grand wedding at the Wankhede Stadium and I had reported on the event. The man, who at any given time would have had at least two dozen films in various stages of production, looked worn out and sad. I felt uncomfortable seeing him in that position.

In October 2003, Judge Bhangale sentenced Shah to one year's rigorous imprisonment on the charge of facilitating extortion activities by the underworld, and awarded six years' jail term to producer Nazim Rizvi and his assistant, Abdul Rahim Allah Baksh, for extorting money from Bollywood personalities. Rizvi and Abdul Rahim were also fined ₹5 lakh each under MCOCA provisions for forging links with the underworld and targeting film personalities. The court ruled that as Shah had already spent 14 months in jail, he should be released.

Shah had challenged the constitutional validity of the stated provisions on the grounds that the state government had no jurisdiction over interception of telephone communications. But on 1 September 2008, the Supreme Court in effect affirmed the constitutional validity of the MCOCA, a state law that empowered the state government to intercept telephone calls and use the results as evidence in cases pertaining to organized crime, including terrorist cases.

This was the first major victory for the Mumbai Police after they had begun to crack down on the Bollywood–underworld nexus a decade ago. A jubilant Sivanandan thanked me after the judgement and said that my testimony against the underworld would leave a mark in police and legal history. Yet I felt the loss professionally; I had lost access to the D Company and now any chance I had of interviewing them in person had been lost too.

Fortunately, that was not so. As I've described earlier, four years after my appearance in court, my phone rang one evening, soon after I had finished recording a show for Star News in Mumbai. I took the call impatiently, but on hearing Chhota Shakeel's familiar voice of on the other side, my annoyance dissolved. I was relieved to know that in the process of giving my deposition my credibility had remained intact on both sides.

Bharat Shah is now back to financing films, and his core diamond business is still going strong. But his conviction in this case was seen as a warning and a tough lesson for all Bollywood personalities inclined to use mafia money in their films. Since Shah's conviction, no mafia names or links have been flaunted by anyone in the industry, but allegedly underworld links continue to be maintained in the shadows.

PART 2
The 'Hindu' Dons

Bedlam in Bangkok

'THE DON IS ALIVE AND SAFE in Samitivej Hospital's special ICU room,' Jelly, a businessman in Bangkok, announced nonchalantly. He looked unassuming at first glance, with his Sufi turban and thin beard. However, what he shared over a cappuccino came as a pleasant surprise. 'Rajan Nikhalje, aka Vijay Kadam (alias Chhota Rajan), survived the attack on him,' he said. 'He escaped with one bullet in his abdomen and another in his right thigh. There were 10 assailants (four Pakistanis, four Indians and two Thai nationals), and five of them were arrested 30 minutes ago.'

I paid careful attention to every little detail.

Jelly's calm and clinical approach brought more gravity to the matter. As for me, I was simply trying not to show my excitement over this sudden rush of information. He pulled out some papers from a white envelope and laid them out on the table. He continued in the same tone, 'These are the sketches of the assailants who have been caught from Robinson departmental store in Bang Rak. They hold Pakistani passports.' I was left speechless for a few moments; it felt like I had hit the jackpot. But being a journalist, I thought it necessary to raise some doubts over the facts. Jelly then made me talk to a Thai official who was handling the operation. He confirmed the news and agreed to meet me the next evening. This was brilliant stuff; to put it simply, a real 'scoop'.

On 14 September 2000, Chhota Shakeel had called the English national daily, the *Times of India*, taking credit on behalf of the D Company for killing their arch-rival Chhota Rajan in Bangkok. The air was rife with speculation over the gangster's bloody end after the daily broke the story on 16 September. The Intelligence Bureau was unsure whether he was actually dead, while the Mumbai Police got busy trying to confirm the news. I reached Bangkok on 18 September, after a frantic call from my editor at *India Today*, Prabhu Chawla, the previous afternoon telling me I was to fly to the Thai capital that evening.[1]

It took me 16 hours to reach the city, flying in from Mumbai via Singapore, as there were no direct flights available at the time. It was my first visit to Thailand, and I did not know a soul in the city leave alone understand the language. The long journey had tired me out, and the impending deadline became pressing with every passing minute. All I had as help was a local reference for logistical assistance provided by a friend in Mumbai who was an IPS officer. Upon reaching the Thai capital at about 4 p.m. the next day, I immediately called the local contact, AA, to tell him I had landed and would need his help to go around the city. His enthusiastic voice was music to my ears. A second-generation Indian living in Thailand, AA informed me that he had booked me a room at the Holiday Inn on Sukhumvit Road.

Around 7 p.m., a smartly dressed tall and lanky man in his forties came to meet me with a shorter man who wore a dark suit and a Sufi turban. AA introduced me to Jelly, the man in the turban, as someone who was 'an influential guy in the city's power circuit'. I noticed a white envelope in his hand which he handed over to me and said, 'You have some breaking news, my friend.'

I felt dizzy and tried hard to control my excitement. I immediately faxed a copy of the documents to the *India Today* office in Delhi, and also to the team producing the news bulletin,

Aaj Tak, which ran as a daily news show on Doordarshan then. *Aaj Tak* flashed the exclusive scoop: 'Rajan alive! Critical in Samitivej Hospital. Five shooters arrested after chase at a Bangkok mall. All were from Pakistan.' I relayed all the information I had over the next hour on the phone to the anchor in Delhi. It was my debut in broadcast news and my first phone-in interview on television that featured my mugshot.

I found out later that a few of my relatives and friends who had watched the show had been horrified to see me on television chasing a gang war story. Some even reprimanded my parents for permitting me to go to Bangkok. My father's friends cautioned him that no one would marry me if I was seen chasing mafia dons. To be fair, some of my friends called to congratulate me as well. When I called home that night, my mother simply told me to be careful in a foreign country. She was, nonetheless, happy to have seen me on television.

However, that first spell of relief was short-lived. A bigger challenge lay ahead of me: how was I to reach a badly wounded Rajan in the secluded ICU ward in the hospital besides verifying the information provided by my sources? My first thought was that Indian diplomatic officers posted in Bangkok could be helpful. I left for the embassy the next day, and there the Indian Ambassador to Thailand at the time, R.K. Rai, was extremely cooperative. He not only confirmed the information that I already had on the assassination attempt, but provided some more.

Rai informed me that the Thai Police had seized a few passports from Chhota Rajan's aide Rohit Verma's flat in Sawan Court, where Rajan had been staying. Both Rajan and Rohit were living under new identities – Rajan was known as Vijay Ramakrishna Kadam and Rohit as Michael D'Souza. Though Rajan had a passport in his own name, Rajendra Sadashiv Nikhalje, he was using another passport in the name of Lipendra Ailib from

Lucknow while travelling in East Asia. Verma had opened a jewellery shop in Bangkok with a Thai partner due to local trade restriction rules. The ambassador told me that Rajan had been operating out of Malaysia, Cambodia, Vietnam and Taiwan in recent years, but had been living in Thailand for the last two years.

When I asked him if he could help me reach Rajan, his response was cryptic: 'You find your way. My hands are tied.' I did not quite understand his words. I knew that the previous night's news on Rajan's survival had generated a buzz in India, and North Block had not been too happy with the detailed reporting. I had been told all of this by a senior official at the embassy. It was only later, when I was back at the embassy the next day that I realized what he had meant. Despite an appointment, the ambassador's office told me that he would be 'busy' for the day as some urgent matter had cropped up. When I requested for an evening appointment, I was told very politely 'off-the-record' that it would be difficult because 'Delhi' had shown displeasure at the ambassador's 'cooperation with the media'.

I was now running out of time, as I had to file a story in a few hours. I called Jelly for help, and he asked me to meet him outside the hospital premises a little after noon. Once there, we went up to the second floor from the back entrance. Jelly obviously knew his way around. We crossed a narrow dark passage and saw two armed guards standing outside one of the corner rooms. Jelly spoke to them in Thai, and then turned to me and said that it was Rajan's room. I had not expected my access to Rajan to come about so easily. Nevertheless, the only thing on my mind then was that I needed to reach him quickly and file my story, based on solid facts, within the deadline.

I had to take over from here, and was now on my own. Jelly left me in the lobby, from where I could see the two guards outside the door. As I walked around the corner, I heard someone addressing me in a familiar language. '*Tum India se ho*? (Are you from India?)', asked a tall, dark man who was standing with three other men outside the room. At the corner of the passage was an L-shaped bench on which there sat a lady with an infant. The four of them seemed to be together. What struck me immediately was the man's Marathi accent. A senior official from the Mumbai Crime Branch had told me that four of Rajan's loyal aides had left for Bangkok from Mumbai. These four individuals matched the descriptions I had of the men.

I immediately replied in Marathi, '*Mee Mumbaikar aahe.* (I am from Mumbai.)' The man's face lit up, as if he had finally found someone to talk to in his language in a completely strange place. He told me ruefully, '*Teen diwas pasoon ekdum ithe baslo aahe pan konala bhasha samjat nahi. Tumala Thai samajte tari jara madat kara. Khayala pan problem aahe.* (We have been sitting here in the hospital for the past three days, but no one seems to understand our language. We haven't even eaten properly. Please help us if you can speak their language.)'

The infant began to cry, and the lady, who had Thai features, turned to pacify the child. I told the group that I was a journalist and was there to report on Rajan's health situation. We continued to converse in Marathi. One of them narrated the incidents of the evening Rajan was shot. He pointed to the lady, Kamla (Rohit Verma's Thai maid), and Verma's child, who had witnessed the attack, and told me that 'Nana' (as Rajan was addressed by his men) had been shot twice, but both the bullets had been taken out during the surgery that had followed. At present there was no threat to his life; but being a diabetic his response to the treatment was slower than a normal person's. One of the bullets had hit his lower abdomen and damaged multiple organs, including his kidney.

The men were happy that Rajan had survived the bloody attack. Then they began to talk about their rivalry and declared vengeance. All of them believed that if 'Nana' killed Dawood, it would be a great 'service to the nation' – and only he was capable of doing the deed. It was here that I heard the word '*deshbhakt* (patriot)' being used for the first time to describe Rajan.

It was clear that I could not enter Rajan's room without their help. I told the men that I wanted to see Rajan and, if possible, speak to him and expressed my doubts about the Thai Police guarding the doors allowing me in. One of them stood up and asked me to follow him. As he led me inside, he said: '*Kalji karu naka. Nana cha layi power aahe ithe aani police aapli je aahe. Suraksha sathi paise aapan jedeto karan nana varkaahi case nahi ithe. Udayla plane suddha aahe.* (Don't worry about that; Nana is a powerful person here as well. His sympathizers look after the Thai police properly, and a jet is on standby to take him away because there is no case against him here. He was paying the Thai Police for his own security.)' It was evident that the Thai Police were also standing guard to ensure Rajan was not attacked inside the hospital, and I figured Colonel Kerkpong of the Thai Police was in-charge of the hospital's security.

I had only seen two-decade-old photos of Rajan from his police dossier, the most popular of which was his wedding picture with Sujata – a stout Marathi groom and a young bride posing happily with Rajan's best friend Dawood Ibrahim and his wife, Mehjabeen, by their side.

Here, inside the hospital room, rested a bulky middle-aged man, wired to various machines and a drip, looking helpless and tame. Rajan turned his face towards me groggily. He tried to focus his eyes. I quickly introduced myself while he mumbled some words. I leaned forward to listen to him. Initially, when I was introduced as a journalist from *India Today*, he spoke to me in broken English. Then he reverted to colloquial Mumbaiya Marathi–Hindi and said that I should wait for him to get better to hear his story. He looked at the ceiling and thanked God for saving his life.

An old photograph of Dawood and Chhota Rajan with their wives, Mehjabeen and Sujata.

Just then, a good-looking, fair-skinned man walked into the room and looked taken aback to find me there. He gave the man who had brought me into the room a disapproving look, and I heard the man next to me mutter, 'Santosh is trying to be the boss.' Then he promptly introduced me to the new entrant: 'He is Nana's *khaas manus* (lieutenant), Santosh Shetty.' Shetty looked displeased at finding me there, and told me unequivocally, 'He is extremely unwell. This isn't the time or place to interview him. It's better that you avoid mentioning this meeting at all, particularly his health situation and whatever he said or has happened inside the room. Please do not even mention that you met me here, as it will create problems for my hosts. They (the Dawood gang) have broken the rules of not targeting women and children in our fight. We will fight back.' He was referring to Rohit's wife, who was fatally shot in the attack.

So anxious was I to get the story that I did not want to leave and tried to convince him to let me stay, ignoring the fact that he was trying to intimidate me. It was an opportunity that I did not want to miss. The very thought of having come so far and returning without an interview was a real letdown. I persisted and kept chatting him up as reporters usually do, but all he did was to concede that I could mention I had visited the hospital and the room without quoting any conversations.

And then, as I turned around to leave, making no secret of my disappointment and reluctance, he seemed to sense something. 'Madam,' he said, as I turned around hoping that he had changed his mind. '*Aap baat samjho na, madam. Likhna nahin jo dekha aur suna, madam. Dekho na, achha nahin hoga. Hum safe to aap bhi safe rahenge.* (Please understand, madam. Please do not report what you have seen or heard today. Please understand, it won't be nice at all. If we are safe, you will remain safe too.)'

The air suddenly tensed up. I noticed the other four men had left the corridor. Shetty softened his tone and said, 'We may do the interview some other time if the situation is more conducive. If Nana won't speak, I will tell you our side of the story.' I nodded my head as I hardly had a choice. He walked me out till the staircase.

I had my story, but I really wished I could mention my brief conversation with Chhota Rajan. From what I had heard from the four men, I had gathered that Rajan and Dawood were locked in a proxy war between India and Pakistan. But what really grabbed my attention was that the gangsters were confident of the then Maharashtra Home Minister Chhagan Bhujbal's inability to effectively push the extradition case against Chhota Rajan. Even as Bhujbal was preparing to send in a team of four officials to pursue Rajan's extradition from Bangkok, these men were talking about the don's safe escape to an unknown destination with the help of some powerful officials. They claimed to have more friends than foes in the Mumbai Police and the IB. According to them,

Rajan was not damaging India but helping the authorities destroy Dawood and his criminal network. They believed that Rajan and his associates could help India fight Dawood and his Pakistani patrons. I realized that the theory that Rajan was being treated with kid gloves by Indian authorities to neutralize Dawood was not entirely baseless.

Nevertheless, I was happy that I was allowed to click a picture of Kamla, an eyewitness to the attack on Rajan. She was inside the kitchen when she heard the gunshots and the ensuing commotion. When she rushed out, she saw Rohit and his wife lying on the floor of the living room in a pool of blood. Horrified, Kamla collapsed on the floor. One of the assailants pointed his gun at her and pushed her inside a bedroom with Rohit's child and locked the room from outside. The manager of the Sawan Court estate later told me that it was Rajan who had got Kamla and the child out of the locked room despite being badly wounded himself.

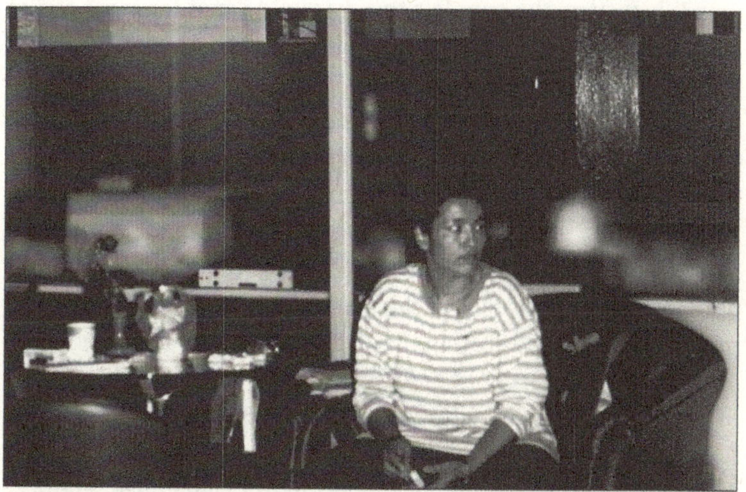

Rohit Verma's maid Kamla outside Chhota Rajan's room at the Samitivej Hospital in Bangkok. Photo courtesy India Today Archives.

I enquired into the events of the shootout, and found that, between 7.30 and 8 p.m. that night, eight people wearing formal clothes arrived at the Sawan Court estate with a big cake. They told the security guard that they had been invited to D'Souzas' (Rohit Verma's alias) party. The guard asked them to wait while he confirmed this with the D'Souzas. But one of the eight pushed the guard through the window grill and knocked him down with the butt of a gun. While four of them waited downstairs in the lobby, four others went up to the first-floor flat. One of the two Thais among them held the cake while the other rang the doorbell. Verma and his wife were watching television, and on hearing the doorbell Verma peered through the eyehole and saw two Thai men standing outside their door with the cake. When he opened the door, the four men barged in and opened fire on him. His wife tried to shield him and died in the crossfire. Verma died on the spot. Kamla rushed out of the kitchen on hearing the gunshots, and one of the gunmen asked her, 'Where is the other man?' Just then, the couple's two-year-old daughter came out of a room, and she was immediately pushed into a room along with the maid and locked inside.

Pushing the couple's bodies aside, they began to scour the apartment for Rajan. Suddenly, in the dark, they saw the silhouette of a figure jumping from a bedroom balcony into a garden below. The four men shot blindly, hitting Rajan in the abdomen and the right thigh. Even as other residents of the quiet Sukhumvit neighbourhood woke up at the sound of gunshots, Rajan stayed put in the garden until he heard the last of the gunmen leave. Despite being severely injured, he returned to the apartment and found Verma and his wife dead. He called his close aide Guru Satam to tell him about the attack, and then made three more calls in the next few minutes, the last to the Thai Police. Minutes later, Rajan was wheeled into the Samitivej Hospital's ICU for emergency surgery.

It was now essential for me to visit the Sawan Court flat, located in an upmarket diplomatic enclave on Soi 26 in Sukhumvit. AA drove me there in his black S-Class Mercedes. The apartment was at the end of a narrow lane in a secure diplomatic area. The manager of the estate took me around the premises except for Verma's flat, which had been sealed off by the Thai Police. It was a plush colony with a swimming pool and a manicured garden. I noticed that Verma's first-floor apartment's balcony was at least 20 feet high. I wondered how a badly wounded Rajan could have jumped from that balcony to escape his assailants. Shakeel later claimed that Rajan had jumped out of the balcony into an open garbage dump and managed to escape. But it was a plush colony and there was no place for a garbage dump below his balcony or anywhere around the colony. The manager of the complex told me 'Mr Kadam' (Rajan's alias) was lucky to survive, and he had called the police himself. 'Mr Kadam' had looked visibly shaken after the attack, as though he had never imagined he could be so brutally attacked inside his own apartment, he said.

According to the guard at the colony's gate, Rajan and Rohit did not own any vehicle and instead used local cabs for transportation. They often walked up to the apartment from the road on foot, about 500 metres away. The obvious question on my mind was, why weren't Rajan and Rohit attacked in the secluded lane? As Shakeel had revealed later, they had been tracked for over a month. Shakeel's squad of ten shooters had hired an apartment at Amiree Court adjacent to Sawan Court. The conspirators had even found a flat that overlooked the front gate of Sawan Court, enabling them to keep a close watch on their quarry.

According to the Mumbai Police's inquiry report published later, sometime in July or August 2000, Chhota Shakeel was informed that Rohit Verma was staying in Bangkok as Michael D'Souza, along with his wife Sangeeta and their two-year-old daughter, and that Chhota Rajan was staying with them. He directed Munna Zingada to visit Bangkok and locate the two of them. On 31 August 2000, Munna Zingada flew to Bangkok on a Pakistan International Airlines flight from Karachi via Nepal. Three others accompanied him to the Thai capital, where he was asked to rent out a hotel room and wait for further instructions. As directed by Shakeel, Munna contacted a man named Cirrac, a local readymade garments dealer. Having learnt that Verma was living in the Sukhumvit area on Soi 26, Munna secured an accommodation in Amiree Court in the same area with Cirrac's help and succeeded in locating Verma's flat. Once Munna passed on the information to Shakeel, the latter arranged for the hit-team to reach Bangkok from Karachi on 11 September 2000, where they were received by Munna and taken to the flat in Amiree Court.

When I voiced my doubts before Colonel Manthan Apaivongs, superintendent of Thonglor police station and the main investigating officer in the case, he said, 'It is more than mere business or gang rivalry for sure. The case was easily cracked because the criminals had left behind a lot of evidence. There are lots of questions, like how could eight people with 9mm guns fail to kill Kadam when they could kill D'Souza and his wife?'

Jelly and AA had come along with me to the police station. Jelly, who was here as my interpreter as Manthan could only speak Thai, then asked him, on my behalf, if I could meet one of the assailants.

Manthan first showed me all the arrested assailants' Pakistani passports, then obliged me by getting the man he called Saleem Mohammed, the main assailant in the attack, to meet me. Mohammed slowly walked into Manthan's office in chains and handcuffs, and was made to sit on the chair across from him – and next to me.

Manthan introduced me, and I interviewed Saleem for about 20 minutes in Hindi. He spoke about revenge and his failure in the mission, and expressed no remorse in killing the innocent Sangeeta, Rohit Verma's wife. He simply said, 'We did not do it deliberately. She (Sangeeta) jumped in front of her husband to shield him. We respect her. She is a very brave woman.' He also said that the attack had been carried out at Rohit's house because Dawood had given them explicit instructions that Thai citizens should not be hurt. I then asked him how the attack was planned. 'I arrived in Bangkok and searched for Rohit,' he said. 'Bhai managed to lure him by promising to make him the next boss of Rajan's gang.' And why was Rohit killed after all this? Succinctly, Saleem said, 'He double-crossed us.' AA took our pictures with Manthan's permission to keep on record.

Later, the Mumbai Crime Branch DCP told me that the assailant I had interviewed was not Saleem Mohammed from Pakistan but Munna Zingada from the Mumbai suburb Jogeshwari. He was a wanted criminal, and had jumped bail and managed to flee the country for Pakistan via Nepal.

Manthan's information on the activities of Chhota Shakeel and his boys in Bangkok added more twists to a simple gang rivalry and revenge story. What was more disquieting was the reason cited by the Thai Police as the immediate provocation for the attack: large stakes in a major arms smuggling racket. They believed that both gangs had bid for the same consignment, and the attempt on Rajan was to keep him out of the game as he had previously sabotaged a D Company racket involving fake currency. The shoot-out, it seemed, had occurred after negotiations for a settlement had failed. Chhota Shakeel had been tipped off about Rajan's presence in Bangkok and had put his team on the job to find their rival. Rajan had eventually been spotted by members of the D Company at a Bangkok hotel in May.

According to Manthan, Shakeel had been visiting Bangkok regularly from July onwards to oversee the progress on the plan.

In fact, Shakeel had been in Bangkok till the day of the attack, and had reportedly met Rajan at Hotel Tara (Saleem Mohammed, aka Munna Zingada, had booked two rooms at Hotel Lucky and Hotel Tara under his own name for Shakeel). However, when I interviewed him over the telephone on 26 September, Shakeel denied having met Rajan; in fact, he said he would have killed Rajan if he had met him at the hotel as had been reported. To quote a part of our conversation:

> **Me**: What was the purpose of your recent Bangkok trip between 11 and 13 September?
>
> **Shakeel**: How did you know? I can't tell you the inside story but I visited Bangkok regularly over the past three months. I left the city just a day before my boys went to his (Rajan's) house to kill him. I had to finalize the operation and escape route for my boys. It was not just an important operation but also a prestige issue for us... We knew that it was a tough task as he was also heavily armed.
>
> **Me**: And yet your operation failed?
>
> **Shakeel**: I am not God. Things went wrong and we made mistakes. But it happens in such operations. He was lucky but a coward. Instead of facing bullets like a good warrior, he ran away. Anyway, better luck next time. My man, Munna Zingada, who is in police custody now is a capable man and he won't miss a second chance. He got caught because he called me from a public booth and his phone was tracked down immediately.[2]

When I asked him why he wanted to kill Rajan, Shakeel simply said they had to eliminate Rajan because 'he is not just a traitor but is instead trying to become a patriot'.

The author interviewing Munna Zingada in Bangkok in the presence of Colonel Manthan Apaivongs, superintendent of the Thonglor police station, Bangkok. Photo courtesy India Today Archives.

'Tell me, what has he done for India? He is just another gangster like us. How can a criminal like him be a patriot, and if he is one of them, what about the *kurbani* of the hundreds of *jawans* who sacrificed themselves in the Kargil war?' Shakeel asked me pointedly. He put the blame for the attack squarely on Rajan, who he said had made the gang wars a communal issue by calling himself a 'Hindu don'. 'He is responsible for dividing gangs on religious grounds... The game should be equal and fair.'

In the same conversation, Shakeel denied being supported by the ISI. Instead, he said, 'We have no doubt that Rajan is supported by Indian intelligence and is protected by Indian authorities.' When I asked him how he knew this, he said they had high-level sources among the police in Bangkok who had told him that Rajan was being protected by Indian intelligence officials there. He confirmed that the reason they attacked Rajan at his house was because 'we did not want to disturb our equation with the Thai authorities', and said they had no businesses at all in Thailand, refuting all reports of the D Company's involvement in supplying arms to the LTTE.

While the accused, Munna Zingada, subsequently told reporters that there was 'enmity between the two gangs' and 'we will attempt to kill Chhota Rajan again',[3] Rajan himself told a Thailand court later on 28 September, 'In Thailand and India, I have no enemies. I am not aware who they were trying to kill. There has been no attempt on my life and I don't know any of the shooters.'[4] It was a blatant lie but Rajan probably needed to buy more time to recuperate and leave Thailand without legal strings attached.

Born into a Marathi family in Mumbai in 1959, Rajendra Sadashiv Nikhalje, aka Chhota Rajan, grew up in the lower middle-class locality of Tilaknagar in Chembur, a suburb in central Mumbai. He started his criminal career in the 1980s by black-marketing cinema tickets; it was at this time that he met his mentor Rajan Nair, aka Bada Rajan, under whom he learned the tricks of the trade. He took over his mentor's gang after Bada Rajan was killed at Esplanade Court in 1983 by their rivals, the Pathan gang. Bada Rajan and Dawood Ibrahim had joined hands against the might of the Pathan gang, and after Bada Rajan's murder Chhota Rajan and Dawood became allies. In the mid-1980s, Dawood frequently shuttled between Dubai and Mumbai for the purposes of smuggling and, in his absence, Chhota Rajan supervised all his operations in Mumbai.

Between 1985 and 1986, Chhota Rajan was facing the heat in a case of assault on police officers near Sahakar cinema, which had come up for hearing at the Mumbai Sessions Court. There was every possibility of him being convicted as most of the witnesses

A TV grab of Chhota Rajan.

in the case were police personnel whom he could not win over. At around the same time, Arun Gawli's elder brother Kishor, aka Papa Gawli, was murdered over a drug deal, and once Gawli found out that both Dawood and Rajan were indirectly involved in the murder, he vowed to eliminate all those who were behind his brother's murder. With enemies and the law on his trail, Chhota Rajan escaped to Dubai, where he met up with Dawood, who had also jumped bail in the Amirjada Pathan case sometime in 1984 and had made Dubai his home. The gang wars that broke out in Mumbai in the following years kept Rajan in Dubai, where he remained till mid-1993.

Rajan's split from the D Company, which finally came about after the Mumbai blasts of 1993, was very dramatic. The genesis of the split explains the complicated relationship they share and its long-lasting impact on the Mumbai underworld.

To start with, Dawood and Rajan were close friends; with his vast number of shooters, Rajan carried out almost every killing on behalf of Dawood. He was instrumental in taking Sunil Sawant, aka Sawtya; Anil Parab, aka Wangya; Chhota Shakeel and Bhai Thakur, among others, to Dubai. However, in early 1992, this very group along with other members of the gang requested Dawood to clip Rajan's wings as they suspected he would pose a problem for them in the future. Sharad Shetty took the lead in vitiating the atmosphere and Sawtya told Dawood that, like Rajan, he too had enough muscle power to organize any killing in India, in essence proposing to replace Rajan. When I interviewed Shakeel in July 2015, he claimed that Rajan had not been comfortable inside the D Company even before the 1993 blasts. According to him, Rajan had embezzled one million dirhams from the organization, but Dawood had forgiven him for old times' sake.

In September 1992, Sawtya carried out the JJ Hospital shootout, in which D Company shooters killed Shailesh Haldankar, a member of Arun Gawli's gang, in retaliation for the killing of Ismail Parkar, Dawood's brother-in-law. Rajan, who would earlier plan all such operations, was kept in the dark about the shootout and found out about it only the day after it was executed. He realized he had fallen out of grace with Dawood. He railed against the caucus, and angered at his reaction Dawood declared that he should be killed and buried in Dubai itself. Noted gangster Bhai Thakur stepped in at this point to broker for peace between the two, and Rajan was asked to either go down on his knees and beg for forgiveness from the caucus or face death. He was given 12 hours to decide.

Rajan reportedly drove around Dubai and Sharjah in his Mercedes for most of those 12 hours, unsure about his next move. Finally, prudence prevailed and he publicly begged for his life before the caucus – on his knees, just as they had wanted. Considering his long association with and contribution to the gang, he was pardoned, but the rift was final. He was no longer given any important assignments. He was kept on the periphery of the Company's activities, but he knew that something big was cooking against him. From late 1992, he and other members of the gang had observed Dawood's new circle of powerful smuggler-friends from Pakistan who frequently visited the don and could be seen alongside Bollywood stars at the lavish parties Dawood hosted. Dawood was secretive about his dealings with the visitors and shared no details whatsoever with Rajan or the rest of the gang. Most of the D Company thought he was strategizing to expand his operations in foreign countries, but they would later find out that he had started a parallel drug smuggling operation with his Pakistani friends.

In 1993, in the aftermath of the serial blasts that rocked Mumbai, Rajan seized the opportunity to get out of the impasse. Indian authorities were actively seeking the extradition of Dawood and his brother, Anees, from Dubai in connection with the blasts and the brothers were compelled to leave the city overnight. With the help of his Pakistani friends, Dawood fled to Karachi and the rest of the gang was paralysed. Over the next few years, Dawood would sneak back into Dubai for quick visits but his mind remained focussed on his own future rather than the gang's business.

One of the four men whom I had met outside the hospital room had told me how Dawood had taken away Rajan's passport in Dubai. According to him, Rajan, like others in Dawood's gang, did not know Dawood was being aided by the ISI in his drug smuggling business. On one of his visits back to Dubai from Karachi Dawood called all his men, including Rajan, for a meeting, where he asked Rajan if he had his passport on him. When Rajan handed over his passport – which he mostly kept on himself, according to the man I spoke to – Dawood received a call on his satellite phone and went out to receive it. When Dawood did not return to the meeting after a long time, Rajan went out to look for him and was told by the guards that Dawood had left for Karachi on his boat – leaving Rajan stuck in Dubai without his passport!

Fearing for his life, Rajan decided to approach an Indian Embassy official whom he had met earlier. It is said he walked into the Indian Embassy late at night reportedly prepared to surrender to the authorities in a worst-case scenario. He would at least be alive then, is what he had figured. This move not only changed his life but also brought with it a new era of intense gang rivalry in Mumbai.

The twist in the tale is that not only did Rajan get a new passport under a new name, but he was also provided a ticket to Kuala Lumpur via Kathmandu. It is believed that, as a quid pro quo, he had to give away the details of Dawood's business interests across the world – legitimate and otherwise, and list his crime associates and all known ISI links.

Chhota Rajan had access to Dawood's networks, his clandestine operations and hideouts across the globe. He also knew enough about the syndicate's key personnel, Dawood's political friends in India, his financial conduits in India and Dubai, his nexus with police officers in Mumbai and other cities, his wealth and assets, his association with various arms and drug mafia organizations and international spy agencies, and also the various fronts that Dawood had floated across the subcontinent. In short, he knew everything about Dawood's strengths and weaknesses, and his information turned out to be very valuable for Indian agencies at a time when they were struggling to combat Dawood's ISI-instigated operations that were damaging India. This tacit support by agencies to Rajan was perceived by him as a reward for his 'help' for the good of the nation. With his rival now clearly marked out as India's enemy number one, his criminal actions took on a new meaning and a new perspective.

He gathered other members of Dawood's gang who were his supporters – among them Gurunath Narahari Satam, Rohit Verma, and Vicky Malhotra – and fled Dubai. Under his new identities, Vijay Ramchandra Kadam and Lipendra Ailib, Chhota Rajan and his newly formed gang then set up their illegal business network in Malaysia, Cambodia, Thailand and Vietnam successively.[5] In the years that followed, quite a few of Dawood's men fell away from the gang or defected to the Chhota Rajan camp, splitting the D Company practically down the middle. Chhota Shakeel, Abu Salem, Sharad Shetty and Sunil Sawant remained with Dawood, while Divakar Churi, Sanjay Raggad, Mohan Kotian and Pradip Madgaokar defected to Rajan's gang. Anil Parab remained within the D company as Rajan's mole and, actively assisted by Firoze Pathan, he passed on information on the Company's activities and operations to Rajan. Parab also had an excellent rapport with the Mohajirs of Karachi, who had migrated to Pakistan after the Partition, as well as the Nepalese underworld, and Rajan put this to good use for purposes of his own business.

With his intimate knowledge of the D Company's networks, Chhota Rajan began to target Dawood's supporters, financiers and gangsters. He arranged the killings of Philoo Khan in Bangkok, Thakiuddin Wahid of East-West Airlines in Mumbai and Sunil Sawant in Dubai, among others, which quickly established him as a force to reckon with. With his vast army of shooters, Rajan practically decimated Dawood's empire, at least in Mumbai. He also attempted to form new alliances with Dawood's sworn enemies or erstwhile friends. Ali Budesh of Bahrain joined hands readily with Rajan as he believed that an enemy's enemy is a friend. Through Dawood, Rajan had some connections with the Turkish–Cypriot underworlds, but it was difficult to be sure of their loyalties in the light of his differences with Dawood. His efforts at winning over Sharad Shetty through his brother-in-law, Prabhakar Punja, a smuggler-turned-hotelier from Mangalore, did not bear fruit and Sharad continued working with Dawood, only to get killed by Rajan later. Among the dons back in Mumbai, Rajan extended a hand of friendship to Arun Gawli, though the association was short-lived as Sada (Pawle) Mama of the Gawli gang was antagonistic towards Rajan. With the demise of Sada

Mama and another key member of their gang, Vijay Tandel, in a police encounter, a no-war pact was later drawn up between the two groups though no alliance grew of out Rajan's efforts. Ashwin Naik has also maintained a lukewarm attitude towards Rajan, though there is no history of hostility between the two.

News of various defections and ever-new alliances have constantly made the rounds, but what is less known about the extreme enmity between Dawood Ibrahim and Chhota Rajan is that between February 1997 and December 1998, Rajan made at least eight attempts to assassinate Dawood in Pakistan. Members of Rajan's gang are known to have acquired Nepalese passports to travel to Pakistan. In February 1997, Rajan's aides Vicky Malhotra and Farid Tanasha travelled to Karachi posing as clothes-sellers. They canvassed the area where Dawood lived at the time – Sea Face in Defence Colony – though they did not approach his house. In March 1997, Tanasha went to Pakistan on his own, rented a room at Al Mansoor Apartments in Defence Colony and tried to acquire weapons. A month later, Malhotra took seven armed men to Karachi, but could not carry out the operation as Dawood's movements were extremely secretive. The fourth time the team visited Karachi, a couple of months later, they took up a place in Defence Colony. But once again Dawood could not be tracked. When they returned two months later, the death of Dawood's daughter, Maria, kept him confined to his house. The team went back to Nepal for a while and returned again, hoping to spot Dawood at the graveyard, but the don had been tipped off and did not make an appearance. Rajan then called off the hit, fearing exposure. A seventh attempt was made in October 1998. One of Rajan's hitmen, Nayan, rented a house in Karachi and watched Dawood for 15 days, but once again, the plan did not materialize. The final attempt was made in December 1998, but Dawood's network averted any bid on his life.[6] (In 2015, former home secretary and BJP MP R.K. Singh revealed that the Indian government under former Prime Minister Atal Bihari Vajpayee had considered a covert operation against Dawood with the help of Chhota Rajan. It was the first admission to such a plan by someone who held a position of authority in the Indian government. Singh said that India had tied up with the Chhota Rajan gang to launch an operation to 'take down' Dawood, but Mumbai Police officials close to the D Company 'landed up at the training camp with arrest warrants for the covert operatives engaged by India'.[7])

With the battlelines finally drawn between the two dons, the rivalry between the two gangs reached its peak. The D Company responded to Rajan's assassination attempts with a vengeance, killing Rajan's financiers, lawyers, builders and political friends, including a few Shiv Sena shakha pramukhs and a BJP MLA from Mumbai. The war took the lives of several builders, advocates, politicians and industrialists in Mumbai, till it met its messy climax in September 2000 with an attack on Rajan himself.

The 1993 Mumbai blasts, in fact, led to a massive shift in Mumbai's underworld alliances. Rajan, with newfound confidence and covert support, not only termed the serial blasts 'anti-national' but also vowed to kill the accused involved in the blasts. As Shakeel had pointed out to me in a recent interview, he gave the split and ensuing gang wars a communal colour and polarized the underworld along religious lines. Rajan's efforts to project himself as an enemy of the Pakistani ISI, determined to avenge terrorism in India, was strategically aimed at winning the support of politicians and authorities, who seemed to believe Rajan's 'Hindu' spin could be an answer to Dawood's Muslim identity.

Over the years, Rajan has repeatedly invoked 'national interest' to justify his crimes and has used it well as a façade for his survival. In 1998 he planned the killing of Nepalese MP Mirza Dilshad Beg, allegedly the lynchpin of the ISI's activities in Nepal and Dawood's point man in Kathmandu. He had Sharad Shetty, Dawood's close associate, killed in Dubai in 2003 and plotted to eliminate Ehtesham Qutubuddin Siddiqui, an accused in the July 2006 blasts, though he did not succeed in the latter and Siddiqui was later awarded capital punishment along with five others found guilty of planting the bombs. Under his new 'nationalist' garb, Rajan called to threaten filmmaker Ram Gopal Verma in 2013 to tell him not to glorify a traitor like Dawood. He wanted to know why Verma was making a film on a 'deshdrohi' like Dawood. In his newfound jingoism, he has not spared the media either. And it was he who allegedly ordered the murder of crime journalist Jyotirmoy Dey in 2011 on the mere suspicion that Dey was helping his rival gang through his writings, and Shahid Azmi, a lawyer representing the terror accused.[8]

Back in Bangkok, I visited the Indian Embassy once more to use their computers to send some exclusive photos of the attack that were given to me by the Thai Police. But I received a somewhat cold response. Ambassador Rai said he was not in a position to confirm or deny any information related to Rajan, and suggested that I approach Delhi for more details on the case instead. The embassy could not upload the photos for some reason. Later, I was told by a senior IPS officer from Mumbai that Delhi had been closely following my reports from Bangkok.

After the bloody shoot-out that had left Rajan gravely injured, efforts had stepped up on the part of the Indian authorities to get the don extradited to India where he would stand trial for murder and other mob-related activities. On 5 October 2000, a four-member police team from Maharashtra visited Bangkok and informed the Thai Police that Vijay Kadam was none other than Chhota Rajan, and that he had fraudulently obtained an Indian passport.[9] Rajan was still in hospital, recuperating. The team questioned him at length in the hospital. The details of the attack on Rajan, and the eventual negotiations over his deportation, are contained in the inquiry report they submitted.[10] The team stayed in Bangkok for a month. One of the officials told me that they had convinced Rajan to return to India and had promised him security; the team asked for his consent in writing as the Thai authorities maintained that he was not a Thai national and was therefore free to go to Mumbai provided he was willing. But the team was to be disappointed, for Rajan changed his stance and decided not to return home with them. Later, the Mumbai Police surmised that Rajan may have consulted his mysterious handlers, who had advised him not to return to India as he would be unsafe in Mumbai.

On Monday, 21 November 2000, my sources in Bangkok called to inform me that Rajan had been driven out of the hospital to somewhere outside the country two days ago. His exit had been facilitated under some sort of unofficial diplomatic pressure. I wrote a small news item for *India Today*'s web edition on Tuesday afternoon after reconfirming the news with my sources in India.

That same evening, Chhota Shakeel called me on my office landline to suggest that my news on Rajan was incorrect. He said he had checked with his boys and his sources in the Thai Police, who had told him that Rajan had been shifted to another government hospital and had not escaped from Thailand. However, I maintained my stand. That Friday, the news agency Agence France-Presse (AFP) proved me right by carrying the news of Rajan's dramatic escape from the hospital. According to a statement issued by the Thai Police, Rajan had used knotted bedsheets to climb down from his balcony in the hospital.

Rajan's lawyer Sirichai Piapichetkul denied the statement and said that the police had been paid off to allow him to escape via an emergency exit. Later, he also named Thai Police Major General Kriekphong Phukprayoon as the officer who took the money. In an interview with Star News in December 2000, however,

Rajan denied bribing the Thai Police and said he was forced to flee Thailand because he feared being killed by Dawood's gang. 'This is a lie. He is not a lawyer; he is a liar. After the period that he was my lawyer, I haven't spoken to him and I haven't given money to anyone,' he said of Sirichai's claims.[11]

In the same interview, Rajan said that a team of professional mountain climbers had helped him escape from his fourth-floor hospital room to his car, which took him to his yacht. He then sailed to an undisclosed port, where his private jet was waiting for him. It would be almost a decade before the story I'd reported on Rajan's escape would be confirmed for me by his aide Santosh Shetty, who had been deported from Cambodia to India in 2011 and whom I had met at the hospital. Shetty told me in an interaction I had with him before I recorded his interview that aired on Star News that a Thai military official had played a major role in Rajan's escape. The military personnel allegedly provided Rajan's transportation till the Cambodian border, from where he was picked up in a chopper by a powerful Cambodian official and ferried to a safe hideout in Siem Reap.

The blame-game over Rajan's escape continued to dominate the headlines in Thailand and in India. The Thai Immigration Police Chief Lt General Hemraj Theerarhai denied that the Thai Police had slowed down the deportation of Chhota Rajan to allow negotiations to continue over the bribes that Rajan had promised to pay. He claimed to have tried to speed up the process but the response from Indian authorities had been slow. According to him, the Thai attorney-general's office had asked the courts to deport Rajan to India on 14 October, but the Immigration Bureau did not hear from India until 17 November.

The blame for Rajan's escape was, therefore, shifted onto the Indian authorities. The situation was muddled further when, in frantic damage control mode, Chuan Leekpai, the prime minister of Thailand, sought an explanation from the police about the allegations of bribery, and an official probe was ordered. An initial probe found that the immigration police official, normally stationed at the elevator at the hospital, had not shown up for his assignment. Seven policemen usually stood guard at the Samitivej Hospital while Rajan was there – four outside the room, two in the alley below the fourth floor room and one at the elevator. The Thai authorities suspended the seven police officials on guard at the time of Rajan's escape. Doubts were raised by the Thai media over the Indian authorities' deliberate delay in pursuing Rajan's extradition, which ultimately gave the mobster time to escape from the country. Subsequently, Munna was arrested along with Sher Khan on 17 September, while two more accomplices were arrested later. Four others, however, managed to flee the city. In fact, the arrest of Munna and others was believed to be a staged surrender, as Chhota Shakeel wanted to earn the goodwill of the Thai Police after the attack.

Rajan's gang had kept a chartered flight ready to move him from the hospital to a safer destination. Meanwhile, due to the information provided by the Mumbai Police, the Thai immigration authorities had detained Rajan on charges of illegal entry into the country. The immigration officer who was contacted by the Mumbai Police team that visited Bangkok was initially cooperative. A letter from D. Sivanandan, then joint commissioner of police (Crime), Mumbai, was handed over to him; however, the officer verbally informed the Mumbai Police team that assisting the investigation was out of the question as the Thai Police had not received any official communication from the CBI, Interpol or New Delhi, about their visit. Under these circumstances, no official communication was possible with the team. At this point, the visiting team explained the implications of the shoot-out to the coordinating officer of the Thai Police and requested him to allow the team to interview Rajan in the hospital and the other suspects in jail. The officer obliged by arranging a meeting with Rajan in the hospital. Colonel Kerkpong accompanied the team, and after the interview he suggested that Rajan's passport would have to be revoked if it was obtained by suppressing any information or furnishing false information. For his extradition, an official request through diplomatic channels was required. Once it arrived, Rajan would be deported. If Rajan gave it in writing that he wished to travel on his own to India, he would be allowed to do so without any further delay.

While speaking to Rajan, the team made an effort to convince him to come to Mumbai, where he would be given protection. Rajan requested he be given some time to think it over. Colonel Kerkpong informed him that in any case he would not be allowed to stay in the hospital for a long time, and immediately after the doctors discharged him he would be detained along with other criminals with no special security arrangements. This was done to impress on him that he should leave on his own at the earliest.

The extradition request that followed was in the form of a letter written by the Mumbai Police team addressed to the first secretary at the Embassy of India in Bangkok, which contained Rajan's personal particulars, such as his true name, date of birth, residential address, his wife's name, and so forth. It was delivered with the request that his passport in the name of Vijay Kadam (which was in the custody of Thai immigration) needed to be revoked. The first secretary, in a letter dated 9 October 2000, informed the team that the revocation of the passport could only be done with the approval of the government of India and the case would have to be taken up with the joint secretary at the Ministry of External Affairs, who is also the chief passport officer of India. The letter further stated that only the original passport-issuing office could actually revoke the passport, which in this case was the Chennai RPO.

On the same day, the Thai investigating officer at the immigration office refused to accept any assistance from the Mumbai Police and declined to give copies of statements by the accused on the grounds that no documents could be parted with according to Thai laws. Colonel Kerkpong arranged an interview between the team and the three suspects in the presence of his officer and jail authorities, with strict instructions that no recording of statements in any form, or photography, or exchange of any material with the team would be allowed. They were allowed to question the three suspects for 40 minutes.

The extent to which communications over Rajan's extradition went back and forth is remarkable. The next day, the Mumbai Police team handed over a letter with the details of the prime suspect, Mohammed Saleem aka Munna aka Sayed Muzakir Hussein aka Munna Zingada, along with a copy of his fingerprints to the Thai Police, with the suggestion that the said suspect was an Indian national, that the Pakistani passport obtained by him was false and the matter should, therefore, be taken up with the suitable authorities. The officer accepted the letter but refused to acknowledge its receipt, with an indirect remark that he was not bound to act on it. The first secretary at the Indian Embassy was informed of this. Later, India did manage to pursue the matter with Thai authorities and thus prevent Munna's escape to Pakistan. India's persistent efforts to bring Munna to Mumbai after serving a 20-year jail term in Thailand could still become a reality.

In Rajan's case, the Indian Embassy informed the Thai Police on 11 October that his passport was being revoked. Rajan was subsequently issued a show cause notice, and on 13 October, his passport was revoked. On 16 October, Superintendent Chinapak, assistant to Col. Kerkpong who was out of the country, was contacted, and he arranged a meeting with the three arrested suspects and Rajan. On 17 October, a letter to the Thai Police requested them to supply the fingerprints of suspect Mohammed Yusuf Haji Abdul, who, though holding a Pakistani passport, appeared to be an Indian national. The result of the comparison of Munna's fingerprints was also requested. On the same day, another letter informing the Thai Police that Rajan's passport had been revoked and he could therefore be deported was personally handed over to the commissioner of immigration of the Thai Police. The letters were acknowledged, but during personal discussions the commissioner asked for a similar request through diplomatic channels.

On 20 October, the team met Col. Kerkpong and requested for one more meeting with Rajan. During the meeting, an officer of Thai Immigration and Rajan's wife were also present. When asked about Rajan's deportation, Col. Kerkpong repeated that the request should come through CBI or the Interpol, and further informed that, in the event of the extradition papers not being received, deportation was out of question. The team in Bangkok received the mugshot of a person who had been arrested in Lucknow earlier by fax for verification. On 24 October, Col. Kerkpong was requested to arrange another meeting with the three suspects in jail so as to identify the person in the photograph, and to find out if the photograph matched one of the accused in the Rajan attack, as the Mumbai Police team suspected. Col. Kerkpong, however, refused permission on the grounds that the Mumbai Police team's visit to Thailand was unofficial, and no further requests would be entertained. Another letter was sent to the first secretary at the Indian Embassy informing him about the latest development and with a request for him to take up the issue with the concerned authorities. However, nothing materialized from this as the embassy did not intimate the team about the outcome of their approaching the Thai authorities.

Under these circumstances, no further meetings could be

arranged with Rajan to persuade him to come to India. The team had to return empty-handed to Mumbai. As expected, a few days later, Rajan managed to escape from the hospital.

The Bangkok episode completely changed my perspective on the Mumbai underworld. I realized that once small-time Mumbai gangsters had become gang lords and global players operating from various countries. They ran their crime conglomerates like corporate CEOs and had established their own criminal empires of arms trafficking, drug-running and counterfeit currency. They were able to generate territorial unrest on demand, and now catered to various international intelligence agencies, giant corporate houses and political and financial establishments. Larger-than-life images created by their patrons had helped them create a formidable brand for themselves in the criminal world. The shoot-out in Bangkok and all that followed was a telling example of the multi-country, multi-establishment power games that constantly took place behind the scenes.

After his escape, the last few years have seen Rajan constantly changing his location to dodge his rivals, across Southeast Asia and even in Australia and South Africa. With age catching up with him, Rajan has developed ailments like high blood pressure and diabetes. Sources in the know have revealed that he has developed kidney ailments that require frequent dialysis.

Though several of his aides are either dead or behind bars, it is said that Rajan still takes good care of their families, ensuring they get a monthly stipend. Over the last decade, like the rest of the underworld, he too is believed to have moved into real estate, with huge interests in Mumbai and Pune. His wife, Sujata, and their three children had moved to India a few years ago. Sujata is currently facing trial under the MCOCA for allegedly helping her husband in his land-grabbing and extortion businesses. Rajan's brother Deepak is a real estate developer and politician in Mumbai who lost his third election as a Republican Party of India candidate from Chembur in 2014 after declaring ₹14 crore in assets in his poll affidavit.

Santosh Shetty's version of the events that he narrated to the Mumbai Police during his investigation (detailed in a later chapter) after Rajan survived the attack in Bangkok corroborates the theory that Rajan had escaped to Tehran via Cambodia. Because he is diabetic, it took a long time for his bullet wounds to heal. With Shakeel pursuing him, he moved from Tehran to Indonesia and in 2003 he shifted base to Harare, Zimbabwe, where he got his new Indian identity as Mohan Kumar and the Indian passport he presently travels on. In 2008 he moved again to Australia and has been living there since, making arrangements to take on an Australian citizenship. In these years, his movements, however, do not seem to have drawn the attention of the Indian agencies that had issued a red-corner Interpol notice on him in 1995.

In May 2015 Rajan is said to have been alerted to a threat to his life, forcing him to consider moving base from Australia as well. Chhota Shakeel had been successful in extracting the information of his whereabouts from one of Rajan's aides in exchange for money. In July 2015 Shakeel had sent a team to Newcastle, in New South Wales, Australia, to find Rajan. When the surveillance team confirmed his presence in the city after spotting him, Shakeel gave the order to shoot him as soon as they could. But Rajan had already moved out.

After this near-miss, Shakeel is said to have posted his team in Australia to hunt Rajan down. Rajan moved to Canberra, but remained in Australia as he had applied for citizenship a few months earlier, and Shakeel galvanized local support on his 'find Rajan mission' in Australia through the D Company's influential Australian business associates who have connections with Australian immigration authorities. Meanwhile, Mohan Kumar alias Chhota Rajan, received an intimation to visit the immigration office for fingerprint and biometric verifications in connection with his residency and the application for a visa extension. Rajan complied, but the routine criminal background check during the verification process on Interpol's crime record files landed him in a soup. His case was put up for detailed verification on suspicion that he resembled one of India's most wanted men, Rajendra Sadashiv Nikalje, alias Chhota Rajan. The immigration office informed the Interpol office and also contacted the Indian mission for further details and sent across a copy of Mohan Kumar's fingerprints and biometrics to clear any doubts. He was also placed under surveillance, pending the verification.

The Australian authorities soon contacted New Delhi through the Interpol division of Canberra around 16 October 2015. All concerned security agencies had been alerted on the subject and were asked to comply with the verification process. When the required documents were sent back to Canberra, hardly any doubt remained that Mohan Kumar was indeed Chhota Rajan. But apprehending him in Australia would mean a long-drawn legal process as it would have to pass through stringent extradition proceedings in court in accordance with the extradition treaty that exists between India and Australia.

Here began the operation on the part of the Indian authorities to apprehend Chhota Rajan under the close watch of the offices of the National Security Agency (NSA) and other nodal agencies including the MEA. It would also involve the coordinated efforts of the CBI, Interpol and Australian federal law enforcement officers. Following sustained surveillance and intelligence-gathering, the three agencies determined in the third week of October that they were sufficiently equipped to move in on Rajan.

During this time, Rajan had been waiting anxiously for the immigration process to be completed; it appeared to him to be taking an unusually long time. It seems that at some point Rajan received a tip-off that he was being watched by security agencies, which is when he decided to flee from Australia to a country from where his deportation to India would be an easy process. It seems Rajan decided that Indonesia was the most suitable place for him. Interestingly, two senior officials were in the region prior to and during the time Rajan was arrested: an officer from internal security, said to have been visiting Indonesia for official purposes, and BJP leader Subramanian Swamy, who tweeted on 26 October, the day after Rajan was arrested, 'Two days ago I phoned [Minister of State for External Affairs] Gen. V.K. Singh and found that he was speaking from Indonesia. Has he negotiated something?' It was subsequently revealed that the Minister of State for External affairs was leading the operation in Indonesia and Australia, while at home the NSA was supervising the overall operation.

Rajan's arrest in Bali on 25 October 2015 was thus a well-planned move by the Indian authorities. The Bali police arrested him as he alighted from a Garuda Indonesia flight from Sydney at Ngurah Rai International Airport.

The Bali police have said that they arrested Rajan acting on information on a 'red-corner notice for a murderer' received from their counterparts in Canberra. The reference is to a 15-year-old red-corner notice issued against Rajan in 1995. 'What we know is that this man is suspected to have carried out 15 to 20 murders in India,' the Bali police spokesperson, Heri Wiyanto, told the media. 'Initial investigations have revealed that he intended to stay in Bali for 15 days.' Another official revealed that Rajan seemed to have come prepared to be arrested at Ngurah Rai International Airport. He had packed light – a small suitcase containing a few clothes and his dialysis kit – and offered no resistance. When he was intercepted at the airport he smiled at officials and showed no surprise. He did not create any problems and readily cooperated with the police.

Those close to Rajan believe that he gave himself up in order to ensure safe passage to India, where he believes he will remain unharmed. At his Tilak Nagar home the mood was one of relief the day after the details of Rajan's arrest became clearer. 'Initially, when we watched the news regarding Rajan's arrest, it came as a shock and we doubted if he had really been arrested. However, after seeing his photograph released by the Indonesian police, we knew it was true,' Yashwant Kharat, Rajan's relative, told ABP News. 'I'm sure Rajan was not caught by the police. It was a well-planned surrender.'

While the arrest itself has been a matter of procedural mechanics, there were several determinants surrounding it that were too suspiciously convenient for them to be coincidental. Rajan's complete non-resistance to being arrested was one such. The photos released by the Indonesian police showed Rajan dressed in a white T-shirt smiling at the camera with a single guard by his side. His mini dialysis kit was covered by his T-shirt but visible if carefully looked for. He looked happy, perhaps because he will be returning home after over two decades.

Television footage of Rajan being swarmed by the media cameras coaxing him to say something on his trip to hospital from custody, have revealed Rajan trying to avoid cameras but he could not resist answering a pointed question: Was he scared of Chhota Shakeel who is out to kill him? Rajan responded, 'I am not scared of anyone. I want to go to India or Zimbabwe.' Zimbabwe was the place where his first passport was issued, in which he is shown as a non-resident Indian from Mandya, Karnataka. Meanwhile, Chhota Shakeel expressed that we was not happy with Rajan's arrest. As he told the *Times of India*, 'My boys were on the job in Fiji last week, and we had jammed him in his hideouts. He was forced to flee to Indonesia, which led to his arrest. The D Company is not happy with his arrest and our enmity does not end here. I want to eliminate him, and I will not rest till I do so. Even if he is deported, my operation against him will continue.'

What had played out until now between the two dons was a typical cloak-and-dagger approach and a fixation with settling scores but their long-drawn battle is bound to have security implications on the region as a whole. In July 2015, India hanged Yakub Memon, an accused in the 1993 Mumbai blasts case. Against that backdrop, Rajan's arrival in India could add to the country's security challenges. Shakeel made the D Company's objectives very clear in the interview I held with him for ABP News, as also in various other interviews with the media after Yakub's hanging: '*Action ka reaction hota hai* (Every action has a reaction)'.

After Rajan's arrival in India, the Mumbai Police have handed over all of Rajan's case files to the CBI in Delhi, which will be dealt with priority-wise by the agency. The CBI has filed fresh charges against Rajan for passport forgery and travelling on a fake passport. Alongside, they have also filed charges against unknown officials who are being accused of helping the don by issuing him an Indian passport based on forged documents relating to his alias 'Mohan Kumar'. Threats from Chhota Shakeel have forced the CBI to keep Rajan under tight armed security, turning the CBI headquarters, where Rajan is housed, into a virtual fortress. The threat seems to be serious enough, for Rajan's medical treatment is reportedly being administered in the CBI cell itself.

Rajan's homecoming and arrest have raised more questions than answers regarding the dynamics within the underworld and the fallout on the ground. Foremost among these are whether Rajan can resist justifying his crimes by reiterating his stance as a 'patriot', an image he has been building for a long time now, and what the CBI will do about the pending charges against Rajan in over 70 cases in which he has been named. Even after his arrest in Bali, whenever he has faced television news cameras, Rajan has reiterated that he will keep up his fight against terrorism and Dawood Ibrahim till his last breath. It remains to be seen if his ranting could turn into a liability for the very people for whom he has functioned as a 'deep asset'.

Many are of the opinion that both Dawood and Rajan have well passed their expiry dates of being useful assets to their mentors. Rajan's arrest is perhaps the first step. The survival or otherwise of Rajan and Dawood now seem to be interdependent. Technically, with Rajan's arrest, his chapter in the underworld has come to an end. What remains to be seen is whether it signals the end of the era of the 'Hindu' don before or after his nemesis, or if his name will continue to wield a power similar to what it had in the past.

The One Who Broke Away

'A MEETING IN BANGKOK IS POSSIBLE but I would not like to appear before the camera.' This was Santosh Pandurang Shetty aka Anna's response to my message asking if he would agree to an interview. He added, 'I am just an hour away. When you reach Bangkok and finish your business, just message me.' I had doubts about him turning up for the meeting as an Interpol red-corner notice had been issued against him in 2002, listing him among the most wanted criminals of Indian origin operating from a foreign land against India, but I was still excited.

I was visiting Bangkok in November 2010 to interview one of the initial suspects of the 26/11 Mumbai attacks. In November 2008 the country and the world watched in horror as Mumbai was rocked by 12 coordinated shooting and bomb attacks around the city that lasted three days and saw close to 150 people killed and many more injured. The man in question was American citizen, George Mapp, who had been detained by the National Investigative Agency (NIA) in India for his Pakistani connection. Mapp had been living with Faiza Outalha, a Moroccan who was the third wife of David Coleman Headley, one of the main accused in the attacks. Mapp was flying from Chiang Mai to Bangkok for the interview, in which he had agreed to talk about his fling with Faiza and her Pakistani and Lashkar-e-Taiba connection. I knew

Shetty used to shuttle between Thailand, Vietnam, Indonesia and Iran, but was based in Cambodia, so I got hold of his number from a source and messaged him. After a long to-and-fro messaging exercise, Shetty agreed to meet me in Bangkok. This would be my second meeting with him in the Thai capital.

When we had first met at the Samitivej Hospital in September 2000, when he politely but menacingly told me to leave the room in which Rajan was being treated for his wounds, Shetty was a confidant of mobster Chhota Rajan, so I was surprised when I heard rumours of a split between Shetty and Rajan through my sources in Mumbai sometime in the middle of 2004. Shetty was now a don himself! Word was that having formed his own gang, called the 'SS Syndicate', with his close associates he was in the process of regrouping.

Around the months of May or June in 2006, one of my sources in Mumbai asked me if I would be interested in interviewing Anna, who wanted to formally declare his separation from Rajan after working closely with the don from outside India for nearly 12 years. I finally interviewed him for Star News in August 2006.

In the interview, Shetty sounded bitter about Rajan's attitude towards him, and pointed to the fact that Rajan's close aides (Vijay Shetty, Farid Tanasha, Bharat Nepali and him) had all left him one after another due to his disrespectful behaviour. He did not consider Rajan his competition, he said. His disdain towards his former boss was evident in his description of Rajan as 'powerless and paralysed', an ailing mobster whose gang had now been reduced to a handful of men.

Of his plans ahead he revealed, 'Since I have parted ways with Rajan I have been regrouping with all those members who have left Rajan.' Shetty had banded together with fellow Mangaloreans such as Vijay and Suraj Shetty to increase his clout. Bharat Nepali joined hands with Shetty after the former broke away from Rajan around 2009.

'I had to leave because he pulled me out of a thriving narcotic business,' he had explained. 'He asked me to forget about it and stay away from it. After we escaped from Bangkok (in 2000), I was handling the same area (narcotics). After a year or two he told me that I should look for greener pastures. He cut me off completely from the business. He started ignoring me. I was very upset and hurt.' He emphatically said that he had separated once and for all from Rajan. 'I have nothing to do with him anymore. I live in my own world and he lives in his. Neither does he know where I am nor do I know where he could be.'

A TV grab of Santosh Shetty. Photo courtesy Star News.

The SS Syndicate's plan was to out-turf Rajan from the Southeast Asian narcotics business. With his extensive knowledge of Rajan's network, Shetty had managed to spread his own network very swiftly in Rajan's territory – Southeast Asia and east

Mumbai (Chembur, Kalyan, Thane and Ulhasnagar). Shetty wanted to prove to his former boss that he should have been allowed to handle the narcotics business instead of being pulled out of it.

Shetty told me that after the attack on Rajan in Bangkok in 2000, when it became evident that information on Rajan's whereabouts had been leaked, he lost all confidence in his close associates, and this had a terrible effect on the business. 'Businesses in our world are run on the basis of trust, and if you lose trust in your own people, then it is tough to work together,' Shetty said. Additionally, Rajan did not recuperate fully from his wounds, which triggered further medical complications. Rajan's kidneys had been badly affected, restricting his movements, and his prolonged medical treatment was perceived as a weakness among the members of his gang. Then, when some of his close aides such as Shetty, Nepali and Ravi Pujari parted ways with Rajan, it hit 'Brand Rajan' hard. From there on, his gang gradually depleted.

I found Shetty to be clever and ambitious. Unlike other gangsters of his time who gave an impression of being rough and tough, Shetty, who spoke English and looked like a corporate executive, gave the impression of being suave and sophisticated in his attitude and dealings. If he had to get into Rajan's shoes, it was necessary that he be perceived as someone who was stronger than his former boss. Shetty could read situations well, and I have no doubt that he had figured out that Rajan's powerful mentors would not mind using his brand of *deshbhakti* as long as Shetty could maintain the myth of the mobster Chhota Rajan or, even better, remain in their good books.

Although Shetty had agreed to meet me in Bangkok, by the time the message reached me I had returned to Delhi. And though I couldn't interview him then, he assured me that there would certainly be a next time.

Although the second interview is yet to come about, following Shetty's activities has been interesting enough for me.

The newly minted don's brazen attitude and over-confidence about operating in the subcontinent proved to be an open invitation to Indian agencies to close in on him. His flashy lifestyle meant that it was not much of a task for them to spot him, particularly with his love of fast cars and his chronic cocaine addiction, which in the end gave him up in Bangkok. His swanky 7-series BMW was among the first things the Thai Police identified when they started their operation to nab him. In August 2011, the Thai Police finally arrested him based on information they had received from the Mumbai Police.[1]

At the press conference held by the Mumbai Police to announce Shetty's arrest, Himanshu Roy, joint police commissioner (crime), said that the Mumbai Police had used every trick of the trade to get Shetty – from electronic and email surveillance to traditional information networks in the underworld and sending decoys to Thailand. The Mumbai Police first sent two people to Bangkok in the guise of businessmen, who got in touch with Shetty. He gave the duo his visiting card, which was in the name of Nikhilesh Sharma. This confirmed his identity for the police as a passport had been issued in that name from Delhi. After over three months of surveillance, reconnaissance and tailing, the Mumbai Police gave the Thai Police specific information on Shetty, including his residential address and details of four fake passports (two Danish, one Indonesian and one Indian) that he used for travelling.

After his arrest, Shetty tried to exploit a legal loophole to prevent his deportation to India. His second wife, Fun, a Thai national, lodged a false complaint against Shetty, accusing him of cheating her of $5 million. This was a plot he had hatched to remain in a Thai jail, which delayed his deportation by a few more days. Ultimately, the Bangkok Police was persuaded through diplomatic channels to refrain from arresting Shetty in the case, and the gangster was deported to Mumbai on 12 August 2011, where he was formally arrested the next morning. Shetty was charged with the murders of lawyer Shahid Azmi and Chhota Rajan's aide Farid Tanasha, along with 12 other offences pertaining to smuggling and the drug trade, and travelling on a fake passport.

What caught my attention after his arrest were his claims regarding Chhota Rajan's escape from the hospital in 2000, certain personal details about Rajan and Bharat Nepali's killing in 2010. Police chief Roy had narrated Shetty's version of the 2000 attack on Rajan at a press conference. According to Shetty's revelations, when the attack on Rajan took place, Bharat Nepali and Shetty were already in Bangkok. They called the other gang members, Bunty Pandey and Farid Tanasha to Bangkok after the attack, and the four of them planned Rajan's escape from the Samitivej Hospital.

Shetty claimed that his paramour in Bangkok was an accomplished mountaineer. She had given them mountaineering gear and trained Shetty and Nepali for two days to bring Rajan down from the third-floor window. On the day of the escape, Shetty and Nepali stayed with Rajan in his room the entire night. The two got drunk with the watchman and mixed sedatives in his drink to knock him out. At around 2.30 a.m., they threw down a rope to Pandey and Tanasha, who tied a haversack with the climbing gear in it, which was pulled up to the room. Nepali carried Rajan on his shoulders in the fireman's position and climbed out of the window. (In an interview with a national daily in October 2015 Shetty also stated that none of Rajan's injuries had been life-threatening.)

Shetty's statement to the police gave more details of Rajan's eventual escape from Bangkok to Tehran and Indonesia, most of which sounded extraordinary. He said that a Thai businessman named Parazane had organized a military vehicle, in which Rajan and the gang were transported to the Cambodian border. Here, Rajan was picked up in a helicopter by a top Cambodian official and ferried to a safer hideout in Siem Reap. From there, Rajan was taken to Tehran for a short while, where he recuperated as his bullet wounds had not healed completely. In Tehran, Rajan and Nepali shared a flat while Shetty and Bunty Pandey stayed in separate accommodations. Rajan, he said, had an affair with a woman caregiver there, who bore his child and for whom he 'bought an apartment and provided financial support'.

Considering the aftermath of Rajan's getaway, the story Shetty revealed to the Mumbai Police does not hold much water. Though the gangsters had iron-clad alibis to cover their tracks, the Bangkok Police first reported that Vijay Kadam (aka Rajan) used knotted bed-sheets to climb down from the hospital balcony and flee from the country. The twist came when Rajan's former lawyer Sirichai Piapichetkul refuted the Thai Police's version. The lawyer claimed that Rajan had telephoned him from somewhere in south Thailand, saying that he had used the emergency exit at the hospital to walk out after paying a bribe of $575,000 to a major-general in the Thai Police. He was also given safe passage in lieu of money.

Unlike Shetty's dramatic story of Rajan's escape, the bribe story seemed to be smoke from actual fire. Thai Police Major-General Kreukpong Pookprayoon, chief of the Immigration Bureau's general staff division, had approved Rajan's request to continue receiving medical treatment at the Samitivej Hospital, overruling a suggestion from the Bangkok Police department that the gangster be transferred to the Police General Hospital, where security was much tighter. Rajan was reportedly scheduled to be transferred there at the end of the month. The *Bangkok Post* quoted the immigration chief saying that he had not wanted to visit Rajan at the hospital out of fear that he would be accused of extorting money from him.

Rajan's escape vindicated the police department's stand. Rajan's lawyer, Sirichari, named the major-general as the officer who had taken the money. Sant Saluthanon, deputy police commissioner of Thailand, had urged Sirichari to present his evidence of Rajan's bribe to Pookprayoon on the record. In an interview to DPA News, a leading German news wire, Sirichari claimed he had received several death threats since his accusation of bribery against the major-general.

Rajan has not yet come out in the open against Shetty. He has chosen to play down the separation between them, possibly because Shetty knows all his personal and trade secrets. While Rajan was recuperating from his wounds in hideouts in various countries, Shetty returned to Bangkok to run the business. He had an edge over other members in the gang as he spoke English and was more tech-savvy. He used modern technology to evade detection and arrest for a long time. The most educated among all the gang members, Shetty behaved more like a chief operating officer than the top man in a criminal gang.

In the 1980s and early 1990s, Shetty was peddling drugs in Mumbai. The south Mumbai boy, a graduate from Mumbai's Siddharth College, was initiated into the underworld when he was jailed for the first time under the COFEPOSA in a gold smuggling case in early 1989. While in jail, he networked with Rajan and Dawood's cronies, and when he was released his close relations with them took him straight to Dubai where he hobnobbed with the big daddies of the underworld. He served another jail term of five years after his conviction under the Narcotics Act, and became closer to Rajan when he went to Bangkok after being released on parole. It seems as though with each jail term he grew stronger and rose to higher levels in the underworld.

An addict of mandrax and cocaine, Shetty's earlier experience as a drug peddler came in handy in spreading his network in the international market. He managed to capture the drug market in Hong Kong, Singapore, Thailand, Macau and other parts of Southeast Asia over a couple of years. Since 2000, he was, it is said, the mastermind behind all of Rajan's operations, including the kidnappings and killings by the gang in India and outside. An enterprising man, Shetty set up his own shop along the way, and the police believe that although Rajan knew about it he chose to ignore Shetty's growing strength and speedy climb. Shetty himself has claimed that Rajan was wary of him, yet he did nothing owing to Shetty's past loyalty towards him.

As a Mumbai Police source told me, the arrangements made by Shetty suited Rajan as long as his share arrived from each deal. Rajan had invested $200,000 in Shetty's mandrax plant in Batam in the Sumatra region of Indonesia. Shetty kept 40 per cent of the profits and Rajan got the rest. After the supply of raw material for mandrax tablets dried up, Shetty claimed that he got into the business of printing fake US dollars on Rajan's instructions. He put in his share of investment and waited for Rajan to send his share of the money. The profits out of his fake currency racket – including getting counterfeit currency from China, South Korea and Indonesia and selling them in Singapore – was routed to buy a restaurant in Jakarta, which Shetty named after his Chinese girlfriend, Nayatali.

Meanwhile, Shetty suffered a huge loss when a consignment worth around $1.2 billion was intercepted by the Singapore Police. When Shetty told Rajan about his losses in the drug business, Rajan agreed to give him some money on the condition that Shetty would transfer his hotel in Jakarta in the name of another gang member, Balu Dokre. This came as a shock to Shetty, especially as he had invested in the project only after Rajan's assurances. It was clear to him that Rajan did not trust him anymore, and Shetty felt he had been short-changed in spite of his contribution to the gang and loyalty to Rajan. Dokre was ultimately murdered in Kuala Lumpur in 2005 by members of Dawood's gang. Allegedly, the information on Dokre's location had been leaked to Chhota Shakeel by an erstwhile member of Rajan's gang.

As in politics, so in the underworld, no two factions stay bedmates forever. In his interview to me in 2006, when I had asked Shetty if he was one of the pillars of Rajan's empire, and whether he was important to the gang he replied, 'Not to the gang, but to Rajan, yes... We were like brothers. He was like my elder brother and I called him "Nana".'

Shetty's return to custody in India begs for a more complicated explanation than what has been revealed by the Mumbai Police. The Mumbai Police's elaborate disclosure of how Shetty was trailed by undercover agents and his capture and ultimate deportation to India sounds realistic enough. Yet, as a senior Indian intelligence official put it, 'There is more to this than meets the eye.' Shetty's exposés on Rajan's transnational activities haven't gone down well with his mentors. This was evident when Rajan's aide Nilesh Shedge, an accused in journalist Jyotirmoy Dey's murder, slapped and manhandled Shetty on the premises of the Mumbai Sessions Court. He apparently warned Shetty not to act smart and to keep his mouth shut. Timely intervention by the cops reduced what could have been a more serious attack to a minor scuffle.

But Shedge's attempt was meant to drive home a point, which reflected clearly in Shetty's plea to the court for increased security. Shetty's lawyer, Rajesh Srivastava told the media, 'Shedge tried to hit Shetty but he did not succeed. My client has already made applications before the courts that he fears for his life.'[2] Shetty was aware that Maharashtra jails are not only breeding grounds for criminals, but also a place to settle the scores between gangs – sometimes by means of murder.

Shetty's disclosures on the Indian mafia's activities in the subcontinent have reaffirmed my belief that the Indian underworld had evolved into transnational mobsters dabbling in arms, narcotics and foreign counterfeit currencies. There are indications, too, that they had aligned with international crime cartels such as the Colombian drug cartels, the Russian mobs and the Japanese Yakuza.

Nicknamed '*Chikna* Hero' because of his looks, Shetty is an articulate, clever and hard-nosed man. He has a knack for convincing people easily about things, which has taken him a long way in his career, from being a small-time gold smuggler to becoming a narcotics kingpin in the subcontinent. He seems to be playing a game with all those who want to be engaged in it – the Mumbai Police, the media and Chhota Rajan's mentors. The information that he has gradually leaked about Rajan's empire and the alleged involvement of agencies in it indicate a soft bargaining trick. These moves signal that he is a seasoned gangster with the necessary skills to hold his own. Almost reiterating Rajan's escape alibi, he has shown that he is still playing on the same side and is game to enter into larger turf wars between rival factions.

The Sports-loving Don

WHAT IS COMMON BETWEEN SACHIN Tendulkar and notorious gangster Ashwin Naik? Strange as it may sound, Tendulkar and Naik shared the same cricket coach, Ramakant Achrekar.

'I played cricket for several years. Ramakant Achrekar was my coach. But ever since I got paralysed by a bullet, I haven't been able to play,' Naik said when I met him on 12 August 2012 for an interview.

Naik had been shot in April 1994 by Ravindra Sawant of the Gawli gang at the Mumbai Sessions Court, where the former had appeared for a hearing. Dressed like an advocate, Sawant had waited till Naik walked up with his police escorts before shooting him in the head at point-blank range. Miraculously, Naik had survived, though the nature of his injury had confined him to a wheelchair ever since.

The attack on Naik was to avenge the murder of Tanya Koli, a close aide of his boss Arun Gawli. The killing had enraged 'Daddy', as Gawli is known among his gang members, and the killer had to pay. On 17 September 1993, Koli was shot while being taken back to Amravati Jail by train after attending court in Mumbai; gangsters from the Naik gang barged into the compartment when it stopped at Kalyan railway station and shot him. A policeman was also killed in the incident, and another was injured.

Police investigations later revealed that Gawli had ordered his lieutenant, Sada 'Mama' Pawale, to arrange for Naik's murder while the latter was in judicial custody. Since this task was a tough one, it was decided that he would be shot at the Sessions Court as that is where he would be most exposed even while in custody. Pawale recruited Sawant and trained him at Dagdi Chawl for the job, but Sawant didn't know what Naik looked like. Nagesh Mohite, who knew Naik, was asked to help Sawant, and Sawant fired the bullet only after Mohite had identified Naik for him. Naik collapsed, and was taken immediately to JJ Hospital.

Naik told me that he had not been shocked or surprised at the attempt on his life. As both Gawli and Naik conducted their extortion and protection-money rackets in the same areas in Mumbai, their interests clashed regularly and a rivalry had already existed between the two. Naik knew Gawli would retaliate after his assassination of Koli, which in turn was carried out in response to the murder of Naik's father-in-law.

Even before I met Naik, I had heard about his interest in sports. In his interview, Naik not only professed his ardent love for cricket but also expressed great regret at having to abandon his childhood dream of becoming a professional cricketer. He told me his heart went out to all those sportspersons who, for want of money, struggled to pursue their careers. The poor financial conditions of many sportspersons reminded him of his own situation – he had to leave his beloved sport and study engineering as no one in his family thought sports could pay the bills. 'I now wish to help needy young sportsmen who can't pursue sports due to the lack of sponsorship. I wish to set up a foundation for sportspersons to help them to seriously pursue sports as a career,' Naik declared.

Ashwin Naik's father, Maruti Shankar, came to Mumbai from

Narayangaon village in Pune district in the early 1970s to make ends meet for his large family. His village did not have any facilities for higher education, and like every parent he wanted to give his children the best opportunities to become doctors or engineers. To him these professions were the only avenues for his sons to pursue in order to pull the family out of financial misery. In Mumbai, Maruti began to sell vegetables at the Dadar market and stayed in a small *kholi* at 386 Patil House, N.C. Kelkar Marg in south-central Mumbai.

Ashwin was a bright student who excelled at sports. He was enrolled into the English-medium Dr Antonio Da Silva High School and later joined the JR College of Commerce in Dadar, which caused much celebration within his family. He was a star player in his *galli* cricket team and played many tournaments at Shivaji Park. His talent landed him at Ramakant Achrekar's training camp, where he showed great promise.

His elder brother, Amar Naik – who had already established himself as a local don – encouraged him to play cricket, but Maruti Shankar wanted him to put his studies before the game. Fearing that Ashwin would follow in his older brother's footsteps and turn to criminality, he insisted his son pursue mechanical engineering seriously and complete his diploma. His worst fears came true when instead of pursuing a career as an engineer, Ashwin too fell into *bhaigiri* – wayward ways to earn easy money.

Bharat Mane, Naik's lawyer had lined up my meeting with Ashwin Naik, and had asked me and a senior photo-journalist to meet him near N.M. Joshi Marg junction. From there he took us to Tenement Compound, which was Naik's residence-cum-office. It was a centrally air-conditioned double-storey building, and we were asked to leave our shoes outside the office before we entered it. The room was furnished in marble and wood. Naik arrived half-an-hour late and we were summoned to his cabin on the first floor. I had not seen him entering the office through the main door. When I enquired about this, Mane showed me an elevator directly opening into Naik's glass cabin. He had cautioned me that Naik hated words like 'don' and 'Bhai'. 'Naik leads a normal life with his children whom he missed all these years,' he said. 'He has decided to give up the world of crime and leave his troubled past behind. He has returned to the mainstream.'

Naik was on the phone for about ten minutes after we entered his room. There was a big wooden table with a glass top between us. I looked around and figured that we were not on the first floor after all but on a mezzanine floor. The wall behind our chairs was made of glass and he could see the entrance on the ground floor. We sat quietly, listening to his side of the conversation. He was talking politely and courteously with the person at the other end. The conversation was about a residential project under the slum redevelopment scheme (Naik had turned into a builder and a real estate developer) and Naik was telling the other party that he would need the consent of all the tenants before he took up that particular project. '*Kahi kich-pich aani lafda nako*! (I don't want to get into any disputed deals!)' His voice became authoritative and the statement was followed by some choice abuses in Marathi. Suddenly, the atmosphere in the air-conditioned room became charged. Mane looked a little tense and murmured, 'He isn't in a good mood.'

After finishing his conversation, Naik stared at us blankly for a few seconds as if we were not in the room at all. At this point, Mane took the lead and introduced us. He nodded his head and pressed the bell near him; someone opened the door and waited for the boss to speak to him. Naik looked at us and asked, 'What will you have? *Thanda ki garam*? (You want something cold or hot?)' The next instant he had made the decision for us. '*Thanda laana* (Bring something cold),' he said. Soon, three glasses of chilled cola arrived on a tray. I waited for a cue from Mane, but he seemed to prefer to sip his cola quietly. Finally, I began the conversation with a question on sports to ease the tension in the room.

At the mention of his love for sports, Naik's mood immediately lightened up. I asked him about the Dhanraj Pillay episode, when India narrowly missed an opportunity to qualify for the semi-finals in the 2000 Sydney Olympics after drawing 1-1 against Poland. Naik told me that he had been so distressed by the news that he immediately called then captain of the national hockey team, Pillay, offering his help in whatever way possible. He was eager to lend a helping hand to sportspeople, he said. He helped Pillay's prodigy and rising hockey star Yuvraj Walmiki by offering him ₹1 lakh, and claimed to have financially helped some more local sporting talents.

His love for sports aside, Naik's history is littered with constant run-ins with the law. As Naik is now wheelchair-bound and was in jail till 2009, his gang has lost its pan-India influence. He was tried for 16 crimes under the MCOCA in Mumbai, including a case pertaining to the murder of his wife, Neeta, over her suspected infidelity in 2000. But he was acquitted in all 16 cases, mostly for want of evidence.[1]

Amar Naik, Ashwin's elder brother, had dropped out of college after reaching the Intermediate level. Lack of means became the justification for him straying into crime. In a hurry to make big bucks, he got involved with local goons. According to police records, he was initiated into crime by Ram Bhatt, who was a leader of the Bapat gang, which operated in and around the Plaza Cinema in Dadar. When Ram Bhatt and some others were arrested and convicted by the CID in robbery cases, Amar took over the reins of the gang.

By the time Ashwin finished his studies, Amar's gang had managed to spread its activities all over the city and had the support of the notorious Walji–Palji brothers from Prabhadevi. Extortion and protection-money rackets were yielding the gang good sums, which were being used to pay its gangsters, finance court matters and acquire properties.

Like all other gangs, the Amar Naik gang also executed contract killings and assassinations of rival gang members. Their first victim was Vijay Gopal Mandlekar, a *mathadi* worker belonging to the Golden gang, in 1990. The D Company; the Thapa gang, which was affiliated to Dawood; and Chhota Rajan's gang, were Amar Naik's rivals, but their fiercest enmity was with Arun Gawli's men. The years 1993 and 1994 witnessed a number of retaliatory killings between these rivals, triggered by the killings of Sunil Dattaram Samel of the Naik gang and Kantilal Trilokchand Nahar, the financier of the Gawli gang. The two groups had several violent skirmishes, not just outside jails but also within jail premises where members of both gangs were lodged, resulting in several deaths.

After Amar Naik's death in a police encounter in Nagpada on 10 August 1996, Ashwin took over the reins of the gang and expanded its base outside Mumbai and Maharashtra, developing links with local gangs in several states. Close relations with the Prakash Ramashankar Sonar gang in UP; Ashok Narayanlal Trivedi in Rajasthan; Hardevsingh Malsingh in Punjab; Rajesh Madanlal Soni in Delhi; Kundan Bhagwandas Sharma and Girijashankar Tejkant in Bihar; Dilkhush Shankar Shetty in Karnataka; Shashi Kunjiram Nair in Kerala; Murali Balsubramanyam gang in Tamil Nadu; Kasturi Laxman Vasa in Andhra Pradesh; and John George Fernandes in Goa helped the Naik gang, now led by Ashwin, to create a truly pan-Indian presence.

❖

After he was shot, Ashwin Naik was released on bail on 6 December 1995, but he soon jumped bail and escaped abroad. Like other dons, Naik began to operate his criminal empire from overseas. Police records state that a fugitive Naik shifted from Dubai to London and then to Singapore, Australia and Nepal, before being arrested by the West Bengal Police while crossing the Indo-Bangladesh border in August 1999. The reports of Naik's arrest were considered to be quite odd when they were released, and his being in custody has been perceived by many to be more of a surrender. While on the run, he is said to have changed his allegiance from Chhota Rajan to Dawood Ibrahim as per his convenience and his mentors' instructions.

Even though I had been told by Mane not to ask any questions about his past activities, I took a chance and mentioned his life in jail to Naik. He could not resist responding and said sarcastically that everything was for sale inside prisons. 'If you have money, you get the comforts.' But he said his five-and-a-half years in Tihar Jail in New Delhi had been stressful. He was constantly dogged by the fear that rival gangsters would bump him off, and the fact that he was paralysed from waist down added to his woes. While he was in jail he spent a lot of time in the prison hospital because he needed care.

After his release in 2009, Ashwin Naik, accompanied by his daughter, went to meet Shiv Sena chief Bal Thackeray and Maharashtra Navanirman Sena (MNS) chief Raj Thackeray. It was no secret that Naik was connected to the Shiv Sena. Ashwin's wife Neeta (whose murder Naik was accused of conspiring) had been elected a Shiv Sena corporator, after contesting and winning the Brihanmumbai Municipal Corporation (BMC) elections twice, in 1992 and 1995. Further, the Shiv Sena had given Amar Naik's wife, Anjali Naik, a ticket for the 1995 BMC elections, though she lost. Naik's arch-rival Gawli's wife, Asha, had also contested the

1995 election from the same area from their own party, the Akhil Bharatiya Sena, but had also lost.

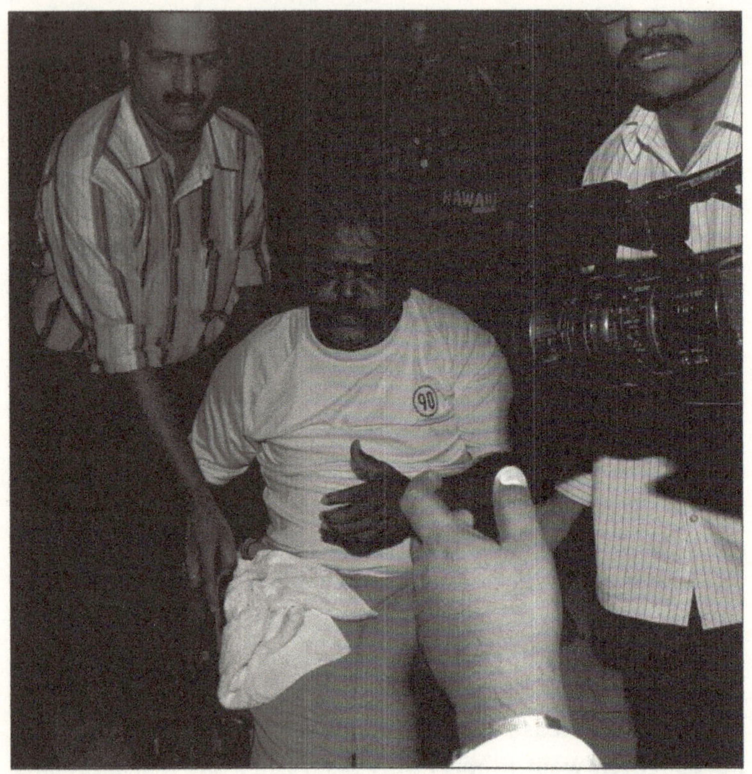

Ashwin Naik outside his residence. Photo courtesy Mahendra Parikh.

A turf war has always existed between the Naik and Gawli gangs in Dadar, Parel and Shivdi areas, all in central Mumbai. Though both of them enjoyed the blessings of the Sena chief for being 'Hindu dons', Gawli fell out of favour with the Sena and had emerged as a potential challenger to the party. Gawli was all set to contest the elections from central Mumbai, where Naik's family lived, and it was suspected that they might take their enmity to the political battleground with Naik too entering the fray.[2] Ashwin Naik's reconnection with the Shiv Sena alerted the Mumbai Police to the possibility of a fresh gang war between Gawli and Naik during the 2009 Assembly elections. When I asked Naik if he had ever thought of joining politics like his rival Gawli, he said in a very serious tone, 'They were merely courtesy calls. I had gone to seek Balasaheb's blessings as I wanted to revive my real estate business.'

An engineer by qualification, Naik is arguably one of the shrewdest criminal minds I have come across. He is known for his quietly efficient management of operations. He has never displayed an in-your-face attitude. Less talked about than the other dons, he is yet known to be highly effective when undertaking any operation. Despite his known criminal past, he refuted it when the topic came up and said he was 'being framed'. He cited his acquittal to qualify his claim. 'It took me a really long time (19 years) to clear my name. Those were the worst days of my life. I have left my past behind and have started a new life with my family,' he insisted.

I was curious to know his take on Dawood and Rajan, and asked him about the D Company's role in India after the 1993 blasts, and whether there was any truth in the rumour about the tiff between Rajan and Dawood on religious grounds. Without blinking an eyelid, he looked at me and asked, 'Are you religious – Hindu? What stand would you take when you see what was done to Mumbai? It is not as simple and straight as the world sees it. But I would support my city and defend my faith. The fight against anti-national forces cannot be abandoned.' As I saw it, he was stating the same patriotic criminal versus anti-national criminal twist that Chhota Rajan had initiated. I was not surprised with his response as he was perceived to be a deep asset for the country along with the other Hindu dons.[3]

Just then, some people walked into his cabin. He spoke to them in Marathi. They were from the neighbouring chawl. I gathered from the conversation that some residents were giving consent for the reconstruction of some chawls, while others were not. He was aware of our presence, and in a concluding remark he announced, 'Come to me when all of you are ready to resolve these issues internally.' Once they left, he told us that he helped rebuild dilapidated chawls as he was in the construction business, though merely as a facilitator.

A young girl, who wore her hair straight in a chic look, walked into the cabin and reminded him that it was time for lunch. She was introduced to us as Reshma, Naik's daughter, and a dentist. Naik seemed to be very fond of her and said, 'She studied in an English-medium school and has come a long way. She has earned her place as a dentist in society.' Ashwin's brother Amar's daughters have also become professionals – one is a doctor and the other a commercial pilot. Naik's son was pursuing architecture to carry on his business of real estate development.

Ashwin Naik seemed aware of the fact that he could not shrug off his past, even if he claimed to have called it a day. He still carried an image of being a formidable don, which was handy in his construction business, a business that is believed to go hand-in-hand with criminality and coercion. He continues to face several charges of coercion and extortion. In June 2012, BMC contractor Dhiraj Gohil accused Naik of assault and extortion. The Sewri Sessions Court granted him an anticipatory bail on a bond of ₹25,000 in the case, but just a few hours after being released on bail he was arrested again for allegedly thrashing a builder. Till March 2014, there were four cases of alleged extortion and threats filed against Naik and his associates.

According to sources in the Mumbai Police, Ashwin Naik is known for working with subtlety. His organization has several qualified people who avoid publicity as much as possible even as they work efficiently and quietly behind the scenes to expand his business. Naik himself has been quite averse to coming on camera for a formal interview. During our warm-up meeting, I was left with no doubt that he already knew about my work in detail. While taking leave, I asked him what he had enjoyed the most in his life. His response was not surprising. He reminisced about the days in his youth when he was an innocent boy playing cricket and scoring runs to make his *galli* team win. At his Tenement Compound house, he now looked forward to the times when one of his old friends dropped by, he said, and they travelled down memory lane talking about the adventures and misadventures that had brought them to this point in the present.

The Resident Don

IN EARLY 1990 I FOUND myself sitting on a sofa in the living room of Mumbai's only resident don, Arun Gulab Gawli, aka 'Daddy' among his followers. It was a somewhat tense moment. I had asked him a question in the form of a rather blasé statement: 'It is said that it is impossible to catch you from inside Dagdi Chawl.' I had heard about his various hideouts, and in my novice's ignorance about how to conduct interviews of underworld dons, had let my curiosity take over.

In response, Gawli sharply said, 'Get up.' I feared I had asked the wrong question and slowly got to my feet. As he came closer, I thought he would throw me out saying the interview was over. But he walked past me and in a sudden movement pulled out the top of the sofa. I was stunned to see the sofa open into an empty space that could easily hide a man. He shut it as swiftly as he had opened it, and asked me to take my seat again.

I felt a simultaneous surge of fear and delight surge through me. I knew then that his hideouts in Dagdi Chawl were not a myth. It was said there were hiding places in walls, cupboards and even a cavity in his bed for him to hide. He had not allowed any cameras during the interview, and all I have are words to describe what I saw. Gawli remarked in his trademark tone, '*Fakt badhaycha, kaay*! (This was for your eyes only!)'. Ironically, later, in July 1990, Mumbai Crime Branch officers would raid Dagdi Chawl and recover a carbine from Gawli's house. Gawli himself would be found hiding in a cavity in one of his beds.

Gawli was the first-ever gangster I met during the course of my reporting career. I had got his number from a senior crime reporter and called to seek an appointment. The person who answered the phone had confirmed that it was his number and told me that I could drop in any time after noon. He had asked me my name, telephone number and the publication where the interview would be printed, and I had simply reached central Mumbai's most infamous address: Dagdi Chawl, Saat Rasta, Byculla. The chawl itself was a cluster of tiny cramped spaces that passed off as homes for many lower middle-class Maharashtrian families. Everyone in Mumbai knew that the iron gates of the chawl sheltered one of the city's most hardened criminals. This was the don's kingdom-cum-fortress.

The address I had was 714/E, Room No. 37. I hunted for it, eventually discovering that he owned an entire building in the chawl. Hailing from a community of cattle-grazers and milkmen, Gawli's father, Gulab Puran, had come to Mumbai in search of work from a village in the Ahmednagar district in early 1960s. Gulab Puran worked at Simplex Mills, while his wife, Laxmibai, also worked in a mill near Nair Hospital for about a decade to fend for their large family of eight, including four sons and two daughters.

Gawli had been born and brought up in Dagdi Chawl, and he studied up to the eleventh standard in a municipal school in Bakri Adda, Byculla. Here, a close friend, Bablya Sawant, introduced him to Rama Naik, his senior in the same school and also a resident of Dagdi Chawl. The chawl has long been famous for its association with criminals. The second generation of the Mumbai underworld

– Rama Naik, Babu Reshim and Chhota Babu – began their careers in crime from here in the 1970s. Naik and Reshim became heroes for the teenage boys and unemployed youth of Dagdi Chawl due to their exploits. Naik ultimately left school without completing his studies, but his friendship with Gawli continued.

Gawli was in the tenth standard when his father left his job. He took up a job in Shakti Mills, Mahalaxmi, as a temporary hand and left school in 1970. In 1973, Gawli, who was by that time working at Godrej Boyce in Vikhroli, began to run his own parallel union and defied the might of trade unionist Dr Datta Samant. Under pressure from Datta Samant, the management of Godrej Boyce terminated Gawli's services abruptly. Shiv Sena activist Bala Mapankar of Agripada then got him work at Crompton Company at Kanjurmarg, where he came in contact with Sadashiv Bhimrao Pawale, aka Sada 'Mama', who went on to become his partner-in-crime and trusted aide.

At that time, would-be gangsters such as Naik, Ashok Chowdhary aka Chhota Babu, Bablya Sawant, Vilas Chowgule and Arun Gawli used to play kabaddi at the Om Club in Byculla. Mohan Chowdhary, Ashok's father, used to run a *matka* (lottery) and liquor business behind Peon chawl in Agripada, where Naik used to act as a strongman along with Ashok. As part of the same kabaddi gang, Gawli accompanied them. This was his informal induction into the gang. Initially, their main source of income was protection money collected from illegal gambling dens and liquor joints and other illegal activities like smuggling. In addition, their own *matka* and liquor dens supplemented their income during the reign of Rama Naik and Babu Reshim. Each gangster had 10 to 15 followers with him, with Naik at the top of the crime pyramid. They began calling builders who were building skyscrapers on the lands acquired by another local kingpin, Bhai Thakur, and extorted money from them. They spent this money on purchasing arms.

In the beginning, the gang ran like a well-oiled machine. Members were remunerated on a fixed basis according to their levels within the gang; important members like Gawli were given ₹25,000 per month, while gangsters at lower levels were given ₹2,000 to ₹5,000 per month.

In 1980, Gawli was detained under the National Security Act, but was released in a month by the advisory board. This brought his some fame, and he expanded his sources of extortion and also entered the *matka* and illicit liquor businesses. The same year, Reshim, Naik and Gawli were arrested for conspiring and killing Parasnath Pandey, a rival who had been brutally hacked to death near the Lambi Cement chawl. However, after three months, all three were released on bail.

After this, there was no looking back for Gawli. The don and his associates started collecting money from smugglers and builders, and provided muscle to builders to evict tenants or clear a site selected for new construction. They also got involved in settling financial disputes, charging half the amount recovered for their services. Since the police could not interfere in such cases in any way due to legal constraints, there was no recourse for their victims. This built links between gangsters and businessmen, who used the former to collect unsettled debts. Gawli also began demanding protection money from jewellery shops in Agripada, Mumbai Central, Kumbharwada, Pydhoni, Parel, Bhoiwada, Dadar, Kanjurmarg, Bhandup and Mulund. Almost all the bars, especially the dance bars, paid huge amounts to Gawli too. During the festivals of Ganesh Chaturthi, Navratri and Holi, the gang started sponsoring cinema or orchestra shows arranged by different *mandals*, who were asked to put up banners showing that Rama Naik or Babu Bhai or Arun Gawli was sponsoring them. These activities gave them respect in the locality, and their followers increased.

The funds were partly spent on court matters. Allegedly, the gang managed to win over a public prosecutor to their side, who kept a low-profile during many bail cases resulting in favourable judgements for the criminals. The staff in various jails were also said to have been paid off to give the gangsters VIP treatment and for allowing extortion victims to be taken inside jails without registering their entries, which is mandatory. In one such case, a hotel owner was taken to Yerawada Jail where Gawli threatened him.

In 1983–84, Gawli had constructed an illegal three-storeyed structure in Dagdi Chawl. The ground floor was rented out to 24 shops, and Gawli and his family lived on the second floor. The vacant area behind the shops was believed to have been used as a hideout for his associates, and the narrow passage leading to it as a firing range to train new entrants. The building was also used to confine extortion victims. In 1995, the then DCP of Zone-II, Datta Padsalgikar, got the shops sealed under Section 39 of the Mumbai Police Act. The action was upheld by the High Court, and the BMC issued a notice with respect to the illegal structure. Deputy Municipal Commissioner Patankar had given the orders to demolish the structure. Gawli managed to avoid the demolition by obtaining a stay from the city civil court. Municipal officials registered a case against Gawli, but they could not secure a conviction due to insufficient evidence. In the meantime, Gawli had managed to form a society of tenants of a dilapidated chawl within the Dagdi Chawl area.

Like his mentors, Gawli soon became a hero for the youth in his area. He continued to cultivate his image of a messiah, a desi Robin Hood. He looked after his gang members – who mostly stayed inside the chawl or in surrounding areas – like his own family. The families of gangsters killed by rival gangs or in police encounters were paid according to their status every month. Even if family members of the deceased had returned to their native places, Gawli arranged for their payments on either a monthly or a yearly basis, or their businesses would be financed so that they could earn a livelihood.

As I walked into the infamous chawl, I saw some women standing near the gate. I asked them to help me spot Bhau's house as I had an appointment with him. The women asked me to show my press ID card and my handbag. One of them searched my bag thoroughly. Professional hazard, I thought. Then two of them escorted me to a two-storeyed house in a corner. One walked ahead of me on a narrow staircase leading up to the first floor, while the other walked behind me. A gentle knock at the door and a female voice called us inside: '*Aat ya ho.* (Come inside.)'

I walked into a rectangular living room where I was greeted by Asha, the don's wife. Born a Muslim, Zubeida Mujawar had changed her name to Asha Gawli after her marriage. She looked exactly like any other married Marathi woman, with a big red *bindi* on her forehead, *sindoor* in the parting of her hair, a pair of *bichiye* (toe rings), green bangles and a *mangalsutra.* The two of them have five children – Gita (who is now a corporator), Mahesh, Yogita, Yogesh and Asmita, the youngest. There was minimal furniture inside the room, just two sofas and some chairs. The walls were adorned with garish pictures of Hindu deities.

The two ladies who had accompanied me stood outside the doors like commandos. From the living room window I could see a Shiv temple inside the high walls of the chawl. After a while, the don walked in like a politician, clad in white and wearing a Gandhi cap, and with folded hands said, '*Namaskar.*' He did not come across as the man who challenged Dawood Ibrahim's supremacy in Mumbai's underworld, but then Gawli is known to be cold, cunning and ruthless.

As we began the interview, he promptly declared, 'Right from my childhood, I was attracted towards social work.' It struck me that he was sticking to the Robin Hood image he had cultivated for himself. I was intently observing his mannerisms, and could not resist comparing them with those of Vijay Deenanath Chauhan, the character played by Amitabh Bachchan in the Bollywood hit *Agneepath* and said to be partly inspired by Gawli. Gawli indeed used the word '*kaaye*' frequently, followed by a long pause during which he would stare at me poker-faced. In the film, Bachchan had replicated the style perfectly, intoning the response as '*haayen*'.

While the interview was in progress, his kids were all over us. One wanted to look into my purse, and the other wanted to play with my tape recorder. I had to request Gawli to hold them back till we completed the interview as it was becoming difficult for me to concentrate.

The clever Gawli spoke in measured words on his past associations with gangsters like Dawood, Rama Naik and others. He cheekily said, '*Te gele...palale, aani mee ithej aahe. Aata sanga, kon hushar aani konachi takat jast*? (All of them fled, and left this city. But I stayed back. So tell me, who is cleverer and more powerful now?)'

Gawli avoided making any comments about the alleged political patronage he had recently received from a right-wing party, simply saying, '*Ashirwad aahe te.* (It's just their blessing.)' When I mentioned over a dozen cases of kidnapping, extortion and even murder that had been levied against him, he said, 'Like my benevolence, my revenge is famous. Unemployment is rampant as many industrialists are closing down their businesses. I want to do something for the jobless youth.' His answers seemed like they were meant to be echoes from his life. He continued playing a victim, despite being one of the most noted criminals of Mumbai at the time.

In the early 1990s in the Mumbai underworld, Gawli continued to actively carry out kidnappings and extortion and was believed to have been supported by powerful bureaucrats and politicians following the vacuum created by Dawood Ibrahim's flight to Dubai. Gawli followed his mentor Rama Naik in aligning with Dawood. They were not friends but they were not enemies either. Gawli claimed that they fell out only after Dawood started selling brown sugar in Byculla. The youth was getting into it and the trade involved big money. Gawli's gang started giving tip-offs to the police, and subsequently a war was declared. Gawli revealed to me that many young boys were killed on either side; so many, he said, that he had lost count. The gang war escalated over a property matter and Dawood got Rama Naik murdered. Since then, Gawli had mostly been confined to Dagdi Chawl and moved about secretly. After his brother Kishore, aka Papa Gawli, was murdered by a member of the Dawood gang, Anil Bambulkar, a bar owner at Naigaum Cross Road, Matunga, had distributed sweets in the area. On 5 March 1990, Gawli's men shot Bambulkar dead while he was sitting at the cash counter of his restaurant. Later, his shooter Shailesh Haldankar killed Dawood's brother-in-law, Ibrahim Parkar, at his Nagpada bastion in 1992.

Police records also implicate Gawli in other killings and crimes. In 1992, a raid on Dagdi Chawl unearthed two underground bunkers along with two AK-47 rifles, seven revolvers, four grenades, and nearly a thousand bullets. Back in 1981, Gawli had met a local videographer Lalit Shah in Arthur Road Jail, where he and Rama Naik were both imprisoned at the time. Shah went to meet Gawli in Aurangabad Jail while he was imprisoned there in the 1990s, along with a lucrative business proposal and a new partner, Raja Jadhav. At that time, Shah is believed to have told Gawli to invest with Vallabh Thakkar, a mill owner, so that the amount would be doubled in a year's time. Accordingly, Sada

Mama invested ₹30 lakh with Thakkar. After a few days, Shah took another client, Pujit Agarwal, to Aurangabad Jail for a job entailing eviction of tenants, for which Gawli took ₹25 lakh. But Gawli was to be shifted from Aurangabad to Amravati Jail at the time, and he asked Shah to stop his transfer. Shah is said to have informed Gawli that his transfer couldn't be stopped because of Jayant Jadhav – a confidant of Shiv Sena supremo Bal Thackeray, considered to be close to Amar Naik, Ashwin Naik's older brother and Gawli's rival. A furious Gawli is said to have asked his men to eliminate Jadhav, and on 30 April 1996 Jadhav was shot dead near his residence in Kamdar Park, Dadar. Gawli was alleged to have received political patronage from the Shiv Sena in the 1980s, when Shiv Sena chief Bal Thackeray had criticized Mumbai Police for taking action against Gawli and Amar Naik. However, after the death of Jadhav, Gawli fell out with the Sena.

Gawli's relationship with the Shiv Sena had begun as a tacit understanding of political patronage by a party that went on to project him as a Hindu don against Dawood's gang. Bal Thackeray had gone on record to announce at a rally in Dadar after the 1993 riots, 'If they have their Dawood, we have our Arun Gawli.'[1] Gawli joined the Shiv Sena in organizing *mahaaratis* on the streets of Mumbai.[2] The dalliance finally ended when Gawli had Jadhav murdered. Ramesh More, another Sena MLA, was killed in 1996, allegedly because Gawli had been ignored by Bal Thackeray. In early 1996, Jitendra Dabholkar – who was an office-bearer in Kamgar Sena, the labour wing of Shiv Sena – approached Arun Gawli while the latter was still in jail over his differences with Sena leaders. Gawli used this opportunity and assured Dabholkar of his cooperation; subsequently, Dabholkar constituted a party by the name of Akhil Bharatiya Sena and started its office at Lalbaug. Gradually, he began to attract disgruntled activists of the Sena.

When Gawli was released on bail, he became the president of ABS and Dabholkar was nominated as its secretary. Asha Gawli became the head of the women's wing of the party, while Bharat Mhatre, a confidant of former Shiv Sena leader Chhagan Bhujbal from Mazgaon, was made the vice-president. During the 1996 municipal elections, ABS fielded its candidates in all the constituencies in Mumbai. They began to threaten Sena workers during the campaign, and gained so much ground that in the constituency of the then chief minister Manohar Joshi, ABS candidate Meenakshi Tandel came in second after the Sena candidate. The Congress candidate was a distant third. Gawli's influence in the area was evident from the results. His political influence and intrusion into the Shiv Sena vote bank had became a sore point for the ruling government.

The Sena had begun to seethe at Gawli's antics and looked for the right opportunity to cut him down. A case was registered against Gawli for harbouring wanted criminals Nandya Sawant and Bandya in 1996, and he was detained under the National Security Act. The ruling government at the time was concerned with the fallout of the perception that it was a Gawli-basher, as he was quite popular in his locality. A strategy was devised to play hot-and-cold to undermine the fallout, and soon after Gawli's detention, Mohan Rawale, a Sena MP, made his displeasure known and staged a hunger strike outside Agripada police station for eight days demanding Gawli's release. He finally broke his fast by drinking a glass of juice given to him by Gawli's mother. Gawli's wife Asha, meanwhile, filed a writ petition in the Nagpur High Court challenging his detention under the NSA. The High Court upheld the petition, fined the Mumbai Police, and released Gawli.

Upon his release, Gawli immediately began opening new branches of his party across Maharashtra. On 18 July 1997, he organized a *morcha* against the state government at Hutatma Chowk. The movement received wide publicity and saw the participation of nearly two lakh people. According to reports, Gawli had spent about ₹1.5 crore to organize the *morcha*. Three days later, there were reports that Gawli had diverted all his funds towards the *morcha* and had not paid his henchmen. The same day, Anandita Ramaswami, a reporter with the *Asian Age*, was assaulted by Gawli's associates in Dagdi Chawl where she had gone to report on the ABS. In her complaint to the police, she mentioned that the attack had been at the behest of Gawli, who was arrested along with Raju Kamlakar Shirsat and Suresh Bhaskar. After being held for seven days, Gawli was released on bail.

Nevertheless, the state government continued to relentlessly keep Gawli in jail by lodging case after case against him. They even found an older resident of Dagdi Chawl to lodge complaints against the don. Chandraprabha Gajre, an ex-resident of Dagdi Chawl, alleged that Gawli and his friends assaulted her and drove her out of the chawl at gun-point after she refused Gawli's associate Sunil Ghate's marriage proposal to her daughter.

But the ultimate setback for Gawli would come later, when the state would come after him with all its might. On 16 August 1996, Gawli's two associates, Chandrasekhar Mirashi and Suresh Yende, died in an encounter with the police near Vithal Mandir, Laxmi Building, in Byculla, considered a stronghold of the gang. This was the first major blow to his empire. He filed three petitions in the High Court alleging use of excessive force by the state; however, the High Court rejected his petitions. The BJP–Sena government retaliated further, destroying his gang in 'encounters'.

❖

I met Gawli for the second time in an obscure village, Vadgaon Pir, in Maharashtra after he had been thrown out of Mumbai under section 56A of the Mumbai Police Act.[3] Politically an outcast, Gawli had been externed for two years in February 1999 from Mumbai and Thane for his involvement in numerous cases of extortion, intimidation and murder. By that time, the ABS had begun to co-opt Sena rebels, flex its muscles and expand its influence.

When Gawli was externed from Mumbai, he decided to move to his father-in-law Shaikh Lal Mujawar's village with his wife and 125 acolytes for two years. I was asked to reach his place around 10 a.m., the time at which he held a public *darbar*. It wasn't difficult to find Mujawar's house – a lone cement building amid thatch-roofed dwellings. I noticed a long queue of people outside, waiting to meet Gawli and that all visitors had to pass through a metal detector installed at the gate. I was led up to the first floor, where a chosen few were already waiting to meet him. Like his own living room at Dagdi Chawl, the guest room where I was seated was also decorated with portraits of Hindu deities adorning its walls, the best of calendar art.

I was told that he would join us shortly after finishing his *puja*, and that he had become a vegetarian for the month of Shravan in the Hindu calendar (June–July). I was given further details about his daily routine. Gawli spent three hours doing *puja* every morning. He would be up at 8 a.m. and his *bhakti* time included reading the Bhagavad Gita. He met his visitors, watched news on the television and took strolls in the onion fields accompanied by his private gunmen while in the village. One of his gunmen told me, 'He has to be careful about security because bullets can come from the police or from his rivals.'

After half-an-hour, Gawli, dressed in a green T-shirt and blue jeans like any other urban resident, finally arrived, but remained glued to his phone for another 15 minutes. It seemed that the

TV grab of Arun Gawli in Vadgaon Pir. Courtesy Star News.

exiled don was learning to overcome geography, even though he looked out of place and restless. As he answered questions, some visitors went through the ritual of touching his feet. Declaring his love for Mumbai and the fast-paced life of the city, he talked about his political plans and life outside Mumbai. Gawli denied he had a hand in any of the murder charges that had been levied against him by the police and the government. He muttered incessantly about *anyaya* (injustice) while being surrounded by a fawning crowd that insisted on calling him 'Daddy' even in the village. He feared the worst not from his rivals, he said, but from the police. He told me, 'I am not afraid of any rival. My only fear is that the police may get me. I have spent over a decade in jail. Now I wish to spend time with my family. But the police want to put me back in prison.' He claimed that it was the fear of his party that had forced the Shiv Sena-led state government to expel him from Mumbai with just a year to go for Assembly elections. Gawli was plotting revenge and promised to use Vadgaon Pir as the base for a political takeover of the hinterland. He had already appointed 20 *taluka* chiefs and enrolled 250 new members, he said. At the same time, he claimed to have over 5 lakh members in Maharashtra and vowed to contest 150 of the 288 Assembly seats in the next polls.

In the Lok Sabha polls of May 2004, Gawli surprised many by bagging over 92,000 votes in the Mumbai South-Central constituency, in a triangular fight against sitting Shiv Sena MP Mohan Rawale and the gangster's nephew and Nationalist Congress Party (NCP) legislator Sachin Ahir. He tasted his first-ever electoral success by winning the Chinchpokli seat in central Mumbai by a margin of 8,000 votes.

At the end of the interview, he changed into black trousers and a half-sleeved *kurta* with a Gandhi cap for the photoshoot. He said, '*Neta aahe tari disayala payje na.* (I am a political leader and should look like one.)'

Despite a long career in crime, each time Gawli was arrested it looked like he would escape conviction due to lack of evidence. There were reports that members of his gang intimidated witnesses before a hearing. Eventually, however, the law was to catch up with him. Ironically, his trusted aides would implicate him in the murder of Shiv Sena corporator Kamlakar Jamsandekar in 2007. In 2012, Shrikrishna Gaurav, an aide who was not involved in the action, gave vital information and Sandeep Gangan, another aide, turned approver for the police. With their help, the Mumbai Police was able to establish that two builders – Sahebrao Bhintade and Sadashiv Surve – who were Jamsandekar's rival-realtors, gave

Gawli ₹30 lakh to have the councillor killed in a land dispute. In 2008, Gawli's shooters, Ashok Jaiswal and Narendra Giri, recorded a confession testifying to Gawli's role in the murder, and he was arrested. First lodged in Arthur Road Jail, he was shifted to Thane's Taloja Jail in 2010 after his conviction.

Gawli was sentenced to life imprisonment by a special MCOCA Court on 31 August 2012 – this was the first time that he had been convicted and sentenced in any case since the beginning of his career.[4] Special Judge Prithviraj Chavan also sentenced 11 others for their roles in the conspiracy and murder of Jamsandekar. In addition, he ordered the convicts to pay a substantial sum as fine, failing which they would remain behind bars for a few more years. Of the total fine, 40 per cent was paid to Komal Jamsandekar, the victim's widow.

Gawli's daughter and now councillor, Geeta, who has inherited his political mantle, has challenged the conviction in the Mumbai High Court. 'Justice has not been done,' she told reporters on the day of the judgement. Hundreds had gathered in Gawli's support outside Dagdi Chawl and the MCOCA Court that day. As the unassuming don emerged from the courtroom in his trademark white *kurta-pyjama* and Gandhi cap, he smiled and waved at his supporters like a seasoned politician before stepping into the police van that took him back to Taloja Jail. For the don who had spent most of his life in prison, it was just another jail term.

Gawli is currently one of the star inmates at Taloja Jail, 50 km from Mumbai off the Mumbai–Pune expressway. It is believed he pays for services within the prison (an estimated ₹1 lakh per month) for special privileges such as meals from outside twice a day. He is apparently surrounded by a fleet of loyal foot-soldiers inside the jail, and his gang is still believed to be active in central Mumbai. In September 2013, he was admitted into the state-run St. George Hospital for treatment of cerebral

Arun Gawli was out on parole for his son Mahesh's wedding in May 2015. From left: Gawli's daughter Geeta, the bride Krutika Ahir, Gawli's son Mahesh, and Gawli himself. Photo courtesy Mahendra Parikh.

malaria. Since then, an ageing Gawli goes for an annual health check-up to the hospital, which is also when he catches up with the outside world, including his family, friends, party members, cronies and even film stars. Though visitors are not allowed to meet him officially, such restrictions have never deterred Gawli from carrying on with his business from wherever he is.

Gawli and his family strongly believe that he has become a victim of saffron political vendetta. He has elaborated in media interviews about his feeling that he has been wrongfully implicated and that it was a deliberate attempt on the part of political parties who wanted him to stay away from active politics.

In May 2015, Gawli was granted a 15-day parole by the Mumbai High Court to attend the wedding of his son Mahesh. According to the court order, Gawli had to report to Agripada police station near his house in Mumbai for one hour on alternate days. Nearly 100 to 150 police officers from the Mumbai Crime Branch kept a close watch on all the attendees of the ceremonies in an attempt to unearth the people close to the former don and get fresh insights into the underworld's forever-changing equations. Gawli audaciously invited Maharashtra's chief minister Devendra Fadnavis and the then Mumbai Police Commissioner Rakesh Maria as well, though none of them attended the function organized on the premises of the Mahalaxmi Race Course.

The area around the Gawli residence in the Byculla-Saat Rasta area of Mumbai, from where the don had risen to prominence, was decked up for the short homecoming of their 'king', as his municipal corporator daughter Geeta described Gawli. A clean-shaven Gawli in his trademark topi and white shirt-pyjama looked sharp and alert as he interacted with the media, sounding philosophical and playing the victim card. 'I will be sad to go back to jail,' he said, 'but I don't want to spoil the present moment of happiness.' He went on to say that he is looking forward to coming out of jail after completing 10 years, or even earlier if he finds himself lucky in the higher courts, and rejoin politics with renewed vigour even at the age of 60. There is, one would suppose, no retirement age as such in politics and the crime world.

The life story of this rustic don has found a new fan in film actor Arjun Rampal, who will reportedly portray Gawli in a film. Two maiden production houses in Mumbai, Pentagram Films and Sunil Mane Entertainment, have joined hands to make a biopic on Gawli. Allegedly, in early 2015, Rampal sneaked into the gangster's guarded room at JJ Hospital where he had been brought for a routine check-up under judicial custody at the time. Rampal was pulled up by the authorities and questioned by the Mumbai Police for this act.[5] This larger-than-life portrayal of Gawli was endorsed by his family, and it goes without saying that the contents of the film were discussed with the family and consent was given with an assurance that 'Daddy's' life would be portrayed with emphasis on the more positive aspects.

Whatever the response to the movie turns out to be, one thing is certain: the film will only add more glamour to the ageing don's profile and immortalize his exploits on the silver screen.

Acknowledgements

THIS BOOK WAS BORN IN the winter of 2013, when I was recuperating from an ankle injury. The real task was to find my old notes, records and reference material, from which I needed to dig out the stories.

First and foremost, I would like to thank Aroon Purie and Shazi Zaman for allowing me to use the *India Today* and ABP News (formerly Star News) libraries respectively to access reference material, my old articles and my old shows. I am grateful to Sujoy Das and Rajesh Sharma at the *India Today* library, and Vijay Shrestha and Naresh Verma at the ABP News library. I am also thankful to Mahendra Parikh for allowing me to use his photographs for this book.

Many thanks to all the sources who have helped me in my coverage of the underworld over the years.

I would also like to thank Nisha Jani, Anupama Chopra, Shankkar Aiyar, Raj Chengappa, Fawzan Husain, Roshni Jayakar, Sangita Jain, C.P. Thomas, Ajith Pillai, M.N. Singh, Rakesh Maria, Satish Mathur, Ahmed Javed, Deven Bharti, Parambir Singh, Mohan Kulkarni, Nitin Pradhan, Shyam Keshwani, Sapna Kanwar, Kamal Jain, Satyakki Bhattacharjee, Rahul Chandre, Dr Rajesh and Dr Firuza Parikh, Swami Chaitenya Keerti, Aparna Sharma, Charu Swarup and all my old and new friends and colleagues at the organizations in which I have worked for their valuable support in shaping this book.

My special thanks to Rohini Salian, D. Sivanandan, Pradeep Sawant and Shankar Kamble for teaching me the most valuable lesson to remember while covering the underworld, and helping me gain a legal perspective and an inside view on the Mumbai underworld and its nexus with Bollywood. I would especially like to thank A.B. Ravi and Preeti Mehra for their invaluable help and support. My work and this book would not be possible without you guys.

I would also like to thank my editor, Amish Raj Mulmi, at Hachette India for his untiring and diligent support. He made it all possible. Thanks also to Poulomi Chatterjee at Hachette India for seeing the book through to completion.

Finally, I would like to thank my family – Tushar, Parul, Snehal, Paritosh and Abhishek – for always being there for me, and members of the Muktaba family and the Wadhwan clan for your blessings and best wishes.

Notes

Enemy Number One

1 See excerpts from Chhota Shakeel's interview with the author and the complete news story here: https://www.youtube.com/watch?v=6aKkXKHc3BI More details here: http://www.abplive.in/india/2015/07/05/article639925.ece/Exclusive-interview-Chhota-Shakeel-says-he-and-Dawood-demanded-a-fair-trial-in-Mumbai-serial-blasts-case

2 Ibid. Also see excerpts of the interview to ABP News at: https://www.youtube.com/watch?v=vsz2LHnjLRA; http://indiatoday.intoday.in/story/dawood-ibrahim-surrender-ram-jethmalani-sharad-pawar-spar/1/449173.html

3 http://www.abplive.in/india/2015/07/08/article643240.ece/We-couldnt-have-provided-5-star-facilities-to-Dawood-Pawar-on-gangsters-offer-to-surrender

4 https://www.youtube.com/watch?v=6aKkXKHc3BI

5 http://www.abplive.in/incoming/2015/07/15/article650518.ece/1993-Mumbai-blasts-convict-Yakub-Memon-to-be-hanged-on-July-30

6 http://www.abplive.in/crime/2015/07/16/article652282.ece/Mumbai-Blasts-1993-CBI-did-not-deal-with-Yakub-Memon-says-Shantanu-Sen

7 *Ziyauddin Burhanuddin Bukhari vs Brijmohan Ramdass Mehra & Ors,* on 25 April 1975, Supreme Court of India.

8 Dawood was granted anticipatory bail to the sum of ₹25,000 by the Sessions Court, which directed Investigating Officer Tambe to visit his residence to verify his address. Dawood deposited his Indian passport no. V057865, dated 3 October 1983, issued by the Passport Office at Mumbai with the DCB, CID, as per the court order.

9 http://indiatoday.intoday.in/story/police-have-named-me-because-i-am-a-good-alibi-says-dawood-ibrahim/1/302050.html

10 Interview with sources within Intelligence Bureau and Ministry of External Affairs.

11 http://www.therichest.com/celebnetworth/richest-criminals/dawood-ibrahim-net-worth/

12 http://www.billionairesnewswire.com/dawood-ibrahim-billionaire-criminal-moves-sydney-buys-mansion-worth-5-million/

13 http://www.forbes.com/profile/dawood-ibrahim-kaskar *Forbes* editors said they went by four broad parameters to make their list: Does the person have influence over lots of other people, financial resources controlled by these individuals, if they are powerful in multiple, and do they actively use their power.

14 http://www.treasury.gov/press-center/press-releases/pages/js909.aspx

15 Gilbert Anthony King, *The Most Dangerous Man in the World: Dawood Ibrahim,* Chamberlain Bros, 2004

16 Peter Dale Scott, *American War Machine: Deep Politics, the CIA Global Drug Connection and the Road to Afghanistan,* Rowman & Littlefield Publishers, 2014

17 'War of the Dons', *India Today,* 2 October 2000

18 'Bangkok's Dirty Secret', *India Today,* 9 October 2000

19 http://indiatoday.intoday.in/story/indian-media-has-already-painted-me-black-dawood-ibrahim/1/293945.html

20 Ibid.

21 Ibid.

22 http://cbi.nic.in/fromarchives/Mumbaiblast/mumblast.php

23 See http://indiatoday.intoday.in/story/police-have-named-me-because-i-am-a-good-alibi-says-dawood-ibrahim/1/302050.html

24 http://supremecourtofindia.nic.in/outtoday/1728.pdf

25 B. Raman, *The Kaoboys of R&AW: Down Memory Lane*, Lancer Publishers, 2009

26 Scott, *American War Machine*

27 A reprint of the original story can be accessed here: http://archive.mid-day.com/news/2001/sep/15398.htm

28 Author interview with Ghulam Hasnain.

29 Amir Mir, *Talibanisation of Pakistan: From 9/11 to 26/11 and Beyond*, Pentagon Press, 2010

30 http://mcomments.outlookindia.com/story.aspx?sid=4&aid=221905

31 Quoted here: http://archive.mid-day.com/news/2003/jul/58446.htm

32 Ibid.

33 http://www.larouchepub.com/eiw/public/2009/2009_1-9/2009_1-9/2009-1/pdf/61-64_3601.pdf

34 'Long Before Sept. 11, Bin Laden Aircraft Flew Under the Radar', *Los Angeles Times*, 18 November 2001; accessible at:http://articles.latimes.com/2001/nov/18/news/mn-5593

35 https://www.globalpolicy.org/component/content/article/165/29634.html; also see Peters, Gretchen, *Seeds of Terror: How Drugs, Thugs and Crime are Reshaping the Afghan War*, Thomas Dunne Books, 2009

36 http://www.larouchepub.com/eiw/public/2009/2009_1-9/2009_1-9/2009-1/pdf/61-64_3601.pdf

37 http://www.firstpost.com/business/economy/from-dubai-to-nassau-dawood-blood-money-is-tainting-banks-686737.html

38 http://www.business-standard.com/article/current-affairs/no-role-of-bahamas-branch-in-dawood-s-money-transfer-bob-113040600390_1.html

39 http://www.dailymail.co.uk/indiahome/indianews/article-2810173/Hunt-Dawood-goes-global-Modi-Obama-s-joint-statement.html

40 http://www.hindustantimes.com/india-news/dawood-ibrahim-on-nsa-talks-agenda-india-has-proof-he-lives-in-karachi/article1-1382846.aspx

The Second-most Wanted Man in India

1 For a detailed transcript of the taped conversation, see 'The Don's New Victim', *India Today*, 20 December 1999; available at: http://indiatoday.intoday.in/story/revelation-of-nexus-between-judge-and-underworld-don-shakes-legal-circles/1/254546.html. Also see: http://indiatoday.intoday.in/story/police-just-doesnt-care-about-the-law-chhota-shakeel/1/256570.html

2 Ibid.

3 The DCB, CID, took over the investigation of the murder of Gulshan Kumar, vide C.R. No. 71/97, and nine gangsters of the Chhota Shakeel gang were arrested viz. (1) Javed Kalia aka Rajesh Javed Abdul Wahid Khan, (2) Rafiq Ahmed Shafi Ahmed Ansari aka Anand, (3) Rafiq Mohd. Issaq Phalke, (4) Imtiaz Dawood Merchant, (5) Mohd. Ali Hasan Shaikh, (6) Adil Mohd. Ali Khan (7) Pratapsingh Sakbir Singh Sakin, (8) Feroz Khan Sultan Khan, (9) Shafiq Ahmed Mohd. Sayyed. Although Ramesh Taurani was arrested on the basis of the information received from the arrested, Nadeem could not be arrested, as he fled the country. He is in London at present. The main conspirator and shooter Abdul Rauf Dawood Issak Merchant was arrested by Kolkata Police in 2014, and a supplementary chargesheet has been filed against him. The trial of the case concluded recently in the Sessions Court. While Merchant was convicted and sentenced to undergo

imprisonment for life, all the other accused were acquitted. An appeal is being prepared against the said order of acquittal. Author interview with police sources and police records. Also see 'Police Farce', *India Today*, 6 May 2002, available at http://archives.digitaltoday.in/indiatoday/20020506/crime.html

The Younger Brother

1 'Hello Brother', *India Today*, 3 March 2003

2 Ibid.

3 http://archives.digitaltoday.in/indiatoday/20030616/crime.html

4 http://archive.indianexpress.com/news/sarasahara-case-dawood-s-brother-kaskar-acquitted/33552/

5 http://indianexpress.com/article/india/india-others/dawoods-brother-deposes-in-case-related-to-drivers-death/

6 http://indiatoday.intoday.in/story/chhota-rajan-owns-up-to-attacks-on-iqbal-kaskar/1/139085.html

7 http://www.abplive.in/crime/2015/02/03/article492246.ece/Dawood%E2%80%99s-brother-two-others-booked-for-extortion

8 http://www.mid-day.com/articles/cops-to-initiate-chapter-proceedings-against-iqbal-kaskar/16303169

9 http://www.mid-day.com/articles/dont-seal-my-house-it-belongs-to-me-not-dawood-iqbal-kaskars-plea/16373160

The Don Who Loved Mumbai

1 For more information see: http://indiatoday.intoday.in/story/drug-czar-iqbal-mirchi-arrested-in-uk-faces-extradition-proceedings-to-india/1/287859.html

2 http://www.theguardian.com/uk/2005/feb/13/india.drugsandalcohol

3 http://timesofindia.indiatimes.com/india/Dawood-aide-Iqbal-Mirchi-dies-in-UK/articleshow/21851878.cms

The Don Who Fell in Love

1 'End Game', *India Today*, 10 July 2002; 'Quiet Lay the Don', *India Today*, 14 October 2002; available at http://archives.digitaltoday.in/indiatoday/20021014/crime.html

2 http://timesofindia.indiatimes.com/india/Abu-Salem-sings-under-narco-test/articleshow/2286455.cms

3 http://archive.mid-day.com/news/2006/mar/133901.htm

4 http://www.indiantelevision.org.in/release/y2k5/nov/novrel37.htm; excerpts from Samira's interview can be accessed here: http://www.telegraphindia.com/1051119/asp/frontpage/story_5495451.asp

5 http://archives.digitaltoday.in/indiatoday/20020506/crime.html

6 http://timesofindia.indiatimes.com/tv/news/hindi/Salems-hurt-over-Rahul-Monica-romance/articleshow/3609613.cms

7 http://www.abplive.in/video/2013/08/05/article27823.ece/Extradition-to-India-still-valid-SC#.VaX67_mqqko

8 http://www.abplive.in/video/2013/06/27/article27058.ece/Abu-Salem-injured-in-firing

The Gangster's Moll

1 See report of the duo's arrest in Lisbon here: http://archives.digitaltoday.in/indiatoday/20021014/crime.html

2 http://www.dnaindia.com/mumbai/report-salems-former-lawyer-attempts-suicide-1151941; also see http://www.mumbaimirror.com/mumbai/others/I-couldnt-deal-with-rumours/articleshow/15787991.cms

3 See http://archives.digitaltoday.in/indiatoday/20021014/crime.html

Interlude: Becoming a State Witness

1 For more details on the *Chori Chori Chupke Chupke* case, see 'Body Blow', *India Today*, 22 January 2001

2 Full judgement available at:http://indiankanoon.org/doc/698472/

Bedlam in Bangkok

1 'War of the Dons', *India Today*, 2 October 2000; available at: http://indiatoday.intoday.in/story/attempt-on-chhota-rajan-life-intensifies-war-with-dawood-bloodbath-in-mumbai-feared/1/244887.html

2 http://archives.digitaltoday.in/indiatoday/20001009/crime2.html

3 http://archives.digitaltoday.in/indiatoday/20001009/crime.html

4 Ibid.

5 'War of the Dons', *India Today*

6 http://indianexpress.com/article/india/india-news-india/2006-mumbai-train-blasts-case-5-convicts-get-death-sentence-life-for-7/#sthash.OO4I0LvR.dpuf

7 See complete interview on http://indiatoday.intoday.in/story/exclusive-india-planned-covert-dawood-operation-says-rk-singh/1/460523.html; also see: http://indiatoday.intoday.in/story/covert-op-on-dawood-compromised-by-some-mumbai-cops-rk-singh/1/460542.html

8 'Bangkok's Dirty Secret', *India Today*, 10 September 2000

9 See http://www.rediff.com/news/2000/oct/05rajan1.htm; http://www.rediff.com/news/2000/oct/27rajan.htm

10 Author interview with Mumbai Police sources; also see http://www.rediff.com/news/2000/nov/01rajan.htm

11 http://www.rediff.com/news/2001/jan/15afp.htm

The One Who Broke Away

1 http://www.outlookindia.com/news/article/gangster-santosh-shetty-nabbed-in-thailand/731160

2 http://timesofindia.indiatimes.com/city/mumbai/Chhota-Rajan-aide-assaults-Santosh-Shetty-inside-court/articleshow/13278082.cms

The Sports-loving Don

1 More details here: http://indianexpress.com/article/cities/mumbai/former-gangster-moves-court-in-extortion-case/

2 http://indianexpress.com/article/news-archive/web/gawli-poll-plan-sparks-fear-of-gang-wars/

3 http://indiatoday.intoday.in/story/inter-gang-rivalry-in-mumbai-moves-on-to-another-plane---communal-wars/1/253881.html

The Resident Don

1 http://www.rediff.com/news/aug/13gawli.htm; Also see http://www.outlookindia.com/article/tooth-and-claw/283066

2 http://indiatoday.intoday.in/story/inter-gang-rivalry-in-mumbai-moves-on-to-another-plane---communal-wars/1/253881.html

3 'Mobile Underworld', *India Today,* 15 March 1999; available at: http://indiatoday.intoday.in/story/thrown-out-of-mumbai-by-the-law-gangster-arun-gawli-makes-an-obscure-village-his-home/1/253467.html

4 http://indiatoday.intoday.in/story/arun-gawli-gets-life-term-in-corporator-murder-case/1/215428.html

5 http://indiatoday.intoday.in/story/arjun-rampal-bumped-into-arun-gawli-during-location-hunting/1/417319.html

Index